W9-AUW-994

CRAZY FROM THE HEAT

David Lee Roth

CRAZY FROM THE HEAT

HYPERION
NEW YORK

Printed in the United States of America. For information, address: Hyperion, 114 Fifth Avenue, New York, New York 10011.

Library of Congress Cataloging-in-Publication Data
Roth, David Lee.
Crazy from the heat / by David Lee Roth
p. cm.
ISBN 0-7868-6339-0
1. Roth, David Lee. 2. Rock musicians—United States—Biography I. Title.
ML420.R882C73 1997
782.42166'092—dc21
[B] 97–21887
CIP
MN

FIRST EDITION

10 9 8 7 6 5 4

THIS BOOK
IS DEDICATED TO
JAURETSI SAIZARBITORIA
WHO KEPT TELLING ME,

WRITE IT . . .

A SUPER ULTRA HYPER
SPECIAL THANKS TO

PAUL SCANLON

WHO WHITTLED THIS
MONSTER MANUSCRIPT
DOWN FROM 1200 PAGES
TO THE GEM YOU NOW HOLD
IN YOUR HANDS.

YOU ARE AN AMAZING EDITOR,

A STELLAR SPIRIT

AND NOW A GOOD FRIEND.

TABLE OF CONTENTS

JUMP!

JAH

TWO STRIPPERS

POLICE STORY

LOOKING IN THE REARVIEW MIRROR

IGNITION

THE GREEN HORNETS

UNTOUCHED BY HUMAN HANDS

BIG ED

M & M'S

PERSONAL BEST

HERBAL

54

HUCK

ROTHING YOUR ROOM

HELLFIRE

GRANDMA ROTH

What Made Classic Van Halen Tick

Personal Interaction

The Engine Room

Roadwork

Censorship

Primary Colors

Night Moves

Business 101

Fans & The Cult Of The Spotlight

Rationalization

Bomb

Crazy Horse

Elvis

Captain Blood

Jolson

A Zen Poem

Meet Helmut Newton

Body Language

Wars & Remembrance

Adventures In Hollywood

Krell Wars

Practicality

Tiaré

Beauty Pageant

Catch The Cat

Nowhere Gets A Name

Puss In Boot

Showtime

A-105

Heidi Fleiss

"Unplugged"

Art & Commerce

A Walk In The Park

Recreation Director

Travels With Dave

Brass Attack

Reunion Blues

Flexible

All The Girls I've Loved Before

Coda

Jump!

I'm always hurting. Hurt my back, somebody says, "Getting a little older?" I says, "I wish." I've hurt since day one. Not three days in my life have gone by in professional music for twenty years that I didn't have a toe that was screwing around with me, a knee that was ungrateful, a backache that threatened catastrophe. Gets very quiet at that moment, you're inside your knee, you go, "Fuck you, knee, I work with you all these seasons, here we are on stage here and you give up on me?" Knee says, "No, man, you just did fourteen nights in a row. I'm going home." I go, "Fuck you. I have Motrin."

I started jumping around on the Van Halen stage in '79 at the Oakland Coliseum. I didn't have my regular platform shoes, and I borrowed some Capezio dance shoes from somebody and just started flippin' around. All of those kicks, by the way, are designed for a specific reason. When they banned weapons throughout the Orient, all of these martial arts really blossomed. So when you see the jump-spinning back kick, that's designed to knock somebody off a horse.

We did some sequential photography with a strobe

light where you see multiple images, and they had a ballerina as my stand-in for all the test shots, and she made a nice, graceful, curved arc. When I jumped, it went straight up and straight across. It looked like it sounded; it was savage. It took so many hundreds of hours of preparation to be able to pull that out of my hat.

I know the floorboards of every major arena, stadium and venue in the free world, from bending over to stretch and stare at the floor for hours at a time before every show. My feet hurt constantly. I would sit in the doorway of the tour bus, and we wouldn't have any water so Big Ed, my assistant, would pour Perrier on my feet, and I'd patch up all the blisters.

All of those moves were not gymnastics; they were martial arts. And I approached them with that discipline. They had to be very real. As a result, every day something would snap. I broke my foot doing the big split jump that's on the back cover on the second Van Halen album. I was jumping off a drum riser onto cement, and I snapped a bone. Inside is a picture of me in a cast with a cane. That's how I sang "Somebody Get Me a Doctor" in the studio. I went to Jack Curran, the trainer for the Los Angeles Lakers, and I learned how to tape up my feet like a ballplayer. I constantly have shin splints. I was in pain, but I romanticized it as my equivalent of a guitarist's bleeding fingers.

Now, I know my engine inside and out. Not to say I don't floor it and drive right off into the hay on more than a frequent occasion. But for showtime, you can't eat six to seven hours in advance, which usually means by 2:30 in the afternoon; you're dangerously low in blood sugar, so you balance that out with some amino acids. Watch the smoking. Warm-up. Do scales in the bathroom—took a lot of singing lessons. It didn't really assist in my sound, but I never lost what I got. And on and on. It's like being the trainer for Secretariat.

I would always push myself to the point of major exhaustion. Would come off stage so dehydrated we'd have to have paramedics there, and they would have to bag me while I ate dinner. I'd sit there with three saline tubes in my arms while I ate; I'd be so dehydrated I'd clench up. Or oxygen on the side of the stage, what have you. I took great pride that I could max it so hard that I would pass out.

One night in Memphis I smashed a guitar on stage, and a piece flipped up, and that's why I have this scar under my eye. Finished the show, and they Band-Aided me up. Everybody was gagging. I finished the show, walked to the side of the stage, passed out. When I woke up, I was on a bed in the emergency room. They didn't want to wake me up so the call-sheet was sitting on my chest. Under occupation the nurse had written "circus performer."

Ultimately to test all this martial arts theory, I joined up with Benny Urquidez, Benny the Jet, kick boxing, full contact, it was in '82. And did full-contact training five mornings a week plus roadwork—my first experience running. Now I can run the marathon. Then I ran six blocks and felt like throwing up. Got in the ring half dozen times, some of the road crew would come down and cheer me on. It was glorious.

I had the time and wherewithall to invest in serious training, so I was always a little bit ahead of the curve. But I played in front of 375 thousand people at the US Festival in pain. My knee was killing me. If you look at the pictures, I had a piece of something wrapped around my knee. Sometimes I wonder if this was not like a defensive maneuver, metaphysically, an unwillingness to go forward? Or provide myself with sufficient distraction that I could burn calories in that area as opposed to just being nervous about a show. Half my calories would go to my knee.

When I played in Vegas, we did ten shows in a row. Direct. And I never left the stage once.

I had hurt my leg weeks before the show, lugging my kayak out of Florida storm waters, and pulled a muscle. What the cowboys call lumbago. Hurt from the small of my back all the way down to my ankle. I would wake up with my whole leg screamin'! I couldn't sleep, I'd wake up five times a night. And this was a month and a half before the actual showtime. Then I get to showtime.

I have several tattoos on my ankle, and one of them is Huckleberry Finn in silhouette, underneath the full moon, with New York City in the background. The therapist put so much electricity through me to get this leg going again, with the electrodes on the ankle, that it burnt a permanent hole in the moon.

One of the best injuries I ever sustained was when Van Halen played at the famous Piper Club in Rome. The Beatles had played there. It looked like all those early sixties movies with the very low ceilings with the old pipes. They were shooting us for a television show. One of these ready-steady-go kind of pop shows. We do a couple of run-throughs 'cause it's going to be for live television. I determined the best way to go is, they start off with black, the lights are off, you count "Uno, due, tre," and I would jump up, and the lights would come on while I was in mid-air. So we run it through a couple of times, and there's this big mirror ball about fifteen feet above my head, everything works beautifully.

We get ready, going to shoot it for real now. The stage is pitch black, we're waiting for live feed, so it's thirty-eight seconds in the dark. Nobody tells me that they're lowering the mirror ball until its like seven feet off the deck. I get down in the crouch and I'm ready, I'm all hunched up on the floor. And they say, "One, two, three, go," the lights come on, and I launch myself skyward. Do you know that feeling when catastrophe is unavoidable, and everything goes into slow motion, and you're just like an innocent bystander watching it all happen? My nose saw the ball first, and said in very slow motion, "Hey, ball" and the ball said, "Hey, nose." Cut instantly back into full-time fast real motion, BAM! I just crunched my nose big time, slammed into it full-speed ahead. Come down on the stage with my head in my hands, bleedin' all over the place, had to discontinue the shoot. They put me in the car, we rush off to the main general hospital in Rome, which is like, I don't know, what, Allied Occupational Forces. "Quickly, boil some water and bring me some fresh towels." Complete with the gurneys with the big wheels, from all your favorite war movies.

Doctor greets me in a private room, he's wearing the surgeon smock, which goes down below his knees and he's supposed to wear it backwards, drawstring it in the back, right? He's wearing it frontways and he's got no undershirt on so he looks like me, with the chest hair poking out. He's got a plunging neckline. He's smoking a cigarette. He puts the cigarette in his mouth, and he tilts my head, and he looks at the nose. He oohs and aahs and he goes, "Okay, absolutely he needs surgery immediately, we check him into the hospital right now, I do surgery, everything's okay in maybe six, seven days." I said, "I want a conflicting opinion." They bring in another little character right out of an Abel Ferrara movie, he looks, says, "You don't have to stay the hospital, surgery is not necessary, but I must pack the nose now, and absolutely you come back every day for four days." I said, "I need another opinion." A third guy comes in, says, "Do nothing. Just rest." By now my nose is swelled up as big as my thigh. Okay. Gotta rest. It hurts to even move. So they pack my nose, they put bandages all over it to stabilize it. We were due to play what's called the Pink Pop Festival in Holland; it's about sixty-five thousand people. I says, "Aw, man, I think we've got to cancel the Pink Pop Festival next week, I'm hurting *bad.*" Okay—downtime. Everybody's off, gig's canceled, everybody goes their own way for a week.

I get on a plane with Big Ed, and we head back to L.A. By now the swelling's gone down. It hurts, but I'm used to that. And it's not long before we're roller-skating down around Hermosa Beach—well, actually, I'm working out. See, there's this pretty blonde who's got to be all of seventeen that I would drag around, she would hang on to my sweater tied around my waist, and I would roller-skate. Gotta stay in condition. I turned to Ed in the middle of a sunny afternoon two days later. I said, "How's my nose look?" "Looks okay to me." I don't stop to think, Ed used to play semipro ball, his nose goes from nine o'clock to three o'clock, depending which side of his head you're standing near. I said, "Great. What is the last possible moment that we could call our manager, who's staying at the Sunset Marquis in Hollywood, and still catch the last possible plane to make the Pink Pop Festival?"

He said, "Four o'clock."

I said, "What time is it?"

"It's about three."

I said, "Great. Let me know when an hour's up."

At four o'clock we roller-skated up to a phone booth, called the manager and said, "I can make it!" Massive hysterical dash to put together the airplane flights, the visas. Phone calls are made, the trucks have to get from Brussels to Holland. The whole thing. When I stepped off the plane I had big pieces of tape over my nose. There's all kinds of press at the airport; they're delighted that we're going to make it, and they're interviewing me, and they're asking me, "So what is this you are wearing on your face? It is like American Indian, no?" They thought it was a fashion statement.

Another time, another tour. There were these stitches over my eye, like a dozen. We had to fly to Europe immediately. The road manager was a cook, he had been through the Culinary Institute, and I figured, well, he's got the best hand. "You're the one that's gonna pull my stitches."

There was no doctor to do it, and it was time. It had been ten days. We were enroute, we were going to meet the press getting off the airplane. I said to him, "Steve, you're the one. You gotta do my stitches." He said, "Great. We got to sterilize the wound area." He's a cook, what else is he gonna use but vodka? He treated the wound carefully. Pulled out the stitches at thirty-two thousand feet, somewhere over the Atlantic Ocean.

Jah

In 1975, the great Bob Marley came to the United States for the first time. He had several albums already, but the one that really just smacked it over the left field fence was *Natty Dread,* and he came to the United States on his first *real* tour, and played at the Roxy on Sunset Boulevard. I had a stack of posters for some show we were doing somewhere, a party somewhere, and I determined pretty much on the basis of the haircut, that Bob Marley would be a good audience for us to advertise at.

So I went down to the Roxy and it was February. It was freezing cold in L.A., and I had all my posters up under my shirt and tape and glue and everything so the cops wouldn't catch me, and I stood outside the back brick wall of the Roxy, watched everybody go in. Ringo walked in; Ike and Tina walked in; the Stones guys walked in. You know, all the local television-movie people, what have you. It was a stellar crew.

I stood outside that brick wall, and there was a big poster of Bob Marley with that haircut, those dreadlocks, Bob Marley with a spliff. *Natty Dread.* I froze my ass off and flyered every car in the parking lot and then listened to the *entire* show. And he would go on forever—major pot-smoker. I was out there for damn near three-and-a-half hours. I listened to every note of that show through that brick wall. And I swore to myself, I swore to myself that some day, some day . . . I was going to smoke joints that big.

Two Strippers

I was with these two girls once; they were strippers up in Vancouver, Canada. They came up to me and said, "Dave, we'd like to go upstairs, the two of us, with you." So I said, "Okay." We went upstairs, and it was August, and I was hot and sweaty and humid, and we commenced delivering the groceries at 138 beats a minute or more. One of the girls had fifteen hundred dollars in singles and fives and tens, her end-of-the-week tips and pay and everything in her G-string. Nobody noticed, you know, when the G-string came undone—well, I noticed—nobody noticed the money, like, floating around. I woke up at some point around dawn, the two of them were asleep, and all three of us were covered with money, every square inch had a dollar bill pasted to it—all exposed skin, and there was nothing but. The whole bed was covered with bills. Our bodies were covered with bills. There was bills in my underwear. Take a little picture of that.

Police Story

New York City, 1986. A pal and I were just coming by helicopter from the Liberty Island Festival. We landed at the 32nd Street heliport, on the East River. And I'm wearing the spandex, with the boots up to the knees and the Prince Valiant haircut. And my pal says, "Jeez, Dave, this is like Pimpville. This is dangerous turf."

I says, "It's cool, man, it's cool."

A few minutes later, a cop car pulls up, throws the lights on us. "All right, you guys, hold it right there." 'Cause we're colorfully dressed—to say the least.

He checks our ID, he says, "David Lee Roth! What are you doin' around here? This is Hookerville, man!"

"Stayin' over at the Plaza Hotel."

Cop says, "Hey, you want a ride? Jump in the car, you guys. We'll give you a ride to the Plaza Hotel." He and his partner were fans. As we're driving along, one of 'em says to me, "Hey, want to play a little game?"

I says, "Sure. I love games."

He says, "Here. Put these handcuffs on. We're gonna walk you into the precinct station."

It's the 13th Precinct, I think. It's Halloween; it's like a *zoo* in there. He walks us through, and every skell, every transvestite, every kind of pimp, hooker, is in there. In costume. And as we walk through the crowd, everyone gets really silent. And the night sergeant, sitting at the desk, looks at me in my striped pants, and my haircut and everything, and says, "What'd you get *him* in for?"

It's *dead* silent, in the whole precinct station, 'cause everybody *knows* who we are.

The cop turns around, and looks at me, and he says, "I don't know, sir. We found him down by 32nd Street. He says he's just a gigolo."

Looking In The Rearview Mirror

I was born in Bloomington, Indiana, October 10, 1954. My active memory starts when I was two years old. I remember sitting in a high chair. I remember I had to wear Dennis Brown splints, braces, on my legs. I had to sleep with them, too. So immediately, I had a major traumatic thing happen; I couldn't crawl around. Wore them until I was four or five.

That was not a happy point in my life, because at the same time, I had every kind of a food allergy you can possibly imagine. Eating sugar is like doing blow for me. You'll get twenty minutes of my best material, and then I've got to go to sleep. Who knew that in the sixties? Jesus, my mother was feeding me Jell-O water, which only increased my hyperactivity.

I paid a lot of attention to the television set. And I also started reading. I didn't really have a choice, there wasn't a lot of running up and down the proverbial field for me.

I had a little stack of records. Vinyl records, *West Side Story, Gypsy.*

So I always paid attention to those records. The Limbo was very popular, Virgin Islands, steel drums. It was very happening because it suggested the tropics. Of course, all the servicemen returning home after the Second World War, everybody that had been stationed in WESTPAC fleet, west Pacific, with Pacific Rim, and so forth, came back with tiki torches, and tiki masks, to put in the backyard. Everywhere you went there'd be a Trader Vic's, or a Trader Joe's kind of thing. So, the whole idea of "going out into the territory," like Mark

Twain put it, was always very relevant to me. I wanted to dance. I wanted to sing. I wanted to make some attention, because I had to lay around in front of the TV for so long.

Got sent to my first psychiatrist when I was six years old, because I was superactive, well off into the creative aspects of things, and at the same time, I was a little jock. I loved to read, I loved to paint, I loved to learn. Learning, to this day, is sacred to me. But you couldn't adjoin the two; you were either a jock or an egghead. Nobody knew what to do with me, plus I was Jewish. Back then in the sixties I was a "minority."

Pop started college, right out of the Air Force. I remember he had his little room upstairs, where he would study, where he had his books, his papers. My mom had no idea what to do with me.

Ultimately, we started moving around a fair amount as he pursued his medical schooling and internship and residency. We lived in the great outdoors. Bloomington, Indiana, is a college town. It still is a college town (John Cougar Melonhead lives there).

We moved to Newcastle, Indiana, which is where my grandparents had settled. All four of my grandparents are Russian immigrants. My great grandfather rode cavalry in the Lithuanian service. Grandpa Joe never did learn to speak much English, and he died in Florida. Plopped down under his mango tree. A lot of us maintain that he was just so pissed at the Cubans.

Grandma Roth kept a kosher house. Separate plates for milk products and meat, and whatever; go over and eat the classic fare, which was brisket, matzoh ball soup, gefilte fish, fruit salad. I hated it. It was scary. There was nothing to do; had to get dressed up, go see

Grandma and Grandpa. Grandma died when she was ninety-nine.

It was a very disciplinary background for my father. I don't know how many uncles and aunts I've got on his side, four or five. Pop's an ophthalmologist, eye surgeon, and they grew up in probably the linchpin of anti-Semitism, the bread basket of the United States. So where do you go?

You go to the movies. Pop was always going to the movies as a kid and dreaming, and losing himself into that—that and reading. There was always many, many books in our house as I was growing up. Ultimately they became my best friends, and I read everything. By the time I was thirteen, I'd already read the Koran, and Lenny Bruce's autobiography, *How To Talk Dirty and Influence People.* It was Lenny who said, "Some day the Russians are going to be gone; they are going to be our friends, and then we're going to turn our hatred onto ourselves and our public people and our own celebrities." It's precisely what's going on now.

Anyway, Pop related to me by movies, books. We would go to the movies together. I think the first picture I remember going to see was Steve Reeves in *Hercules Unchained,* and I think I was five years old. So I said, "Great. I get it. I'll be Steve Reeves when I grow up. I'll be Hercules."

Mom had sensibility and the sense of humor. My dad always taught me "Stay cool." Mom always told me "You can do it."

When I was seven, in Indiana, Pop got an old farmhouse to live in, as kind of a caretaker, some kind of rent scenario. There was crop land all over, two-lane blacktop leading to it, horses, a great big lake in the back with swans in it.

There was a foreman named Gene, the kind of guy that put Vaseline in his hair, smoked Camels, would roll the pack up in the sleeve of his T-shirt. He was great, became my mentor. Taught me how to spit. Seriously. The kind of guy that, when it was raining, would put on his rain slicker jacket and his rain slicker pants, but no hat, and run to the door and say, "I got to tend to the horses!" And he'd be dripping wet from the rain, with his hair all in his face. I thought that was just the greatest thing, man. Gene never didn't have to wear no hat, man. He was a man's man.

I also began to develop my own sense of fashion. I remember I had a little ring from the bottom of a Cracker Jack box. I showed Gene, while he was baling windrows of hay one day, and he told me, "You know what? I knew a little guy just like you, once. In fact, he had a ring much like that one."

I said, "Yeah? Could he bale good?"

He said, "Yeah, well, he could up until he caught his ring in the thresher, and it tore his arm off."

To this day, I wear no jewelry, ever. And I got all my digits.

Gene and I would go down to the lake and hunt muskrat. Ugliest damn creature on God's earth. It was great. I was a man, just like in the books, went hunting. And I would run. Running was always my thing. As soon as I got those braces off, I was running. And I got my taste of the great outdoors, which has always been important to me.

I remember determining that work was the way up. Because everywhere I turned was folks working. Pop was always studying. The foreman was always digging a hole or filling it up. The whole story of the Roth family was one of travel and industry. Picked up on that early on.

We moved to the East Coast when I was about six years old. We lived in Swampscott, Massachusetts, little town, right by the ocean. My only best pal was my sister Lisa. She's three years younger than me.

Several things happened at that point in time. First, and most memorable, my folks sent me off to the Child Guidance Clinic. Instantly, I realized that there was something wrong with me. Nobody else I knew had to go to the Child Guidance Clinic and talk to a shrink. I would sit in the waiting room and hang onto the chair for all I was worth. The psychiatrist would have to come upstairs and say, "Now, Dave, why don't you just come on down, we'll just play some games, or something, we'll just draw some pictures."

I was onto him early. I knew that something was up.

Ultimately, after almost a year of that, I did go downstairs into his office and sit there silently. They might have thought I was autistic, because I would just sit there, silently, refusing all his ministrations, all of his questions, anything at all.

One day he said, "I'll tell you what. We'll play a game of catch. We don't have to talk. We'll throw the ball."

I know how to throw a ball, and I can remember, quite vividly, that first ballgame. It was called, "He throws me the ball, and I throw it at his head as hard as I possibly can, and he would try and get out of the way." That was my introduction to sports.

I had my own personal self-esteem vibe coming into play: the kid who had to wear some braces, couldn't run around for a while, being Jewish, being new in town, what have you. I didn't get along with the other kids very well.

I remember playing chase in the school yard—that would have had to have been second grade—and I fell down and tore off the whole side of my face. I still have little scars. Just completely burgered the whole side of my head. It was common kid shit, you know—everybody made fun, but I did a noncommon kid thing. I signed everybody off. I was six years old, and I remember the day I did it. Right then and there.

I got home, and they had to hold me down, rubbing my face with the old surgical scrub brushes. Man, it was the most painful thing I ever experienced. I had a bandage covering one side of my head. I walked out onto the front porch, and I built a little boat out of the top of a picket fence, and used pencils and paper to make the sails. I put it right on the edge of the stairway, and I said, "This is me," and I kicked it off, into the street, and never affiliated with a group of steady friends again in my life.

That same day, I went in and I got my roller skates, the kind that you needed a key to tighten up, and I went down the street on Rockland Boulevard, right near Fisherman's Beach in Swampscott. There was a convent there with a big parking area. I had on black Converse tennis shoes, and I put my roller skates on, and went skating by myself. To this day I do just about everything by myself. When I kicked that boat off the porch, I fuckin' meant it.

So books became my best friends. There was an old couple who lived upstairs. I called him Uncle Sol. Uncle Sol gave me an old raincoat that was four-and-a-half sizes too big. It was huge, it dragged on the floor when I wore it. It was perfect for shoplifting books. If I saw a remotely interesting cover of a magazine or paperback, it went right down the left sleeve. Every day I would go out and steal books, magazines. If it had an interesting looking cover, I nabbed it.

Soon I had amassed a collection of paperbacks, hardcover books, girlie magazines, comic books, it was across the board. It was everything from *Babar the Elephant* to *Lusting Babes.* There were these little pamphlets, that were done up like Lili St. Cyr–style black-and-white print. The letters were cut in white into a black background, so it just burst out at you. Titles like *Souls in Pawn.* There would be girls dancing, and chicks starting to lift their tops.

I was onto everything, and Uncle Sol discovered my stash in the basement. I had accrued a huge stash. It was half the size of a Volkswagen, it was piled up, and I hid it under whatever debris I could find, but he discovered it. Knowing he had me over a barrel, in terms of my parents finding out, I was forced to strike a deal with him.

That was that he would not rat me out as long as he could borrow the girlie magazines.

Anyway, on my seventh birthday—by then we had gone to Brookline, Massachusetts—I remember my pop being admonished by my mom to go see *Robin Hood,* the Walt Disney version. I remember driving right past it, and my pop said, "Ah, it's such a long line, let's go see another show."

I said, "What show is that?"

He said, "Have you ever heard of Marilyn Monroe?"

I said, "No, I haven't. What's the movie about?"

He said, "Don't worry about that, it's called *Some Like It Hot.* I'll tell you the story of Robin Hood," so that I could tell my mom, later. We sat through *Some Like It Hot* two-and-a-half times and got home just in time for dinner.

It was pretty evident that we hadn't gone to see *Robin Hood.* But right then I determined that I was not only going to be Hercules, I was also going to be Marilyn Monroe.

I also decided that I was going to make movies, because I knew who Cecil B. DeMille was and I had a real good idea of how movies were made.

Which I have come to do, in video form. They're little movies. I wrote and directed, edited, cast, and color corrected *California Girls, Just a Gigolo, Hot for Teacher* and *Jump,* among others. *California Girls* and *Just a Gigolo* are the *Wizard of Oz* of pop video. And a dozen years later, they're still very, very popular. There are hardly any videos by other artists that you can name; made, say, from ten years ago, that are still popular today. Go ahead, try to name some. You can't.

Brookline, Massachusetts, was very racist. It was not unusual to see swastikas painted on the front door of the Jewish temple. I became Jewish in a militant sense, but not so much in a "church-going" sense. That only added fuel to the fire, insofar as a Dave-against-the-world sense. That was my door. It was not a happy time for me, because that's when you have to start going to Sunday school, Hebrew school, confirmation class.

But I did learn to sing. I am waterproof. Nothing drowns me out. Going to temple, getting involved in whatever it was, the glee club, or Friday night services, or whatever, I had a starring role. I belonged. I had the attention, and I could do no wrong. I had a pretty little falsetto voice, before all those hormones kicked in. I made my grandma cry with alarming regularity. For the right reasons. Now I sound like four flat tires on a muddy road. But I could sing sweetly then, and there wasn't a thing I couldn't sing.

This would have been 1961, when two magazines became hyper-relevant to my development: *Mad* and *Playboy.*

Mad's publisher, William M. Gaines, was the first one to start pointing the finger sarcastically in comic format at that time. What I learned from *Mad* was to find falsehood, or recognize it, to find facade or pretension wherever it exists and crucify it. Just like all the Marx Brothers taking on old Margaret Dumont. It was Ray Bolger, the Scarecrow from *The Wizard of Oz,* taking on the Wicked Witch. *Mad* was a very healthy, balancing factor in my life. For me comedy has always addressed perception and reality way better than drama.

The other magazine that was absolutely pivotal in my development, spiritually, was *Playboy.* All you had to do was open the magazine, even a little punk like me who could barely read. All you had to do was look at a picture. There's that guy Andy Warhol standing next to that guy Cassius Clay, standing next to that guy Picasso, standing next to that guy Hemingway, standing next to that guy Carl Sandburg, standing next to that guy, that professor from Harvard who was taking the drugs, and so on.

And those girls! They were part of the crew too! Oh man, I was going to join that. You'd better believe it. I was going to do everything that was on that page.

Show People. I use that term because it reminds me

of burlesque and vaudeville. Show people is the little lady who takes the ticket and the old guy who sweeps up, with the one white lightbulb on the pole on the stage, after everybody's gone home. Show people is singers and dancers; show people is the guy who paints the advertisement or the photographer, you know what I'm saying? These were all show people.

I didn't know any other way to get into that magazine, except to be show people. I couldn't paint. I couldn't write.

Playboy was so important to me. Most people would never get past looking at the finger pointing to the moon. They'd just crack it open, they see tits and ass, the joke page, the fold-out. That's as far as they ever got. They got as far as the tip of the finger.

If you looked farther, where Hugh Hefner was pointing, it was the universe. Here was the map. Full-blown color and everything. He had an editorial opinion on everything, in a day and an age when opinions were somewhat frowned upon. Opinions caused dissension; opinions caused political foment.

I still read *Playboy,* looking for that same seed, and much of it is there.

There was a very high grading curve for those magazines at the time. Perhaps the descendents of *Mad* magazine were *National Lampoon* and *Spy.* Both very alternative, but cut from the same stone.

I remember opening a *Playboy* magazine and seeing a Miles Davis interview, 1961 or 1962. You didn't see black people in white magazines a whole lot, unless it was Aunt Jemima on the cover of a pancake box.

Lenny Bruce was up and coming at the time, and making big-time waves. Nobody had ever seen a routine like that. Nobody had ever heard of such a thing, and it wasn't just pure comedy—it was reportage, it was social critique, social commentary. It was very left of center. It went hand in hand with the *Mad* magazine and the *Playboy* magazine kind of ethic.

He was at the height of his powers, then, even though he was already legendarily speeded out of his brain.

He made some incredible waves in what we perceived in our culture, in what we perceived as a sense of humor. He was at that party at *Playboy* magazine as well. They called what he did "sick humor." Now he would be a National Affairs editor at *Rolling Stone.* Back then we crucified him, and ultimately killed him, or at least provided a route for him to kill himself. Put him out of business.

In 1962, my Uncle Manny owned a club in Greenwich Village called the Cafe Wha? His wife, Aunt Judy, was the original Indian madras lady. Judy never walked anywhere. She wafted. Manny was the oldest of the Roth brothers. He left Indiana and went to the Village. It was the age of the coffee shop and the cafe.

Manny had a flat over the famous Cafe Reggio, where Hippolyte Havel, the first freewheeling anarchist, held court in the twenties. I would waft up and down MacDougal and Bleecker Street with my Aunt Judy while Manny would tend to his business. It was Judy who scoped me to what New York City was all about.

Pop was in school the first time I went to New York. I guess I was about seven years old. We had flown down from Boston, and I was sitting in the backseat of a taxi, looking out the window. It was 11:30 at night, I was still awake and so was the rest of the entire world. There it was, right outside the window. It was even better than the magazines.

We was freewheelin' then. There's a famous Spanky and Our Gang episode where Buckwheat and Spanky are selling ice out of the back of a horse cart. There's a donkey, there's a stick with a carrot. A tire bursts on a car, and the donkey breaks free. The cart starts careening down the hill at breakneck speed. Spanky turns to Buckwheat, yells, "Hit the brakes!"

Buckwheat turns to him and yells, "Brakes is gone! We's freewheelin'!" (which was the name of the episode, "Freewheelin' ").

The first time I saw New York I commenced freewheelin'—brakes were gone. It was the first time I'd ever seen a magazine store where you needed a stick to get the magazine off the top rack because it was up so high. I'd never seen so much paperwork on one wall. This was heaven. I only really knew two magazines. And lo and behold, I stepped through a doorway, and there were five hundred new friends.

It was right across the street from Cafe Wha? where Manny was the Duke of MacDougal. Manny coined the name by walking from couch to couch one night, saying, "What shall we name our new coffee house?"

And somebody would say, "How about 'The Ever-Arcing Spiral of Transcendence'? "

And Manny would go "Wha?," like Grandma would.

He'd walk to the next couch and say, "What do you think we should call our new coffee house?"

The reply: "Call it 'The Electric Purple Soft Machine . . .' "

And Manny would go, "Wha?"

So he eventually named it the Cafe Wha?

And I took passage through all of those bars, the Cedar Tavern, the San Remo, whatever. Judy took me to all of these places. I got to see lots of fistfights. These painters and writers would get drunk and go at it. Great, I decided I was going to be a painter too. I already knew how to throw a punch. It was a simple conceptual leap for me.

So it was a great, great mix, there. It was just like those magazines I was shoplifting. The whole Village scenario taught me not to be afraid of anything with two legs in pants. Indeed, if it moves, I ain't scared of it; it's the stuff that doesn't move. There's a few mountains I won't go near again.

There's a few pools of Atlantic water that I'm not terribly interested in rejoining again. But if it moves, and it's got two legs in its pants, I've seen it. I ain't a-scared of it, mainly because of that experience in the Village at such an early age.

Lenny Bruce performed at the Cafe Wha? Bill Cosby, Rich Little, Joan Rivers—Bob Dylan got fired three times for being late. Manny was a hard case. Allen Ginsberg did poetry readings there. The place had the classic characters with the soul patch, the goatee and the beret with the bongos, the French black tobacco cigarettes, the espresso coffee and a lot of " spoken word."

I saw every kind of person and character and sex type in the Village at a very early age. I saw lesbians and knew what they were about, I saw the transvestite bunch and knew what they were about. I saw the Bensonhurst jock crowd, I saw uptown socialites, I saw debutantes come through the Cafe Wha? I saw royalty, and I saw junkies. I saw prostitutes, and I saw senators . . . that's not a big leap.

But I developed an appreciation—not just a tolerance, but an appreciation—for all types of people.

It was also a super lively time because everybody was taking "diet pills." Diet pills—amphetamines, methamphetamine, amphetamine sulfates, whatever. Oh yeah! *Everybody*—everybody from the Kennedys to the Beatles, to the Detroit Lions. Everybody was rattled out of their teeth. Everybody stayed up very late in the early and mid-sixties, and I knew what those were all about, as well—those little, triangular Dexamyls. Eat one for breakfast and you could be Bob Fosse too!

Everybody was radiant. Everybody was going to the diet doctor, getting a fist full of diet pills every five days. Or, you'd get a "vitamin shot," which, of course, was laced with every kind of "go-fast" that you could think of. I knew people, friends of Manny's and Judy's. You'd see them at clubs, who you *knew* were three days out from their last vitamin shot, were getting a little cranky.

Andy Warhol read it as, he was not sure, if so much was happening in the early sixties, that nobody wanted to go to sleep, or, if so much happened because everybody was awake so much. Well, I was there and I still can't figure it out.

A lot of my appreciation for the pyramids, and going out upon the burning sands and looking up at the sky, came from my dad. My sarcastic sense of humor came from Mom.

Moms always had a colorful sidebar on just about any subject. She was a valedictorian, Northwestern sorority gal, played violin, spoke Spanish. She was a high school teacher for a while. And so I think that probably mixed with Pop's general workmanlike approach. See, my mother was always there. Pops was the one who was always working on something else. So I guess you start to take that for granted after a point. It becomes an influence that you take for granted. That's Mom.

You know what? Over the years, whatever I pursued, people would say, "What do your parents think about that?" Both my parents were very supportive of just about anything, as long as I did it with some kind of a code in mind. With some kind of self-respect and a certain amount of fury and passion. As long as it was colorful and dynamic. Then they were very content with what I was pursuing, *especially* music. Working in bars, whatever.

My first starring role was Mr. Bookworm, in 1961. My class play. Not that I'm such a great actor. I did play Hamlet one time; Hamlet lost. Mr. Bookworm was the lead in the grade school play, and I was the only one who could remember all the words.

Nineteen sixty-one was when "hipness" entered into my overall consciousness, as well as everybody else's on the planet. It was largely because of President John Fitzgerald Kennedy. He was hip, he was young. He had a cool haircut, he had a babe-o-rama for a wife. He was cultured and educated, and she was society.

Now there might be many people thinking, well, he wasn't hip, or he wasn't cool, or he wasn't whatever. I have no idea, frankly. I don't know what his political policy was at the time, I can only tell you what happened socially, what was going on in the apartment complex. He was a rebel, which meant a lot to me, even at that young, young age.

The Cuban Missile Crisis: Were we going to go to

war? I didn't really know quite exactly what "nuclear war" meant. I knew what regular war was, from television. But nuclear war, all we knew was that the teachers would have "duck and cover" drills in school, you know, where out of nowhere, the teacher would slam a book on the table and scream, "Drop!" Everybody would have to crawl underneath their desk and cover their head and neck.

We would do those drills, and then we would get up and file into the basement. And everybody would stand against the walls, in the basement, or in the hallways, with their hands covering the back of their necks. Now that I think of it, it looked like an after-hours raid in Brooklyn. I remember this from second, third, all the way up through sixth grade.

In the face of all of this was a guy who was really kind of hip, kind of cool, and kind of young, and so was his wife. The contrast made both colors just stand out dramatically, in my mind. A hipness kicked in, in a general kind of a way.

And the Twist was it. Everybody was twisting.

It was everywhere. It was in the commercials, it was on TV sets, it was on the dance shows, it was Chubby Checker. I have since met Chubby, and he's still twisting. When I think about it, this was a conjoining of uptown and downtown. I am visualizing what the TV shows looked like. You had hosts of shows wearing black tuxedos, Frank Sinatra wardrobe, twisting with the little go-go girls. And there'd be guys in jeans, the Marlon Brando Wild-One approach. Everybody was twisting.

What does it mean when everybody was twisting? It means there was mutual acceptance. There was a tolerance developing among people, and I was sensitive to it. Could I have articulated it back then? I would have told you I could. But I who knew not that I knew not, now know that I know not, and that's progress.

In 1963, we moved to Los Angeles. Pop graduated school, finished his residency. Moved to Altadena, right smack into the middle of the lower-middle-class multicultural hodgepodge.

It was not a terribly traumatic time for me, whereas a move like that might be for many kids. I was in fourth grade, Mrs. Pitt's class, and it was the first time I had gone to school with Latino kids, black kids, and every other color and combination. I was already a part of that. I was already a part of the hip jet stream in my mind, via the music and what I was reading. It didn't have a whole lot to do with my parents, as I figured it; the Twist, even though they were twisting, belonged to me. I started to see myself as a black person.

Nineteen sixty-three, Major Lance, Little Anthony, Diana Ross and Marvin Gaye. Everybody kicked in, really, at that point, particularly in Los Angeles. Because we had Wolfman Jack, screaming from the Mighty 1090 XERB! From over the border in Tijuana, I mean, he was just humpin' that stuff.

I remember when Mrs. Pitt announced that President Kennedy had been shot, and we all cried. I vividly remember crying at my desk because he belonged to us. He was not Eisenhower, he was not Nixon; he was not anybody you'd ever seen on American currency. He was cool.

Then the absolute ministers of cool entered the scene, and there were five of them: John, Paul, George, Ringo, and Cassius Clay—all of them representing acts of social terrorism, unparalleled in any book I ever got forced to read.

They had haircuts that weren't cut; they had suits with

no lapels. Do you know what that meant? Do you know what a statement that was? That was my statement. That was an entire generation's statement. The Beatles were black guys, too. If you listen to their first three albums, there's a lot of coverage of old Motown songs. And of course you had the amazing Cassius Clay, soon to be Muhammad Ali, a loud-talking, aggressive, in-your-face black man, who made good in the most dramatic fashion.

One of my most precious possessions was a little black-and-white radio, one of the original made-in-Japan items, when "Made in Japan" meant it was going to break tomorrow. When it was a joke, when *Mad* magazine wrote "Made in Japan" on all kinds of little things. I listened to Cassius Clay whip Sonny Liston for the heavyweight title in 1964. Summer. I remember it was warm outside.

All of these were ingredients that I began to bake with. I started acting out the steps that I saw on the television shows, on "American Bandstand," and what have you. I started singing the songs, learning the lyrics.

Skateboarding entered the culture for the first time. We built them out of a piece of signpost and some roller-skate wheels, or you could buy one for fifteen bucks up at the Thrifty Drugstore. There was a special kind, the best. It was called a Bun Buster. Because you would bust your buns.

This was L.A., and car culture came slammin' in. Who was one of the original greats? A Roth! Ed "Big Daddy" Roth. These were the first times that the idea of exaggeration really became the way to go—big, fat slick tires on the back, little tiny 421s on the front, and a giant hemihead engine with the drag pipes coming out. Big Daddy Roth also drew those wild-eyed monsters, like

Rat Fink, with the big bulging eyes, and the jagged teeth. His rat body barely fits into this minuscule little engine compartment, and the engine is as big as his fuckin' head! There were cartoons about it, and comic books about it, and magazines about it, and he designed these futuro, read: George Jetson, Jetsonmobile kinds of cars, with names like "Road Agent."

I was totally into car culture. Drag racing had always been around, but, in the mid to late sixties, let's go from '64 to the end of '69, drag racing really took off in the public consciousness. America was going the quarter in six flat. We were Road Agents!

That was us. That was the attitude. That was the spirit. England became hip. The Beatles came burgeoning in, followed by a whole other train of thought.

Right on the heels of this pop, hysterical affront to your Pat Boone school of thinking, came the "I'm bored, so fuck you," school of thinking, represented in stellar fashion by the Rolling Stones. Mick will tell you that one of the most critical ingredients of that approach is the boredom: a dispassionate discourse. Sunglasses at night. You're so cool, yet so bored, that you don't even really need to see.

Music got cool. At the same time it was revved so hot that you would watch "The Ed Sullivan Show" and one week see the Beatles and the next week see the Rolling Stones. Now, the Beatles had matching suits without lapels, the boots with the pointy toes. Christ, the last time we saw anything like that was in *West Side Story;* the Puerto Ricans were wearing them. But then Mick and company would show up, in an old white sweatshirt, a pair of jeans, and it looked like they hadn't brushed their hair in three days. Oh yeah!

You knew instinctively, if not cognitively, that these guys never, ever cleaned up their room. The Beatles looked like, at some point in their development, they would clean up their room, and do their homework. The Rolling Stones looked like they ran away from home.

I respected both duly. I completely enjoyed the sounds of hard work and attention to detail that the Beatles represented—that kind of music only comes from distance, it only comes from forethought. I also adored the Rolling Stones for the "who gives a shit?" foundation upon which they built their castle.

They jammed. And there were a number of bands who followed suit, in both fashions. The Monkees came on their heels, and they were celebrative and lively. You also had the Kinks. Or the Standells singing about Boston, "Well, I love that dirty water." You could tell from the tone of voice, this guy is cool. Dirty water, talk to me!

I was into the Beach Boys completely. There was all forms of dissension and foment, and there were quite a few school-yard fistfights over who were better, the Beatles or the Beach Boys.

Oh man, grade school was a hotbed for discontent. Black music was just accepted because we all gotta twist. Or, at that point, we were Mashed Potatoing, we were Frugging, we were Watusiing.

Now, wait a minute, let's just stop right there, Jake. We've just entered African territory. Watusi? Our kids are doing an African dance called the Watusi? The whole element of what was hip, what was cool, what was now got more and more dense, got more and more colorful. And people started letting their hair grow.

Fourth through sixth grade, I was constantly sent to

the school shrink because I was a show-off, in a theatrical sense. My version was to put a whole tube of Brylcreem in my hair, go to school, and do headstands during recess, leave a cool spot on the cement. Everybody would get a great kick out of that. Or I'd make a big Alfalfa cowlick with Vaseline and wear that to school. This was the time when you saluted the flag, said the pledge of allegiance, and sang "My Country 'Tis of Thee" every morning, before you commenced learning. I was like the guy in those live jazz recordings, where somebody's always coughing in the background. You know they're doing it on purpose, so they can say, "Hear that? That's me!" But I was not the class clown.

A class clown is somebody, who, because of a self-esteem problem, is looking to be an interruptive force and attract attention, if for no other reason than that may give you the only impact you can have on the rest of the gang. I was a court jester, a venerated and ancient, traditional, highly respected role, hired by the king himself, a healthy and absolutely necessary influence in our culture and all other cultures. My job was to find the falsehood, the facade, the pomposity, and skewer it—even at the expense of the king. The only one in the entire kingdom allowed to do that!

But the school perceived me as class clown, just trying to be an interruptive, invasive kind of an influence on the class; just to disrupt, for the sake of general hilarity or foment.

It's hard to know when you're in an era until it's over. When you stand back, take a close view from a distance; you see so much more. At the time, I was in the ultimate Taoist state of mind: No mind. No distraction. I floated free.

For children, the psychological term is "primary process"—the desire to pursue, to see, to experience, to touch—but that is beaten out of us, over the years, as we grow older. I never lost that. And it upset a lot of people.

So I was hustled off to Mrs. Buck, the school psychologist, and I would get swatted for misbehaving. All the yelling and what-not, you were made to feel bad. Nowadays, they might have said, "This is a special kid," been sent to special kind of classes. But then you qualified as purely "out of line."

At the same time the world was stopping twisting, altogether, and it was beginning to polarize. You could begin to see this with Big Daddy Roth and Eric Burdon and the Animals and the Beatles versus Lyndon Baines Johnson and the Great Society. Our political involvements, at the time, were a major construct of that deterioration. The Vietnam conflict expanded by leaps and bounds between '63 and '65. In '65, they finally gave it a name, and called it "escalation," and we led with our faces. That's when the dissension began.

The drug culture entered into the picture—beyond the acceptable diet-pill scenario. Now there were alternative drugs; marijuana was smoked by the mods and the rockers. Mods and rockers were taking depressants as well as uppers. The word *meditation* became available to America for the first time. We'd never heard the word before. We were surfing, we were busting our buns, we were doing zero to sixty in five-and-a-half, we were all black guys from London, who wanted to "hold your hand."

In fifth grade, I stole a copy of Harold Robbins's *The Carpetbaggers.* I had to hide the book under the dresser so my parents wouldn't see it. This was the first time I'd ever read anything of any real sexual content. I knew how everything was supposed to work, but this was the first time I'd read it in lurid, luscious terms, extreme stuff. I'm not sure if it was the actual story content, or just the idea that I wasn't supposed to be reading it—probably both. Just turned me on. And opened my eyes to the wonderful world of human interaction in its infinite variety—accent on the word *infinite*—right from the second chapter. Look out! Now I really had a reason to shoplift. Now I had what Dad always called "a focus."

In 1966, the first truly underground free-form radio station, the first alternative radio station, was started in Pasadena, California, by a big guy, a three-hundred-pound DJ named Tom Donahue.

I still had the little black-and-white radio, and I was literally under the covers just dialing around to anything that sounded remotely interesting. One night I arrived at this baleful, off-key—one voice and an acoustical guitar. It was Bob Dylan. The DJ played the whole side of the album! Now, let's take a reality check here. Let's freeze the frame. This was the era of screaming Top-40 disc jockey. Guys like Humble Harve, you know, on KFWB, channel 98: "Hey, baby, hoppin' and boppin' and poppin' with the best top of the pop smash boss beat with the timeless tunes, for those with the textured tastes."

Now here comes a guy with this slow delivery, a half a kilometer in between every word: "Hey . . . that was, uh . . . the, uh . . . new . . . *Quicksilver* album . . . can't . . . wait . . . till it . . . comes out in stereo."

Tom Donahue, KPPC, 106.7. Do the numbers sound familiar? Because today it's KROQ. It is the alternative, the Chili Peps, the Morrisseys and the Rollinses. This was the blueprint from which all rock radio that we listen to today was struck. This pointed the way toward the identity of the disc jockey, to the approach, the laconic tone of voice, that kind of homey touch instead of the screaming introduction for a drag race. "Sunday! Sunday! Sunday! Nitro-burning funny cars!"

We'd go down to the basement of the Unitarian Church on Colorado Boulevard. It was just a big empty room with some couches and black light posters of Jimi Hendrix and The Doors. You could lounge around in your moccasins and your jeans and your Pendleton shirt. Worker-oriented clothes, you know, that was the hip thing. And we listened to the radio. Before long, other stations would appear where the DJ shows up with a milk crate of his own personal records and plays Bob Dylan for four hours.

In 1966, the first underground comics came into any real public awareness. R. Crumb's Mr. Natural . . . anything that was subversive, political, sexy. The whole free-speech thing was on the top of the "topics to be talked . . . to be 'rapped' about" list. And we started seeing, like, Gilbert Shelton's Wonder Wart Hog, and the Fabulous Furry Freak Brothers.

The Fabulous Furry Freak Brothers were Cheech and Chong with an extra guy. The Three Stooges, but they smoked dope. Almost every single episode would start with the two guys handing ten dollars to the one who was essentially Curly, the dummy one, and telling him to go out and cop some pot, and—in big, bold letters: **DON'T GET BURNED.**

But we all knew, of *course,* he was gonna get burned. He'd waylay himself somewhere and waste the money in some bizarre fashion, or it would be stolen, or he would lose it. That would constitute the next two months' worth of misadventure: trying to either get the pot or get the money back. Every episode. Comics were cool again.

Superheroes stopped being squares. Marvel Comics' the Fantastic Four, the Hulk, Spiderman, all became very hip. Even when they were fistfighting, they'd be making all kinds of colorful, hip comments: "Whoa, looks like a little fist-to-face confrontation," as he's knocking out three thugs. This, of course, appealed to me major time. This was very visual, it was very much an attitude. It was *exactly* cut from the lifestyle we all wanted to lead—wise-mouth kids.

We saw every Blaxploitation picture, and those movies were a *huge* influence on me. *Trouble Man, Superfly, Foxy Brown, Shaft, Cleopatra Jones, Blacula,* Rudy Ray Moore doin' his Dolemite Vibe—I saw *all* of those.

Blaxploitation was a white term. It obviously means to exploit blacks. Or blackisms. I don't think it was so much exploitative as time come due. All throughout the sixties all we saw was black people getting sprayed by fire hoses and dragged out of the bar-and-grills and Civil Rights marches and whatever.

All of a sudden you have liberation. You've got blacks in all of their finery, whether that's the Afro, the bell-bottoms, the platforms. Their cars, their slang, their ordnance. Alternately living out a reality and a fantasy that was every bit a part of Civil Rights. You've got Muhammad Ali returning to reclaim his title. He'd finished his gig as outcast for refusing to go to war. You had blacks living out their vision of prevailing.

If you were any part of any subgroup that had a self-esteem difficulty or a "I'm not part of a large clan" mentality you could relate to these pictures big time. Same way that most rap records sell to white kids.

Dolemite—Rudy Ray Moore—was one of the originals. He was a blue comic, doing blue humor. Like Redd Foxx did on early party records. So he was the most perfect to play a new secret agent. His answer was not "Bond. James Bond." His answer was: "Dolemite, motherfucker!" We would wait for that line in all of his movies. "Get Whitey" would show up in every single movie at least once, and we would wait for that, too.

They had the cars. They had the shoes. They had the guns. The haircuts. The slang. And the scams. And we all knew that all those beatific resolves at the end of the movie were white bullshit. He's trying to feed hungry children but he's actually a pimp . . . bullshit. That was designed to make it palatable to our moms and dads so they'd let us go see the picture.

It still rings true. But it was the first time that blacks in cinema really had a position of power. Of strength and authority. So we adopted all of the slang, all of the style of dressing and walking and so forth. There was also a tremendous sense of humor in those pictures. The actors knew that some of this was deeply superficial. And when something's deeply superficial you're talkin' about reality.

So when it came time—not terribly much later—to start getting on stage and doing what I do for a living, I took elements of comics and soul. I took Superfly and introduced him to Spiderman. I took Sly and the Family Stone, welded them together with the Human Torch. And I flamed on a whole fuckin' generation. Dolemite, motherfucker!

Right around that same time, several things happened

to me, or for me, that gave me an overview that I wouldn't have had otherwise. The first was '67, about half a year before I turned thirteen. I got my first job in an effort to buy my first real stereo. I shoveled shit at a local horse stable, in Pasadena, all three months of the summer vacation for a hundred and fifty dollars. I worked with a group of fellas who spoke *no* English. They were all Mexican illegals. I began to explore that culture a little bit, from the inside out. These were all cats who were makin' fifty dollars a week and living over the horse stalls, communally. So I got to see the working blueprint of the real workin' man. Not the way the working man's been depicted, or at least *had* been depicted, but the working man the way he is in most of the world.

The stables is where I learned to roll a cigarette, because there was a foreman—a guy who used Vaseline in his hair. The single most impressive scene I had ever seen to date occurred during my first season at the stable: He rolled a cigarette with one hand, on horseback. This was the ultimate mark. If I was Watusi, I would leave with a spear and come back with a lion. At Eaton Canyon stables in Pasadena, I'd be able to roll a cigarette with one hand.

Anyway, I had signed a contract with my father. I borrowed the money to buy the stereo, and I was to work for the summer to pay it back. This was to teach me to be independent and responsible. Well, it did. I didn't want to lose that stereo. *And* I had to buy my own records. The first two records that I actually *bought*—not shoplifted—were by Creedence Clearwater and Blood, Sweat and Tears.

Now I purchased this stereo after what was perceived as a racial incident in my junior high school.

Essentially, everybody was getting along. It was during gym class and we were playing flag football. Our team was all white, except for one black kid, and the other side was all black, except for one white kid. There was some conflict about a call, as far as how much yardage was actually gained, so I dutifully marched across the line of scrimmage and belted their white guy. They were then duty-bound to select one of their finest to come and belt our black guy. Half of us got tossed out of junior high school—for publicity purposes.

Indeed, we had *great* respect for each other. We knew where to draw the line. I didn't see it as racial at all. It's part of sports, man. It's Chinatown, Jake.

But the principal was right out of "Beavis and Butthead," and, in a grandstand play, threw half of each team out of school. Much to my parents' chagrin.

This happened right before Christmas, I was made to take a variety of entrance exams for private schools of the college preparatory nature, like Choate and Thacher, military schools, the works. Also the Webb School for Boys—it's now co-ed, has been for a number of years—back then, it was just for guys. It's a private boarding school in Claremont, California.

It was super-selective and exclusive. Lo and behold, on the entrance exams, I scored the highest in the history of the school on their humanities/reading comprehension/language skills, et cetera. The quintessential 99 $^1/_2$ out of 100. And I scored the *lowest* in the history of the school in the mathematics department. It was a 23 out of 100. Well, there was an instant flag on the play, there was a special case confab and I was allowed to go to Webb School.

I entered the world of rugby coaches, with names

like Ossery M. Butler III, late of the British Navy, who smoked a pipe on the field. The great biologist, Raymond Alf, was the biology teacher there. My classmates included the Prince of Thailand, the son of the Boeing aircraft fortune, the fella whose father had invented the Learjet, four-syllable white Anglo-somethin' names. I got a really good taste of what that lifestyle was about, what happens to a person when your family owns a yacht or two. I also learned what it meant to smoke Marlboros.

This was the kind of place where you had to wear a blazer, with the school emblem, to chapel every morning at seven-thirty, while they checked your rooms to see that they were cleaned. You would receive a little note in your mailbox when you needed a haircut. There were instructions. I remember a little yellow piece of paper that said "Your hair must be cut so that: 1) it is one-half inch above the ear, on the sides, so that, 2) it is half an inch, or more, above the collar of your shirt.

I lasted a semester. I was always in contest with the teachers, or whatever—I loved class . . . and if you wanted to see what that school was like, *exactly* what that was like, what the teachers were like, what the students were like, what I was like, just go rent *Dead Poets Society.* That was it.

We would have assembly three times a week. There couldn't have been more than five hundred guys there, if *that* many. There would be guest speakers; I remember a senator called the Silver Eagle, because of his silver-gray hair that was swept back and because he was so adamantly pro-Vietnam, pro-military. We sat and listened to him give his speech, and watched him bang his hand on the podium, about how we were going to "Bring the Vietcong to their knees." While Mr. Hooper, the

Headmaster, would kind of move around the edges of the assembly seats and check on our haircuts.

I came home on one of those seven-week breaks—after seven weeks, you got a three-day pass to go home. The fellas like the kid from Thailand just stayed at school. I remember coming home and watching the riots at the 1968 Democratic Convention; Mayor Daley's battalions were slugging it out with the demonstrators.

Big source of controversy when we got back to school, 'cause you either were a hippie or you came from a very well-to-do background, American nobility. Of course most of the seniors were very much established. They were all headed for Harvard, Princeton or Yale, at *worst* U.S.C. Us eighth and ninth graders were pretty much opposite. That conflict would represent itself in colorful ways.

For example, each grade of students had a monitor; it was like military school. It was a senior who was in charge of that dorm. There was a senior in charge of the eighth graders, one who was in charge of the ninth graders, and one who was in charge of the tenth, and so on. If you got too many demerits, you would lose privileges. Normally on the weekends for an afternoon, you could go down into the town of Claremont, go shopping, hit the record store, McDonald's. These weekend passes were critically important to us, because we would go sneak off into the orange grove and smoke cigarettes. If you got a certain number of demerits, you were either looking at lock down, which meant you couldn't go into town that weekend, or you could get a swat from the senior who had a paddle that was passed from senior to senior, each year or each semester. You could get a swat and go downtown, or, you could not get the swat and stay in your room.

I *still* have marks.

But twice a year, there was a day—I forget what it was called—it was like a Sadie Hawkins kind of thing, where everybody could dress as wildly and bizarrely as they absolutely wanted, especially at meals.

We would put toothpaste on our faces, like warpaint, and make our hair into three hundred little braids. Wear funny sunglasses, wear pillowcases to class, and so forth. And you were allowed to challenge your dormitory monitor, the senior, to an exchange of swats. Okay? You could challenge him. He didn't have to take up the challenge, but this was a true test of manhood. No senior would pass on an exchange of swats with a ninth grader. That would be a fall from grace that could never be reversed. We all had to take a craft class once a week; it was on Wednesday nights—metal shop, outdoorsmanship, sculpting . . . I took wood class.

Two of my other pals and I came up with a piece of wood that we found in the orange grove one weekend. It had to be an eight-by-four. It was eight inches wide and four inches thick. It took almost a month to create it. 'Cause this thing was a monster. It was a paddle as long as a Louisville Slugger, and it took two hands to wield it. I drilled holes through it, so that the air could escape, so you could make more impact upon contact. I didn't even want the thin layer of air to buffer the emotional content that I was preparing to deliver.

I painted it gloss black, put white adhesive tape all up and down the handle, for the no-slip grip, and we painted "The Annihilator" in white letters, from end to end. All the underclassmen knew about it.

Came the big day, the entire underclass turned out for the challenge. I marched out in the little area; the building had three sides to it, like a horseshoe. You would go out into the little clearing, and call up to the senior's room—they always had the same room—and you would call him out. Everybody stood around in a big circle, and I called him out. The senior came down.

I challenged him to an exchange of swats. He laughed. Now, he had brought his paddle, which was wafer-thin. By then, I had become numb to his ministrations. Then I unveiled The Annihilator. It was under a bath towel. And he refused to exchange swats. Everybody went silent. This had never happened, to anybody's recollection; fable-wise or otherwise—that a senior would refuse a swat from an underclassman. And there was dead silence. We all knew that his life had ended. That he had committed hara-kiri, that he would never be an acceptable, heterosexual human being in the eyes of any other senior. And that in biblical fashion, I had destroyed everything he'd stood for, without even drawing my sword.

I received a letter, at home, several weeks later asking me not to return for the next semester. The words used were "failure to adjust" to the Webb School lifestyle. I learned that Scott and Griff, who were my two partners, received the same letter.

So I went back to public school.

What's curious now, is I've been asked—on several occasions—to come and talk to the school, to be the guy at the podium. Particularly when Van Halen was at its peak years. I must have received three, four different requests, to come down and lecture the school. 'Cause now its co-ed, and I'm *certain* that it's a bit more liberal. But for me it was still the Dead Poets Society. It was military school. The only thing missing was the uniforms.

Drugs are always included in descriptions of the mid-to-late sixties. Up until that point, seems like everything was medicine cabinet. It was rare to run into somebody with some pot. The pot party was something for parents to be terrified of, at all costs. We couldn't *wait* to get invited to one. Especially since none of us had ever *been* to one.

May 14, 1968, I smoked pot for the first time, during the Old Fashioned Days Parade in Altadena, with my buddies Bob and Larry. Bob got some grade-C reefer from his older brother, and we smoked it behind the First National Bank building while the parade passed by.

I went on to smoke a lot of pot with Barry, over the years. I remember the first time he got his driver's license, sixteen years old, borrowed his parents' car. We were driving along on a pretty empty suburban street in Altadena. I dropped the roach down on the floorboards, Barry went over to pick it up, and we crashed.

This was not the "go" point for a drug-fueled existence from that first joint. The trappings, the ritual of it, were way more important.

Things like LSD, magic mushrooms, mescaline . . . these all had social trappings way beyond "Hey, this is a lot of fun." We junior high schoolers, we were already aware of the downsides of that kind of life—of burnout cases and acid flashbacks, and what have you.

That same year, I came home very late from work at the stable. I'd been smokin' pot with some of my co-workers. I was already a workin' man, to my way of thinking. I'd worked all day, shoveling shit, made exactly nothin'. I came home, and I was feelin' a little low key. My mother said, "What's the matter? You look a little pale. Look tired."

"Mom," I said, not thinking, "I smoked a little pot after work. I'm really tired. I think I'm just gonna go to bed."

She started screaming. This is 1968. They're still showing movies like *Reefer Madness* at movie theatres. I don't mean like, midnight movies at the Nuart, where it's cool to go and mouth the words 'cause you've seen it ten times in a dormitory when you were a fraternity brother. She starts screaming, "Oh my God! Oh my God! Nate! Nate!" Calling my father. "He's been smoking pot! He looks sick! He says he's tired, and he wants to sleep! Should we let him sleep, or should we keep him awake?"

"I don't know, Sibyl, try and relax, I don't know. Son, how do you feel?"

"Oh, I'm a little tired, and I'd like to go to bed."

"All right, let's go upstairs."

Went upstairs, pulled my boots off, laid back on the bed. My father's just kind of watching me. I don't know what he's looking for—eye movement? I don't know. I must have appeared at least in stable condition, to a surgeon. But *nobody* knew what pot was about. It was a *drug*. Like LSD, like heroin! Who knows?

I was laying on the bed, with my hands behind my head, just kind of staring at the ceiling, feeling very mellow, ready to go to sleep. My mother is crouching behind my father, with her hands on his shoulders, she's going, "Oh my God. What are we gonna do? Should we let him sleep? He says he wants to sleep."

My father got a little irate at that point, turned around, and he said, "Sibyl, you've gotta relax. Look. Let me handle this. Take the girls," meaning my two sisters, "and go to McDonald's and get 'em some dinner."

As she started to walk out of the room, with her head in her hands, I remember sitting up, like Dracula out of the coffin, going, "I'd like a couple of Big Macs, a large fries and a large pop."

She came *running* back to the bedside, and they were both staring at me in the face, and she's going, "Do you think it's okay for him to eat? Do you think it's okay?"

I remember my father saying, "I think it'll be okay."

All the early sixties drugs were not hip, because they didn't have the right social connotations. If it wasn't consumed at a love-in with five other people, it wasn't cool. But there was a *huge* market developing for uppers and downers amongst junior high and high school students in the mid-sixties, just because the whole drug culture was at the forefront. It was as evident and depicted as it is today. You hear about it on the radio, the TV, you read about it.

Two buddies of mine in the neighborhood were in on the program—let's call 'em Wayne and Garth. Garth was a party pal; not a real good home life, kind of a lost and wandering spirit, at an early age. He was about a year or two older than me. This is around eighth, ninth grade. Wayne was super academic, the kind of kid who had a chemistry set when he was in sixth grade, okay? He figured out a way to short-circuit the burglar alarms on the local pharmacy. He and Garth broke in one night, and showed up in *my* garage, where we had a little clubhouse, with probably eight-and-a-half pounds of pharmaceutical *everything.*

Every kind of upper, downer, morphine, cocaine—cocaine came in these big Mallincroft bottles. A *quart* of cocaine, pure pharmaceutical. I really had no idea what to do with *any* of it. It scared *me.* Scared Wayne. Garth? He was ready to climb every mountain.

But that whole drug awareness culture was just kicking in. The idea of how popular it was, or wasn't, gonna be, was not yet upon us as a nation. Teachers were just becoming aware of it. These two fellas sold every single ounce of everything that they had stolen. They had the best record collections you could possibly imagine—the best stereo equipment, best everything.

They went and knocked off *another* drugstore in the neighborhood. An even *better* record collection followed.

One day, Wayne's mom is going through his closet, for some reason or other, and discovers a five-pound bag of every kind of pill you can spell. Now, keep in mind, except for Garth, Wayne and I were still waiting for somebody to sell us some pot.

When Wayne's mom discovered a five-pound bag of pills, she took it back to the drugstore, gave it to the druggist.

Over the years, Garth had been shipped off to half a dozen foster, psychological care homes, had run away from home, was living in back in my garage, on a mattress, for some months, this sort of thing. He disappeared into the abyss. Wayne owns a security company that installs burglar alarms and security systems for corporate concerns, internationally. I swear to God, wild or what?

I had another friend . . . let's call him Bobby.

Bobby left high school early and went to Kathmandu, in Nepal. In the late sixties, early seventies, it was not anything like it is now. It was right out of the 1300s. It was Constantinople in the 1300s. Bobby brought back almost six thousand pounds of hashish in the hull of a trawler that leap-frogged out of Nepal. He had made literally over a million dollars. That was his cut. There were three other guys involved in this. He'd made over a million bucks by the time he was twenty-four.

That was standard. That was so constant, because it was considered hip, it was considered cool to do. These weren't cocaine connections, per se, although cocaine was hip as well, because you knew the Rolling Stones were doing it. You knew that a variety of popular musicians were getting involved in that. It was considered a cool thing to do.

I'm at the age now where I know a whole lot of dead guys, a lot of whom were involved in all of this back in the mid-late sixties. This is where we all kicked off, and as I tell you the story of Wayne and Garth, and I tell you the story of Bobby, you can see how we steered off. There's more than one off-ramp on that highway. And I've seen a whole lot of people go down both off-ramps.

Everybody might tell you that. But they're horse-shitting you. They haven't seen it. They read about it. Or they heard about it by proxy. These are guys I actually went to school with, guys that I would sit and listen to records with.

What's curious now, after wandering around inside and outside of the "drug culture," since I was basically twelve, thirteen years old, is: Look at me. I'm a multi-millionaire, my name is as known as the guy on the dollar bill. I'm Mr. Fortunate—I wrote a couple of Beethoven's Fifth Symphonies, and they'll pay my way, they'll pay for my dance lessons and my Mexican cigarettes for probably the rest of my life. It's already done that.

"Ple-eeze sta-aay off-ff the towers-ss an-and, don't take the bro-own aci-id."

"Hey, man, you got any papers?"

I was there when that shit was invented.

An important balancing factor for me, throughout all of this party-referencing, drug culture, hippie-dip Haight-Ashbury whatever, was the martial arts. Karate and kung fu were every bit as tightly woven into the general social fabric as long haircuts and bell-bottom blue jeans. Every movie had kung fu karate in it, whether it was James Bond or Foxy Brown, whether it was Blaxploitation, or whether it was Secret Agent Man, whether it was Green Hornet or Quinn Martin Productions.

It was a discipline that carried me through. *All* of it. I participated in everything, to one degree or another, but throughout all of it, I followed a two-thousand-year-old art form.

I was involved in Ed Parker's kenpo karate. Four times a week Mr. Parker was *not* my best friend. Mr. Parker was considerably more based—I think it was called "the Palama ghetto"—in Hawaii, having trained with all of those characters coming out of there, way more than he was relating to a middle-class thirteen-year-old saying, "Hey man, do you know who Hendrix is?" He was schooled at the end of a stick, and so was I.

Shinai! That means . . . it's like a false sword, it's a piece of bamboo, about four-and-a-half, five feet long, and it's split down the sides, and then tied, at maybe four-inch intervals, with twine, so that it doesn't split any farther. And you can really whack somebody with it and not have it split apart. You use it for sword training—when you see kendo class, you know, with the helmets, the breast plates, and the skirts, they're using shinai.

It's also a training tool. It's the equivalent of the teacher whacking you on the knuckles with a ruler. But if you screwed up in karate class, you got hit with the stick. It wasn't the human hand in a gentle, re-supportive touch that guided you down the path of proper whatever.

That was always my contrast. It was the antithesis of what was hippie, or what was populist culture, what our haircuts looked like. I'm so thankful that I did it.

I still do it, every day. *Every* day. I do the same stretch that I learned the very first day I went to train with Mr. Parker, as a young teenager.

In tenth grade, that's right about when we all started turning "of age" to get driver's licenses. Fifteen-and-a-half for your learner's permit, a '57 Chevy Bel Air was the ultimate. That's what the white kids drove, and you could get one for about eleven hundred bucks. Then you'd go to work on it. You'd put slicks on it, and you'd raise it up, and get the hood scoop, and take it down to Tijuana and get a fifty-five-dollar diamond-tuck upholstery job. The diamonds would be two different colors, like pink and purple.

Or you'd get chocolate and ivory. Pink and black. What else? Yellow and black was an incredibly white set of colors to get. It would cost, literally, fifty-five bucks, and they'd be done at the end of the weekend. You'd take it, you know, like on Friday night, you'd make the trek, and then you'd drop the car off Saturday morning, and stay out in Tijuana, and hang out all night, and come back Sunday afternoon and pick up your brand new used car.

You would take the baffles out of the pipes, so it would be much louder and much throatier.

At that point in time, of course, not everybody had a car. But everybody had an older brother, whatever, who was up in eleventh, twelfth grade, and you would ride around, six and eight to a car.

That year, for me, can be summed up in three songs: "Whole Lotta Love," by Led Zeppelin, Mungo Jerry's "In the Summertime" and Alice Cooper's "I'm Eighteen." "Eighteen . . . and I don't know what I want!" Killer. Those were the songs on the car radio.

So '57 Chevies were baad. Let's just stop, right at that word. 'Cause right around tenth grade was when that word started to become part of the mood. Up until then, you didn't really use the word *bad. Bitchin'* was used up through the sixties—that's a surf word, comin' out of, you know, '63, '64. Or dare I say it? "Groovy." But, even then, we laughed when we said it.

The idea of being "bad" didn't really kick in until like, 1970, and it was part of an overall attitude change. Instead of a bunch of people at a love-in, and everything was "groovy" and "cool," bands like Led Zeppelin showed up. They weren't about "fun," in a "I'm a Pepper, you're a Pepper" sense.

Well, in tenth grade, there was a day off from school so we could all attend the demonstration out on the girl's field against the bombing of Cambodia. A couple of bands played; Carl Donaldson's band played Jimi Hendrix's *Band of Gypsies* stuff, and some old Cream stuff. The government was sneaking around, there was another acceleration in the war.

Jimi Hendrix died that year, Janis Joplin died that year.

And the mood turned from love-in into more of a rally kind of thing. Things got a little more unfriendly. Led Zeppelin was not "friendly." Alice Cooper was not "friendly." Grand Funk Railroad, Black Sabbath . . . these were not friendly attitudes. The predecessors to punk rock, grunge, whatever. There was a lot of discontent. And visions of a beautiful, utopian future—the Age of Aquarius—turned into Cambodia. And Jimi Hendrix turned into a poster.

The music reflected that. And the stage shows reflected that. Suddenly, there was a little more of a violent edge to things. Or at least the attitude of violence. The ultimate compliment was if somebody called you and said, "You 'baad.'" Now, this had been part of old black jive, on and off, a long time. "Bad-ass." Yeah, but white kids didn't use it until the late sixties.

Remember the Chicago Seven Trial? Abbie Hoffman, Jerry Rubin, and the others. And they gave 'em to a guy named Judge Julius Hoffman, who had the *ultimate,* right-wing, old-school, Eisenhower-era legal attitude. So I remember he had one of them bound and gagged during much of the trial.

Every one of them was a cartoon, right out of the Fabulous Furry Freak Brothers. And they behaved like that in court—made fun of the judge, wore clown suits to the trial, that kind of thing. It was a pop trial. When they were acquitted, they all threw the power salute. But that was political. In tenth grade, people started throwing the power salute at rock concerts. It was something besides political, it was bein' baad. Bein' baad together.

Right around tenth grade buying a T-shirt of your favorite band was crucial. Same thing for football teams, baseball teams and so forth. I don't mean just a shirt that said "Dodgers," but a *person.* A picture of Sandy Koufax. Or a picture of Jimi Hendrix playing the guitar, with the flames coming out the back.

It became just as important to get the T-shirt as it was to actually have gone to the show. If you couldn't go to the show, you had your friend get you a T-shirt.

It totally bespoke of who you were and where you were going. You saw somebody with a Black Sabbath T-shirt, you knew *exactly* who that person was. Somebody with a Led Zeppelin T-shirt? You knew *exactly* who that person was.

By the way, in tenth grade I got my first blow job. It was from a girl named Cheryl, who was very advanced in a number of ways. She was a big, busty, very mature gal. Great lookin', in a Jayne Mansfield kind of way.

She was always up helping the biology teacher, who was also the swim coach, who looked like Remington Steele. So you kinda knew somethin' was up. And it probably belonged to the swim coach. Cheryl and I just fell in together one night, at Frank Sousa's party, when his parents went off to Mexico to go scuba diving. We went around the corner from his house, and stood in a driveway, just around inside of the hedge. She got down on her knees, and I remember looking right over her head. The shades were open in the living room of this neighbor's house. You could see the back of the owner's head—he was a little bald guy—and he was watching Johnny Carson. Buddy Hackett was the guest.

Well, maybe it's not much to you, but I like to think back.

Ignition

There was a blues revival from 1967 to 1969, and nobody really got it. If you go back through the Stones and Eric Clapton, most of these people were art school students. Who else is gonna dig up dead guys like Blind Lemon Muddy Someone? *Only* an art student. Or a philosophy major, what have you, but nobody who *works* for a living. They just served it up direct. You had the Paul Butterfield Blues Band, Mike Bloomfield, James Cotton, but The Doors played blues. If you listen to most of their songs they're blues format: One-four-five, twelve bar repetition.

But nobody really thought of it as that.

Jimi Hendrix was unique—to a degree. Lonnie Mack, B. B. or Albert King, and others were all of Jimi's references and inspirations, where he learned to play. Now, go back and listen to that music, with that in mind, and you'll hear he's playing classic blues licks. Yes, he got involved in distortion as a means of gainful employment and feedback—great! But it's just not far off from classic B. B. King, Albert King kinds of riffs.

But nobody knew it. There were blues musicians. . . . "Blues band" was a great thing to have attached to the name: The Steve Miller, The Carlos Santana Blues Band, you know. But most of it was classic blues. That's the way the singers sang it, that's the way guitar players played it, and then, moving on, in 1969 when Led Zeppelin came out—and nobody thinks of them as a blues band—that was hard rock, that was heavy metal. Bull. It was classic, quintessential blues. Most of that stuff: "You Shook Me All Night Long," et cetera . . . are old Muddy

Waters blues songs. They did a different arrangement, but if you listen to Jimmy Page play with that in mind, you hear it's *nothing but* classic blues riffs. Changed the sound of the amplifier, changed the sound of the guitar, gave it his own emotional tone. I've purchased those records and I salute them. But it's blues. The son of a frog is also a frog.

Right at the end of the eleventh grade, there were a lot of hormones in the air. And nothing represented this better than the first ZZ Top album. This is classic blues. You listen to it, it's just blues, but it's played with force, and it's absolutely American. Texas. It's *beyond* American. American was a chip off the Texas stone. All you ever had to do was see a John Wayne movie and you knew that. This is the first time Texas became hip.

And this is the same blues that we were listening to, in terms of the Stones trying to imitate John Lee Hooker, you know, "Little Red Rooster." They're tryin' to sing like Muddy Waters. And, in '71, '72, right in there, ZZ Top opened for the Rolling Stones. And just like the Persuasions before them, got kicked off the tour.

Lead bass and drums. The only thing that had been even close to this was the Jeff Beck group. Listen, it sounds like old Jeff Beck. But Jeff was just stealing old black guys' stuff. Listen to that ZZ Top bass player. He knows barbecue sauce. This band comes from the land of the hubcap and the clothesline, and they're both in the *front* yard. And the hubcaps are there for the kids to play on.

Another band that really swarmed was Grand Funk Railroad. It didn't have the substance of the blues, yet it was a blues band. Grand Funk Railroad kind of veered from that, didn't convey so much of a lifestyle. This was a place that you wanted to go visit. You wanted to go to a roadhouse bar where this band was playing.

We must have learned ten songs by Grand Funk. This is where Van Halen cut a lot of its forceful identity. These guys were obviously havin' a good time. These guys would do the thing, with two guitar players dancing back and forth, which was essentially Paul Revere and the Raiders doin' steps all over again but better.

ZZ Top represented exactly what reggae came to represent a few years later, when Bob Marley landed upon these shores, that was a kind of music that you could dance to and not spill your beer. You're thinkin' that through your head right now, aren't you? Your version. But you already know the step. Just hold it out in front of you . . . there you go. Now groove.

You gotta remember, the operative word now is "baad." That's what it meant, when you went out in your '57 Chevy Bel Air to drink a beer, when you went out to smoke a joint. It stopped being that kind of quasi-political peacenik love-in thing. It became the ritual of Saturday Night-ism, the kind that required police presence. Or at least a higher police presence.

Excuse me, I have to groove. Backyard parties. You'd do it just the way you'd spell it.

Backyard parties. What traditionally would happen, somebody's parents would take a vacation. It starts that simple. The great journey *always* begins with a simple step. Living around the Pasadena area, there was everything from lower-middle-class welfare daddies to upper-middle-class daddies, who belonged to the Allendale Golf Club. Houses that have a guest house. And the kid lives in the guest house.

So it's tenth or eleventh, twelfth grade, right? Junior now has moved out of the house. Lives in the guest house. He lights candles. A little black light, maybe, some Allman Brothers. He's always got the reefer—which he rolls on top of an album cover. Later on, I liked to tell people that Van Halen album covers were specially engineered. They'd say, "How do you mean?"

I'd say, "Well, you'll notice, if you take it, and you just hold it. You put one corner in your mouth, and—you need a partner, you know, Van Halen's partner music—and you hold the nine o'clock and three o'clock corners in your hands, get your partner to hold the other one. If it's a she, get her to hold the other in her teeth, so you're kinda lookin' at each other. You put your reefer right in the middle, and just kind of crumple it, make your thumb go up and down on your middle finger and the other one, and you get it right in the middle, okay? With your right hand, you kind of, like, you know how you tink somebody on the back of the head? You take your thumb, and hold back your middle finger and you go 'tink,' very, very gently right underneath the album cover, and you tilt it ever-so-slightly, and all the seeds will run out."

You would visit the kid who was now living in the guest house, by the little kidney-shaped pool. His parents would ultimately go on some kind of a vacation and you would have a party.

Now, the low end of the spectrum was a house party: stereo playing, somebody spinning records—it would usually be a gal, at that level. I say "gal" because to say "girl" means, like, too young, and to say "woman," well, it's too early to say "woman." Really. "Gal" was right in the middle. To be a woman takes distance. So it's purely complimentary, you know, as well as descriptive.

So it would be a gal, one who had the wherewithal to put a bowl of chips next to the bowl of dip. Whereas a guy wouldn't do either one. A *guy* would count on another guy to bring the stereo and *that* wouldn't happen. There would be a fight, ultimately. Which isn't saying that that was a bad party, but the gals tended toward the contrary. Makes the world go around. Fills the proverbial dance floor, if you know what I'm saying, and I think you do.

We would dance to Sly and the Family Stone, a little Rolling Stones, a lot of Marvin Gaye. 1970 to 1972, that's high school for me. Marvin Gaye, "What's goin' on?" was happenin'. James Brown, absolutely.

We could end the book right here and I would feel spiritually validated and fulfilled as a man, as a philosopher and a competitor in the rat race. Hot pants. Quote the great James Brown, "Use what you got, to get what you want/hot, hot pants!" Oh my God. Her hot pants started late and ended early. And you had the matching go-go boots. "These boots are made for walkin'," Nancy Sinatra kind of white marching boots. Wow. That just focused everything.

We started going to backyard parties that had more of a barbecue element, a gathering of the tribes, "une grande fête." And at these parties . . . they would hire a *band.* The premiere party, every year, was at my pal Stan Swanteck's house on Michigan Street, just below Washington. Right down from the Washington Theater, starring the Mack . . . "He's full of lead an' he still ain't dead!"

Stan had three brothers. His oldest was a few

years older than us, so when we were in tenth grade, Stan's brother Joe was in senior year. Squeezin' the best-lookin' tenth grader, of course. Sandy, I think, was her name. Oh my God. If you look in the dictionary, to this day, under "hot pants," there's a picture of Sandy.

Joe would throw the Swanteck party once a year, toward the hot months, somewhere around May or June. It was always very well attended. You bought your Budweiser malt liquor a month in advance for this one. You started to ice it down two weeks in front. You began to starch your jeans.

When I say, "starch your jeans," it means you get regular jeans, and you iron them yourself, and you use the entire can of spray starch. Okay? And you gotta let it dry, and then you iron it again, let it dry, and iron it again. This was, like, a half an afternoon kind of vibe. You would go over to the kid who lived in the guest house at his parents' house now, and there would be an ironing board and an iron. We'd smoke pot and listen to records, and we'd take turns ironing our pants. Or the girlfriends would iron the pants, and the guys would be there. This is cut right out of the side of the river in Senegal or something. The women are beating the shit with rocks, and the guys are sitting around smoking and bragging and telling lies.

The girls would iron the pants until they were like a *board.* You could tell when you were thoroughly starched, when your shit was right, in that you could hold the pants out from about four inches *above* the knee, and they would stick out, straight. You'd have these razor creases, you know, in the front and the back. An option was to make a cuff, and starch the cuff into place as well. You used the *entire* can of spray starch. Can you dig it? It was quite a ritual.

You'd be waxin' up the car, and pullin' out the baffles to get it to sound that baritone groan, you know, pickin' out the tapes. You would rewind your eight-tracks, because with eight-tracks, you couldn't just hit rewind. You had to know the song on the other side of the tape that corresponded with the song that you wanted to hear, fast-forward it *all* the way to the song on the other side, and then flip the tape. So it really paid, especially if you connived a girl into your car, to have the tape ready. Precious moments could be lost while you're searchin' for the right song.

Of course, your command over the tape deck indicated just how much of a man you were. So you would have to rewind the tapes to get 'em near the top of the song—but not right at the *top* of the song, 'cause that showed that you had a *plan*. You did about thirty seconds of the song before, you know, like it was all uncalculated. As you were driving to the party you had your tapes set. You put 'em in order and shit, 'cause if you move right to Barry White . . . okay, man, your cards are out in the open. You would have to play something like, "I don't care, we're all just havin' a great time, isn't that right, sugar honey?" You know, the Allman Brothers live at the Fillmore. Some Van Morrison. Kind of ease into the program. Put on a little Marvin Gaye, still heavily rhythmic, but hey now, "What's he singin' about?"

"Don't worry, baby—he's black."

Can you dig it? And you wind up with Barry White or Roberta Flack. "Killing me softly, baby. . . . " Yeah. Kill me, baby.

Backyard parties developed into an art form. J. C.

Agajanian, the famous auto-racing promoter, had a nephew who lived in a house with five bedrooms and a big pool, and lots of space. So when his folks would split, two, three times a year, there'd be a *massive* party. Well over two hundred people would show up. This was right about the time, going to one of these parties, that I first saw the Van Halens. It's the brother and the brother, you know, the guitar player and the drummer, with the bass player, doing note for note, *verbatim* renditions of The Who, *Live at Leeds,* or Deep Purple, "Smoke on the Water," or shit from Woodstock, when Alvin Lee comes out and plays "Goin' Home" faster than any known human being on earth, or at least up until that time—Edward could do *that* lick. You know, it was *amazing* stuff.

Playing at those parties got competitive fast. 'Cause I got into a band the last year of high school, right in there, '72, and we made the impossibly forward-thinking move of *renting* a little stage from Abbey Rents. It was about nine inches tall, with little risers, like they do at union meetings.

We set up the band on this little stage. Oh, nobody'd *ever* seen anything like this, God. We took some of the money from the proceeds, and rented a little PA system. Altec Lansing 15/20s, I think. With a horn and a fifteen-inch speaker in each cabinet. Well, a horn and a fifteen-inch speaker on either side is what Dr. Dre is sitting on when he takes off down Whittier Boulevard today. But back then it was impossibly cutting edge—we had upped the ante.

I got into a band called the Red Ball Jets, named after a sneaker. We played "Johnny B. Goode" for twenty-five minutes at a time, some Rolling Stones songs. And our musicianship level, our musicality, between a one and a ten, was a solid five, a solid six on a good night. There was no signature sound to it, but we *had* a helluva show. 'Cause I was already Diamond Dave. I had pants with the pleats and the little sweater, little sleeveless sweater that just goes right to the top of the pants, you could see a little bit of belly button, maybe some suspenders—that was a little bit aggressive, but can you dig what I'm sayin'? Shag haircut that I drove down to Balboa Island to get, little Cuban heels—not two-toned shoes in a gangster sense, but a stripe that ran right down the middle, from the laces to the toe. Blue and tan.

Halfway through singing at a party, I'd take my suspenders down and let 'em hang around my butt, and that really showed I was workin'. We were a pretty big hit on the backyard circuit. We entered into *immediate* competition with the Van Halens, who at the time were called Mammoth, a typical kind of rock band name—nondescript. (It would be my idea to call the band Van Halen. They wanted to call the band Rat Salade, named after a Black Sabbath song. I said, "No." I felt the name Van Halen was like the name Santana.)

There was conflict and rumormongering between bands. During their set, the Van Halens stood around like the guys in Nirvana. They wore Levi cords with the boxer shorts stickin' out and a T-shirt, and just sort of stood there, but their music was spectacular. Chain-smoked Camel filters. They had girlfriends, Alex's girlfriend would sit behind him on a little packing case while he played drums.

We Red Ball Jets were in belligerent competition with Mammoth.

We'd compete for whose parties were the best and

the biggest. There were a couple little park gigs, in the public park. The Youth Community Center, the recreation center of the Pasadena Youth Organization, would have some bands playing. People would gather on the field at sundown, and some rock bands would play—just beginning rock bands, you know, high school, junior college. But these gigs were to be *fought* over venomously.

That was the first stage of "I'm gonna be somebody!" I was bound and determined to go places. Playing at the Agajanian's party was the first place you had to get to.

Youth Club dances . . . they weren't an alternative, they were chaperoned, they were screened and controlled. People were watching you—they would follow you outside to see if you were smoking Marlboros. You weren't allowed to kiss the girls and make them cry.

All those gals from Alverno Heights and Saint Francis, the Catholic girls' schools, the thoroughbreds, I suddenly had entree to. If I could perform in a band, at one of these parties, well, *all* those girls were in attendance. Suddenly, it became what later on, during the Gulf War, was known on CNN as "a target-rich environment."

Okay now, I'm leaping ahead here, in the party schism, because I didn't actually join the Van Halens until probably late '74. But we began to play the backyard parties, as well as dance clubs, Top 40 cover-band, dance clubs or whatever. But the first critical step, first base, was to play the backyards.

In Van Halen, we were the first to get lights. We'd go and steal floodlights from the lawns of little apartment complexes all over Pasadena, at one in the morning. You know, those little red and blue and amber and green floodlights that sit in those little Formica cones?

The ones that shine on two palm trees or against the wall where it said something like Winston Apartments. You would take an Ironboy work glove, 'cause the lamp would be really hot by one in the morning; you could unscrew it manually. You'd carry a paper bag to put it in.

We made three boxes that would accommodate five colors: Red, blue, yellow, green, and off. "Off" being the most important color, because then you knew it was the end of the song. You *knew,* man, 'cause we'd hit a note . . . boom! Very cool.

Your color green served as white; you'd throw that light on, you'd know you were into the next little episode, the next little segment. This was run by a foot switch that the bass player, Mike Anthony, worked. As well as doing backup vocals, he ran the foot switch for the lights.

We would stack these, two banks of each, on either side of the stage, on the little PA system, on this little bar stage. Nobody had ever seen anything like this. This was full-scale production value. Talk about bang for your buck!

Just to complicate things, same time period, somewhere in '71, if you read magazines, and you were plugged into underground radio, you became aware of a fellow named David Bowie. Bowie was not anything like the David Bowie that you can think of today. He was Ziggy, the spider from Mars, the thin white duke. He was every bit that zero percent body fat, wasted lifestyle, superhero, bizarre.

You would read stuff, in *Circus* or *Creem* magazines, "David and his wife Angela Bowie's makeup hints." Nobody even gave it a second thought. They would describe the rice makeup that he would use to get that Kabuki vibe. What he had done was mix Kabuki with science fiction. Platform shoes, vacuum-packed spandex, the butch haircut that all of my lesbian girlfriends adopted instantly, if not sooner.

David looked like he was from Neptune, forget Mars. That old saw of "I come from a planet far, far away, Darlene," could well have been tattooed across his anorexic butt. He caused a fury and a slew of questions and outrage . . . wow. And the word *unisex* slammed into our public consciousness. I asked somebody at a club the other night, "Excuse me, where's the men's room?"

He says, "It's unisex."

I get it. He's being kitsch and shtick, by referencing an old early seventies word, because that's hip, just like early seventies pants—bell-bottoms. And early seventies haircuts. So, now, they say it's a unisex bathroom. I get it. Early seventies. How very pop.

The idea of unisex pants came into vogue because women started wearing pants, for the first time, to the workplace, to a party, to the beach, in 1971 and 1972. Until then—no, no, no. You might run into Marilyn Monroe being a tough guy in a pair of dungarees or chinos, outside a pickup truck in *The Misfits,* but it was not acceptable, standard fare. You'd catch one of my butch girlfriends wearing pants, absolutely. But not Pat Nixon.

Probably the most popular cartoon variation that you would ever see would take a little Martian talking to a garbage can, saying, "Take me to your leader." This is how we felt talking to our parents, our teachers, our probation officers. The way David looked is the way we *felt.*

It was at precisely this time period that I was

"allowed" to go to concerts. My first concert was late high school, Humble Pie at the Long Beach Arena. Up until then, I had to sneak off to concerts. Because, just like when *West Side Story* came out, I was forbidden to go see it.

When *Easy Rider* came out, I was not allowed to see it. I remember hitchhiking in the pouring rain, in 1969, to go see a double bill of *Woodstock* and *Easy Rider.* I saw both twice in a row because I knew I probably wasn't going back again in real short order.

Right at the end of high school, my parents gave in, and this is based on arguments at the family dinner table that revolved around things like, "When I'm able to, I'm gonna grow sideburns."

"No, you're not."

Until then, I had to crawl out the window, literally. Join up with some pals to go see Alice Cooper open for Led Zeppelin at the Rose Palace. To go see Janis Joplin and Iron Butterfly at the Pasadena Civic. That was in eighth grade. I *knew* that I was going to be missing a point in history. And I never got caught. Master of deception. Master of disguise. David Roth, at your service.

That's when I really signed off family existence. I discerned early that that really didn't exist geographically—it's all inside your head—or your shorts. I just discerned—correctly or incorrectly—that if I was gonna really maximize who or what I was as an artist, that I really had to live it. And breathe it. Well, it's that old climbing philosophy. If you cut the rope from below your feet, you're more apt to submit than retreat.

I graduated John Muir high school in 1972. They played "Samba Pa Ti" by Santana on a loop, over and over again, as we walked up to get our diploma's at the Rose Bowl. The Whispers played at our school prom, one of the black step bands, five guys who've been around *forever.*

I started heading out to Hollywood that year, to go to dance clubs, the most important being Gazzari's on the Strip. There was a band there called Thirteenth Hour. And they did Rare Earth's "Get Ready."

I would say, "Man, this is even better than backyard parties. I wanna get in on *this*. This is *great*! This is where all the heat's comin' from, this is where all the light's coming from." And Bill Gazzari had all these dancing girls, the Gazzari dancers, go-go girls. I determined that hey, this was the next step, my entree to Hollywood.

Never even stopping to think that I might have a potential to get into the Rainbow Bar & Grill, which was a full block down the street. That was just like, whoa—Led Zeppelin hung out there, the Rolling Stones hung out there.

A couple years later, when Van Halen kicked in, first place we headed for was Gazzari's on the Strip. We auditioned once, didn't make it; auditioned the second time, made it. Played "Smoke on the Water," by Deep Purple, "Hangin' Around" and "Free Ride" by the Edgar Winter Band. You know, the song goes: "Drivin' around with my stereo on, feelin' good . . . " and even then, I was being left of center: "Drivin' around with no underwear on. . . . "

But Bill Gazarri, the old codger, dug my sense of humor. For the first two years we worked there, he called me Van. It's a good thing I didn't come from a band named Pink Floyd. He would come up to me and he'd say, "Hey, Van. Boys did good pull this week. Here's the hundred and twenty-five dollars I owe you, for the last four nights, and here's twenty-five bucks for you."

I dutifully would go and split up that twenty-five bucks with the other guys in the band. Leaving Bill, of course, to think I was completely on the take. We bonded heavily.

Bill was a video pioneer. These *huge* cameras mounted on tripods, with these *huge* tape decks the size of a suitcase. Can you dig it? He would stop me as everybody was filing out to pack our equipment into our cars, and he's stop me. "Hey Van, hey Van, wanna see some of my films?"

I'd say, "Sure." He'd show me these films, and they'd always be cut off from the tits down, and here'd be this little dick, surrounded by gray pubic hair, with some hot little go-go mama just gorgin' herself.

"Hey, Bill, I didn't know you were an actor."

Bill would make a big production, after everybody else had gone, and they'd feature some of the girls, the dancers, the groupies, the bartendresses, whatever. He'd put a little piece of wood in the little windowlet, in the back door, and I knew that we were gonna commence education. He was gonna school me. He'd say, "All right, I wanna teach ya a lesson about the music business. First off, gimme your watch. Gimme your watch. Come here. Put it here."

I'd take my watch off, and he'd put it in his pocket, and he'd say, "You just learned a lesson."

Right after I graduated high school I attended Pasadena City College. Took theory and orchestration, music theory, these kinds of things. Talk about a fish out of water. Mathematics completely befuddle me. I can spell the word eight in nine languages, and *recognize* it in twelve. But I can't add it with *anything*.

I was in classes with the Van Halens. It was at this precise moment when all young new musicians are making that decision, "Are you going to go commercial? Are you going to be a sellout? Are you going to be a cloying, result-oriented infidel, making money?" Or are you going to pursue the classic Left Bank, "I come from nowhere, I go home to no one," kind of approach?

The Van Halens—as Mammoth—had been playing backyard parties for a number of years, were very adept at what they played, but they couldn't get any *jobs* at dance clubs. Now my band, Red Ball Jets, had broken up, and I had a little PA system that again I signed a contract with my father for, and worked to pay it off. A little club-size PA system. The Van Halens would come over to the house to rent my PA system when they'd play these parties.

But they *weren't* getting the shows in the bars. They couldn't understand why. I explained to them, one day, "It's because you play all twenty minutes of 'I'm So Glad' by Cream, complete with drum solo, live, note for note, and it's very impressive, but you can't dance to it." That's not "Excuse me, do you come here often?" music. The club owners described it as "too psychedelic." The band couldn't get arrested.

I said, "Now *I* can dance. And since you're always renting my PA system, and comin' back frustrated, *I'm* in a position to assist." I said, "I will personally check every song for danceability. And we'll play rock tunes, but ones that you can *dance* to." Like "Walk This Way" by Aerosmith. ZZ Top's "Waiting for the Bus." Or one of those songs, "Just Got Paid," that's a very *danceable* song. It's rock; you can dance to it.

They consented begrudgingly. Lo and behold, we started getting club gigs. We started working forty-five-minute sets a night, running the dance contest and so fourth.

What's more, they didn't have to pay me rent for the PA system anymore. It's what, in business, is called "an inducement."

At the same time, we were in junior college, Pasadena CC—theory and orchestration, music theory, harmonic structure, et cetera. I learned a tremendous amount, but was flunking out duly.

Ed Van Halen and I took vocalization class, learning to sing, learning how to use vibrato. For our final exam—it was a one-semester course—you had to do a song. And Edward played acoustic guitar, and did the Blind Faith tune "Can't Find My Way Home."

He played the guitar *exactly* like it was on the record. It was very impressive. I sang, "Go Away, Little Girl," the Donny Osmond version.

Alex Van Halen was knocking out eighteen-piece rock jazz ensemble arrangements for *West Side Story* that nobody could play, in 11/14 time—eleven beats per bar, and had to go from instrument to instrument, showing these befuddled students how to get to the first coda.

One of our teachers' claim to fame, at the time, was that he was a professor of music and Frank Zappa had studied under his tutelage. Now he brags that he trained the great Van Halen. From him, I learned a singular phrase that I use to this day: "If it sounds good, it *is* good." Two rules to music. Number one: If it sounds good, it *is* good. Number two: There ain't no other rule.

Well, I quit—auspiciously. But I did learn a handful of cool harmonic structures, a couple of hybrid chord structures, the basic theory of melody. Just little elements, bits and pieces. Played saxophone. Also took piano lessons. Got exactly nowhere, but still gleaned little elements here and there. More than anything, it taught me to make a commitment to what you were doing in music, because it was my first experience with detractors. My own colleagues were my detractors!

"Ehhh, you guys play ZZ Top and KC and the Sunshine Band and you get paid for it—you're a *sellout*!"

I had conviction behind that. It forced me to stand my ground, to reconnoiter my own position, in the face of harsh, critical assessment from my peer group.

We played the bars, religiously. As often as they would let us. We learned *hundreds* of other people's songs. James Brown, Ohio Players, Led Zeppelin, ZZ Top, didn't matter. We learned them. We played in places so small that Alex would have to tape his wallet to the skin of his snare drum with gaffer tape, because the owners would complain his snare drum was too loud. We would have to hang blankets in front of a single amplifier case 'cause the guitar was too loud.

This is where my pitch was first developed. "Hey, don't forget, ladies in free before nine, two for one, dance contest Wednesday, division finals twice a year, Happy Hour from five till February . . . " and on and on. You had to keep up the rap. And I would personally check every song for danceability (by dancing to it).

A totally hip car that would run effortlessly was eleven hundred dollars. A pair of *amazing* killer platform shoes, with boot tops that went up to your knee, from Fred Slatin's, cost sixty-five dollars, top of the line. A pair of pants, brand-new designer jeans, were about thirty bucks. Forty with tax.

I bought a little Opel Kadett station wagon for eleven hundred dollars; you could fit one PA speaker in the back compartment and one PA speaker on the top. All of the gear, the brains of it, you know the controls, in the passenger side.

I remember one day the passenger side window became unglued form the ratchet inside the door, and the glass fell inside, so I pulled the glass up with a pair of pliers, and plugged a couple of number two pencils into it, to keep the window up.

Ultimately, of course, the pencils popped out, going over the speed bumps where the Pasadena Freeway turns into the North Hollywood Freeway. The glass fell inside and smashed into a trillion little pieces inside the door; it sounded like a giant maraca. So on my next visit to the Salvation Army, I bought a big wool blanket, kept it in the backseat in case I went on a date. Girlfriend at the time would complain, "When are you going to do something about this?" her little haircut getting blown to pieces out on the freeway.

I said, "Honey, something's bein' done."

She says, "What's that?"

I said, "Summer's on its way."

Bumpered somebody coming home from the beach that summer. Wasn't looking, rolled four feet into the car in front of me, lunched the front bumper, dented the hood cover so hard they couldn't get the hood open. So for the next two years, I carried a shovel in the back of the car, in case I needed to open the hood. You'd have to get out there with the shovel and get some leverage.

I would come home from club gigs, and getting the PA speaker out of the back of the car was easy; getting it off of the top of the car, read: Six-foot-two, and I'm only six feet, in my stocking feet. So I'd pull it off of the edge, and start to fulcrum it, it would start to get off balance, and I'd get the base of it onto my chest, and start to lower it to my legs. I'd get the speaker comin' off the top of the car, and onto my chest, get it positioned, and then start lowering it, using my legs, bending my knees. You didn't want it to roll onto your side and break something—that meant money spent. I would routinely spend a half an hour in that bull-frog position, with a three-hundred-pound speaker sitting on my chest, trying to figure out, "Okay, where do I go from here?"

Today, I have the front of that car. A friend of mine, Ted Rosenthal, is an artist. I'd had the car sitting in the backyard ever since 1969, all the way up into the late eighties. Ted worked a lot with an acetylene torch. I had him cut off the whole front engine compartment, with the front tires and the grille, plus the whole front windshield. And in the hallway, in my house in Pasadena, at about five-and-a-half feet up the wall, we *bolted* the whole front engine compartment—sticks out of the wall by six-and-a-half feet, with the tires, and the grille, and the front window—and then we went to Ellis Mercantile, who supplies props and such for the movies, and bought a stuffed deer in full, bounding gait. Sawed it in half, right past the whithers, smashed out the driver's side part of the windshield, and stuck in just the ass and the back legs . . . like we drove the car and hit it and then somehow careened through the wall. The title of it is My First Deer.

* * *

Back to early Van Halen:

When I first joined the band, tried to sing some of the songs, there was Grand Funk Railroad, as well as Black Sabbath. The music was pretty alien to me. I didn't even own those records. I had to go to the Thrifty Drugstore to buy them. Did my best, which was awful, at the time, and the Van Halens were shocked and horrified. There was a conflict from the beginning. Now I perceive it as par for the course.

When Zeppelin got together, Jimmy Page *hated* Robert Plant, couldn't wait for him to be out of the band, figured that the band would be over in two albums. That's how they did it then. There's always constant shift and change, because all of your cool players, like the Jimmy Pages and Jeff Becks, were session guys as well. That's how they fed themselves, that's how they paid for their—ooh, here's a good group therapy word—proclivities. Show me a couple of yours and I'll show you one or two of mine. By the way, how do you finance yours?

These guys were all working sessions. The most you would expect was two albums, and then they're gonna be off somewhere because of schedule difficulties, going on the road, which is considerably more wearying than anybody lets on. It's a magnificent magic trick, and yes, it is absolutely the Emerald City times Henry Miller and Kiki's Paris with a Helmut Newton photograph and the Bee Gees on the stereo. At the same time you better learn to sleep in your clothes. Enough said for the time being.

Anyway, a couple of albums with the band, a couple

of tours, hey, it's going to take you a couple of tours' worth to recover whatever is left of your medical constitution. A lot of these guys are running on fumes and that may be what fuels their music, that desperate kind of "put your belts on, I think we can make it, but I'm not really sure"-ism.

I'm certain it's fueled some of my favorite rock epics, regardless. Zeppelin got together, they hated each other. Clash of the Titans. Mick and Keith? Their constant to-and-fro and reconciliations are a matter of history. It is part of the breakfast discussion. If you're important enough, you wind up at the breakfast table with everybody in the world. "So what do you think about such-and-such and—Roth?" And everybody knows what you're talking about. That's how you know you're breathing that rarefied air.

So, cut right from the classic stone, we had conflict right away. We were suspicious of each other, not exactly accepting, the sound was not there but the look was. Jesus, how do we get this all to match up? A lot of very opinionated cats, at least three of us.

Had an original bass player named Mike Stone, was more academically set to go to school and follow a more dependable path. But between the two Van Halens and me, we were very opinionated. A *lot* of argument. Created a competitive atmosphere. We really wanted to just have everybody undeniably go, "Okay, wow." When you got one of those happening into the air and up and surfing, everybody's egos were big enough and strong enough to also say, "Okay, that's—that's a wow." I mean, we accepted each other's "Hey, dude, that's a wow," more often than not.

Went in to play the parties. It was the first time I

really became aware of how possessive an audience could really be about a given artist or a given band. Way beyond "this is great music," it was almost as if it was football team time. "Hey, this is our band, they represent *us*." I came from another side of town, so to speak. The first time I sang with the band in a backyard party the audience hated it! So unanimously in fact that I knew I was onto something big.

They didn't have a singer before, really. Ed Van Halen sang the traditional tunes. Black Sabbath, Deep Purple, Grand Funk Railroad, et cetera. And he held down the fort fairly well. I remembered seeing him at youth club dances, you know, high school things. Singing was just an addition, just to get it up and going.

When I got into the band, I was ridin', I was up. I went ballistic right off. Completely confounded, confused and baffled and amazed and stunned and astonished their backyard party audience, which was large. A good backyard party would easily pull six hundred kids. Charge a dollar at the door, band would get one hundred and twenty-five bucks. Kegs of beer. You knew right about ten o'clock, you got a little tired of playing, you just turned the volume up a tad, the police would show up with the new helicopter part of their "Eye in the Sky" program. Wow. A lot of police officers were vets, and so things were particularly athletic, but there was never any serious injuries or conflicts, just a lot of running after and being chased by. Eleven cop cars show up parked in a line, all with the flashing lights and a lot of flares. It was all very exciting and kind of scary, and you might go to jail, and your parents might have to come get you out, and even maybe pay for a friend or two. It was great.

One night, the Van Halens are playing in a pool of beer, and we had rented a Trooperette spotlight. You'd plug it into a wall, didn't require a generator, little Trooperette, it was fifty-five dollars for the night. We'd put it on top of the workshed, which is on the other side of the swimming pool, and shine it down on us. You'd open it up wide enough that you've got the whole band until there was some singing or a solo or something like that, then you would make the spot smaller so you could bring some focus to the proceedings.

We had the PA hooked up where you would tape the microphone to the stand that held the snare drum, and if you got it tuned up just right it would pick up the sound of all the other drums so you actually had drums in the PA system. All of this never before seen in back-yard parties.

The actual party commenced at about two, three o'clock that afternoon, 'cause you'd have to show up and you'd set up. That's when the first kegs were cracked. And everybody hung out and, you know, the band would tune up and play a few songs, and that was very cool.

Much, much later the helicopter would fly in with the spotlight, and the cops made big announcements about unlawful assembly and order to disperse, and everybody would be running. The cops would come bursting in, in a great big line, kind of like football style, onto the field. They would run in and split into a "surround and pound" strategy, you know, surround everybody, move everybody out but also contain everybody.

We would all sit up on the stage and say, "Man, we're with the band. This is our equipment. We don't know nothing about this, man. We were just hired to play what we thought was going to be a normal party. There's nothing fucking normal about this party at all. All we want is out. We're with you, man." So they would leave us alone. We also said: "And she's with me, man. And so is she."

The cops would clear the place out, and they'd all be outside on the street cleaning up the kids, making the neighborhood safe for whatever. We would wait till everybody was gone, then break out our flashlights that we kept specifically for this purpose. Big plastic flashlights with the giant lens that had more throw.

We'd fan out and go over the backyard inch by inch and pick up all the loose joints and unopened little bottles of booze and stuff everybody had thrown down when the cops charged in. We'd come up with little baggies of pot and papers and pipes, whatever your "proclivity" was. We had roadies by then, of a sort, people who would lend us their truck or drive a pickup to help us get the PA and the amplifiers and extra drum stands and help us set up.

After combing the grounds, we would sit up on that stage till four in the morning just samplin' everything.

It became an art form to strategize for the parties, and when we would play them and schedule them so that we had a routine. I had determined early on that there was to be a campaign.

I had read a book called *The Advance Man* by Jerry Bruno. He was an adviser to JFK during the 1960 election campaign. I read this book in maybe 1964, sixth grade at the latest. It made an impression on me.

It explores the idea of continuity, what people would call "exposure," routines, just to be there, to be available. Like on some of my favorite Latino radio stations in Miami, where I get to hear the song "Siempre"—very aptly named, it means "always"—every twenty-eight minutes.

If you're good enough, people will tell friends and they'll want to come back and see you. And then you must be available. You have to be there to be seen. And, yes, that does take strategy. That does take thinking academically or sportingly. It's like playing chess. And one of my fortes in the band was to provide that manner of thinking.

There was certain rituals that were critical to the success of the show. First was sharing Camel filter cigarettes; that's what we all smoked in the band. That was important. You had to share 'em.

We had to drink Schlitz malt liquor, 'cause that was Alex's favorite. For a while there Budweiser malt liquor was still around but it was like a designer toy. Schlitz malt liquor was much more direct.

Once we started playing parties and clubs in Hollywood, Pink's chili dogs became part of my ritual. I would have to stop and buy one with extra mustard and onions on the way to every Gazzari's gig or every Starwood gig. As a direct result, I went on to sell over fifty million records and traveled the world. Just kidding.

Backstage at these little beer bars and clubs became one of my favorite places on earth to be. It was a clubhouse. It was a tree house. It was always some little back room with a couple of filthy couches and cigarette burns in the rug and graffiti on the walls. And that was your place, that's where you hung around, that's where you held court. I was part of what you were working for.

The greatest backstage of all was at the Whisky-A-

Go-Go. By the time Van Halen started playing there, which was right around 1975, they had not yet erased all of the graffiti that covered every inch of the ceiling in the famous main dressing room upstairs. You had poems by Jim Morrison written on the ceiling, complete paragraphs, Morrison's signature, and the signature of everybody in The Doors. The signatures of everybody from Led Zeppelin to Johnny Winter to ZZ Top, Alice Cooper, Jethro Tull, the Mahavishnu Orchestra, Jeff Beck, Santana, Janis Joplin, Jimi Hendrix, and on and on. They covered every square inch. You could spend—and I did—many, many hours just checking out each little quote.

It wasn't until probably the early eighties when they painted it over and commenced the tradition anew, but by then the Whisky had changed. This was one of the first landing spots on the West Coast for any band. And when we in VH first started playing there, that was the first testimonial that we had arrived. We were going to write on the walls, right next to the guy in Led Zeppelin, somewhere in between him and Aretha Franklin.

What made Van Halen's backyard parties different from anybody else's backyard parties was that we really perceived them as little concerts, and we advertised them as little concerts. We put out flyers, we started to take the profits, whatever it was that we could barely make, and use it to rent a little stage and get a little better PA system. There was this store in the Monterey Park–Alhambra area, which is south of Pasadena, called Johnny Roberts Music.

Johnny Roberts Music was the coolest place that you could ever go to rent or buy your equipment. They had little pictures of everybody who had been through town from the late sixties to the early seventies: a picture of Jimmy Page buying a guitar, or maybe Tina Turner buying a microphone . . . nah, you wouldn't have seen that, Ike was in charge of the equipment.

Coming up with a better and better PA system was an important issue because we were pulling more and more people, so you need more and more volume just to get the music across. Bought some big Altech Lansing speakers—it's a big horn, a fifteen-inch speaker, and it put out great sound. And we started dressing up a little bit. What was popular then were the bell-bottoms.

The bondage element was just kicking in, and there was one little store in Hollywood that custom-made all of this leather gear. I don't think any of us were really sure exactly what bondage was, we just knew that the leather belts looked cool. You'd get a black leather belt with some studs on it and a big silver belt buckle, that was your prize of the three-month period, whatever it took to afford the thing. You had to wear it low, gun-slinger style.

There weren't many places that you could buy black leather pants. It was still a left-of-center statement. You had to go to some underground place, who would custom-make them for you. I had a pair of black leather pants with drawstrings in the front and the back made super low-cut. You could never sit down in them; you'd pop right out. They would dye my legs purple black. They were unlined, just raw leather. Some little guy with a Marlon Brando motorcycle hat and a hand-cuff belt made these for me. He had some little slave working for him behind the counter, with his little dog collar and everything, the guy that did all the sewing and shit.

These damn pants stained my legs every time I'd go to sing, 'cause I'd sweat in them, and I couldn't get the dye off. I went to more than one doctor, because at first I was terrified. I thought, wow, I'm going to have some kind of toxic chemical reaction to something in the leather. Now I'm permanently tattooed.

If I stopped wearing the pants, then all the dye would come off on the hotel room sheets in four day's time. It would be okay for me to drop trou in front of you with the lights on, four days later. Till then, we didn't turn on the lights. I looked like the Toxic Avenger, about to put the triple whammy on you.

I was black—except where my little underwear was, from my legs to up above my belly, all you'd see is my little wiener glowing in the dark because of the contrast. Look at the first Van Halen album, on the back cover, I'm wearing those damned pants. Every morning on tour I'd have to bundle up the sheets, put them in the corner of the bathroom so housekeeping wouldn't see the dye had come off. The sheets looked like the Shroud of Turin.

Anyway, Edward and I picked up the gauntlet first, and we eventually became as much fun to look at as to listen to.

We started to improve on the production. We painted a sign on a bed sheet, and *this* had never been done before. The bass player at the time, Mike Stone, knew the way to make a gridwork on the sheet so that the lettering would be right, and then we taped it off with adhesive tape and spray-painted it. It was the first of many signs to be hung behind the band. Whoa, this was *amazing*. This wasn't a sign, it was a *backdrop.*

The banners that we hung behind the stage merely

showed the name of the band, Van Halen. But it was an *effort at production.* And production was always a part of Van Halen, that it would look like it sounded. Alex would spruce up his drum stage, you know, figure out things to hang in front so it wasn't just milk cartons. We went on to build backdrops made out of plywood and pieces of mirror and such that we found.

A very important part of the Van Halen show were smoke pots, which were completely illegal, and I certainly don't recommend fooling with them. You get little empty tins, say, cat food cans, and you bolt them to a little piece of two-by-four. You run a plug, a double-headed plug, up the middle of it, and you run an electric wire over to a little switch system. Next you go down to the local gun store and buy a can of 4F black gunpowder; this is for people who load their own bullets. They would only sell you two cans of 4F per person, especially if you're a nineteen-year-old longhair. So we would each take turns and go down and buy our allotment of 4F powder until we had eight cans. Put a little gunpowder in the tins, and then when you hit the foot switch, it sparks it off and you get a great big colorful "fooomm!"—a smoke bomb.

We would set them up on top of the PA and on the sides of the drums and behind the amplifiers. I would scream, "Ladies and gentlemen, please welcome the amazing Van Halen," and we'd hit the first note and fire off half the smoke pots. It looked like Tiananmen Square. People would be running, gasping, crying from all the smoke. If it was an indoor dance and we'd miscalculated the ventilation, it was like playing in a cloud. You couldn't see three feet in front of you. All of which was immensely cool. It was all too much, it was all over the top. And then, of course, at the end you would fire off the rest of the smoke pots to signify the big finish.

Just setting up and loading the smoke pots took hours. And we would get burned. You'd have a few beers, you're dancing around, you say, "Hey, thank you, have a good night!" and somebody would fire off the smoke pots, and you'd be leaning a little too far to the left and blow off half of your haircut, take off an eyebrow, lose a sleeve, what the hell. Regularly, something on stage would catch fire and have to be put out.

We became known for it; that with Van Halen you got a full-blast show, a real show. This, of course, all carried on into bigger and bigger elements. Once we started to play on the road, we took all of this stuff with us. It was all fiercely illegal. Otherwise, you'd need a fireman and a court-appointed expert in pyrotechnics.

But in the seventies things were looser. People weren't screwed down quite as tight. Vietnam had just ended, nobody even thought of all of these party favors as addictive, you didn't have AIDS, you didn't have Moms Against Drunk Drivers with AIDS, you didn't have Ethiopians with AIDS, whatever. There was sort of a big long halftime going on.

Pretty soon, the smoke pots alone took up half the car. They were all run by the bass player, who also ran the lights. Had a lot of foot switches that boy, *and* backup vocals. Sometimes, of course, just like the Space Shuttle, you go for the lights and hit the smoke bomb. Somebody would lose a sideburn and their sense of humor, but only briefly.

I think you can hear elements of our most classic smoke-pot caper on a bootleg tape of Van Halen's last real show before we went on to make a record and go on the road in 1977 at the Pasadena Civic. We saved all the smoke pots for the grand finale, hit the last song and fired off all twenty-five at once—in a forty-five-hundred-person exhibition hall with the windows closed, and it just smoked the place out. It looked like the Tet Offensive, from what I read. I was afraid to move because I thought I would fall off the stage. I couldn't see two feet in front of me, the smoke was so acrid and thick.

And it, of course, set off all of the smoke and fire sensors in the building, and fire departments from seven cities showed up. It was like right out of the movies. All the doorways flew open all at once, and all you can see was those rolling red lights on top of the fire trucks and all of these guys with gas masks and hoses and full-blast fire boots and gear—from the movie *Brazil*—bursting through the door to throw forty-five hundred of our closest friends out of the building. "Hey, I'm with the band, man. And so is she. And her, too."

One of the vice presidents from Warner Brothers had heard of the band, came down to see the show, sat behind the amplifiers and watched. When those firemen showed up, I knew we had it in the bag.

But I'm getting ahead of the story. There were beer bars. We started to play the beer bars, some of the tops were Barnacle Bill's, which was over near Arcadia, it's more inland than Pasadena. Pasadena is one full side of a cassette tape from the beach. Those of us who live in an automobile, you know exactly what I'm talking about; just put your cassette in, when the side's over you're there. Barnacle Bill's was one-half of one-half tape, a quarter side—going more inland. It held maybe a hundred and fifty people, just a little stage, you could reach up and touch the ceiling from the stage. No dressing room. It was a buck fifty for a pitcher of beer. And there would be a dance contest.

We would play at Walter Mitty's Rock and Grill, which was in Pomona, out in the middle of nowhere, right across from the huge Naval chemical processing installation. Walter Mitty's had been obviously a shop or a store that they'd turned into a beer place. And on one side was a foursquare Gospel Baptist meeting hall, and on the other side was a porno shop. And we would play five forty-five-minute sets there.

The jukebox had two songs on it; one which I don't recollect and the other I'll never forget: It was "Jim Dandy to the Rescue" by Black Oak Arkansas. Whenever they would play it, you would hear glass breaking. People would wahoo, and you'd hear pitchers hit the floor. And we would play everything from old Rod Stewart to Ohio Players.

It was the first time I saw somebody get killed on the dance floor. Bikers frequented the place, and it was during our fifth set, toward the end of the night, and there was a sprawling fracas in the corner. I remember seeing somebody reeling toward the drums. He was holding his stomach, and I thought he was spilling soda pop out of a cup. He flattened out on the floor, and they turned the lights on. Somebody had knifed him in a brawl; two opposing bike gangs. We didn't play anymore that night. But the next night it was all the fear and rumor of, "Wow, the such-and-such guys are coming back to exact revenge, you know, to look for payback." But we went on to play. We simply pulled the amplifiers a few more feet away from the wall than usual in case we had to jump behind the amps if there was a shoot-out.

One night we were out having a cigarette during one

of our fifteen-minute breaks. I was leaning against a pickup truck, which was parked a few cars down from the front of this little place. All of a sudden I was feeling the pickup truck move, and I thought somebody else was leaning against it. Nobody leaning. Looking in the back of the pickup truck, and there's a guy and his gal getting it on like crazy. They'd been drinking, you know, carrying on. So we stood around the edge of the truck and watched and finished our cigarettes and cheered them on. When they were done, they both sat up and gave everybody five and accepted their applause in a dignified fashion.

We told them, "Come on in. Have you been inside?"

"No we haven't been in yet. I don't think I have enough money."

"Ah, come on, you got to be our guests," like that.

He went on to just drink himself silly at the bar, and his little girlfriend spent the rest of the night standing right in front of the stage. This was a tight place; we were packed in there like sardines. And she stood right in front of the stage and just looked me right in the eye and danced for the rest of the night with her blue jeans on backwards. I don't think she even noticed. I guess she was so excited she was going to get in free, she just pulled her clothes on lickety-split and that was it. She was in there making little drunk sexy faces at me, raising the eyebrows. And she didn't know her jeans were on backwards.

It's good work if you can get it.

This was a place where if you were new, you didn't know that the ladies' room was right off to the righthand side of the stage, with one toilet and one sink, and if you just opened the door, you could see the throne. It was like Capone's tomb, you'd get it all in one glance. We would finish a song and everybody would be cheering.

I'd be going, "So you want more? You want more?" And people would go, "Yeah, yeah, we want more!"

I'd signal to one of the roadies, and he'd throw the door open and there'd be some princess sitting on the toilet, and I'd yell, "What about her? Should we give her more?" Everybody would cheer and scream, and we'd hold the door open, and everybody would take a look and cheer for her. You had to wait until somebody who didn't know any better would go into the ladies' room.

In the middle of the song, I'd quiet it down after the solo, "Okay, folks, I want to talk a little bit about love." I'd say, "You know what, I've done enough talking for the night. Let's get some other opinions here."

I'd walk over to the ladies' room and these two big gorillas would open the door, and there'd be a little Doreen taking care of her business. And I would walk right up to her on the toilet, I'd say "Honey, what's yo' name?" Sometimes they would scream and try and hide, I'd go, "No, no, no. We're all friends here. You know, and we all want to talk—we just want to get your ID. Are you listening to me, Doreen? Doreen, I'm going to interview somebody else if you keep this up."

Beer bars! Once again, five forty-five-minute sets, that was the standard, and it was all cover tunes. There are many, many clubs and bars now where you can go and hear original material. You open up the *L.A. Weekly* or the *Village Voice* or anything in between, there's a *lot* of places with original material but *very* few, if any, that play cover songs—as in "Excuse me, would you like to dance?"

The standard until the end of the seventies was beer bars, playing cover tunes. This is where all of the bands until that period have learned to play music. It was a traditional approach. When I first saw the Van Halen brothers play at a backyard party, it was cover tunes. It was not original material at all. You only knew part of the alphabet.

And the ambition was to play the coolest beer bars. The coolest beer bars being in Hollywood.

We started playing two of the best. One was Gazzari's, which I've talked about. That was the first step.

The second was the famous Starwood, which had started off in the late sixties as PJ's. The Starwood was the be-all, end-all: They had the Rock Room, which accommodated a thousand people.

Then they had the Folk Room, which had folk music. There were three different bars, and the upstairs was the most important 'cause it was a labyrinth of dressing rooms and bathrooms and corners and closets. Everything you'd ever read about in *Circus* magazine transpired up there. So it was critical that you become a fixture at both places.

You didn't play cover tunes at the Starwood. So it was like a one-two punch. Now, the Whisky-A-Go-Go was fully functional and had been since like 1965, but that was if you had a recording contract. If you had a deal, or you were about to get a deal.

The one-two punch was: You play Gazzari's and then you explain to Bill Gazzari why it is you have to move to the Starwood. And you would be threatened and banished to the seventh level of hell, but a relationship would be maintained.

Eventually we were a fixture at Gazzari's, playing once every four weeks for two, three years. We knew two hundred songs by other people.

Every song had two solos in it. The first would be played just like the record, and the second solo would be a combination of all the other solos, of all the other songs, and I would also change the lyrics of that last verse. After a while I never even bothered to learn the real lyrics of any of the songs. So we would play something like "Saturday Night's All Right for Fighting" by Elton John, and somebody would come up and say, "Those aren't the lyrics," and I'd say, "I know." I'd catch the gist of the chorus and do the rest of it phonetically: "And that na-na-seena-na-na-ianna motor machine, and that was-ana-na-na-na-na if if you know what I mean." I was free-formin'. Brakes is gone—we's freewheelin'!

It was my idea to take those gigs, and make them real shows. Make some advertising. Publicize. Campaign. Build a following. Let's have a routine, so that you don't just, oh, haphazardly appear here and there, but would play the same club on a time frame every three weeks, every four, five weeks, whatever the case was, so that a following would build. People would know what to expect. They would show up again. They would tell a friend.

We had a list of fourteen high schools and junior high schools within driving distance, an hour in any direction. We would go out and wait for bad weather so that we could have free run of the schools. In every outside locker we'd put a flyer in. We'd flyer the place.

Or we would figure out which shows that other people were tossing, legit shows, that were applicable to ours. If you saw Aerosmith at the football stadium, great, that's perfect, we'll flyer them. You could get, I believe, four thousand flyers for forty bucks at the Instant Press, and we would break it into teams. Ultimately, we had little walkie-talkies because the police would stop one team from flyering cars at the football stadium, and you would know that that was happening so you'd go into overdrive on the other side of the stadium so you could flyer *every* car. This built up a tremendous following for Van Halen on a very, very grass-roots level. On the flyers we'd write "The People's Choice." I got it from Muhammad Ali fight posters, "The People's Choice."

The standard call of the wild from local bands is always, "Gee, if I only had a manager, I'd be great." "Gee, if I only had an agent, then everything would work out fine." "Gee, if I only had, if I only had . . . " I maintained that if the band was good enough, then we would step out. We would be thrown to the front, but that we had to advertise. There were so many little bands cruising around, how do people know when you're going to show up again at the same place? So we made a concerted effort.

There were probably a dozen friends, many of whom later became road crew—who would assist. Whoever had a car, whoever had a pickup truck, was conscripted. It would not be unusual in the pouring rain to have six, eight people flyering a given school. It wouldn't be unusual to flyer six, eight schools in one night—junior college, junior high, whatever. It had a great effect. More and more people showed up. Some local folks who had a little bit of cash, who had—read: steady jobs—got together to promote concerts; rent Pasadena Civic Exhibition Hall, and we'd put out the flyers for it and would charge like $3.50 to get in. And it would not be unusual for us in the beginning to pull between 1,500 and 2,500 people. Ultimately, just before we were going to make our first record, we were pulling 4,500 and 5,000 people.

Never did take a demo tape to a company. Never

did solicit a manager or enlist the assistance of an agent. It was all based on if we're that good, then it will work out great. If it doesn't work out that great, it's 'cause we're not that good.

Standard operating procedure was always, you know, to make a little demo tape, send it to the record company, it winds up on the guy's shelf, and his secretary doesn't answer your calls, and he gets three hundred of these tapes a week.

Again, my mind-set was if we're that damn good—and we thought we were—then every time somebody sees the show, they're going to go tell somebody else, and they're gonna both come back.

But even word-of-mouth can have its drawbacks. There was a brief interlude in 1977, when Gene Simmons from KISS came to the Starwood and saw us play to a sold-out audience and thought we were absolutely spectacular, and said, "I'd like to make a demo tape." He was thinking of himself as a producer. He had a couple of artists that he was producing, doing whatever in the studio. KISS was at an all-time high, they were at their zenith. We said, "Sure. Let's make a demo tape." We didn't have a clue. He flew us all to New York City, we made a demo tape, four songs, some of which later wound up on records—"Runnin' with the Devil," I believe was on there, "House of Pain" wound up on the *1984* album.

We had a big meeting with his manager, Bill Aucoin, who was riding very high on the hog at the time. It was at his Madison Avenue office, high floor of the building. We sat in front of his mahogany desk, and he had his shoes polished by a little Italian man while he spoke to us.

And he said to us, "Guys, I think the music is great but I don't think the vocals hold up. I just don't hear the melodies, the hits that are required in this day and age." He said, "Dave, maybe there are a couple other acts that I can handle that we could get you to work with. Guys, you and the band, maybe another vocalist would work. But otherwise, Gene has his own career, he's in KISS, and barring any other permutations, I don't think I can work with you." Like so.

We walked out of that office, and I felt terrible. Wow—had I let the band down? This was my first experience with somebody getting his shoes polished by an Italian guy on Madison Avenue. I didn't know what the Van Halens were thinking at the time; perhaps they were buying this load of horseshit.

Turns out that Gene Simmons's true interest was in conscripting Ed Van Halen into their show in some form or another, get him to play on a record, get him to help write guitar solos, get him into the band. So this dismissal was followed up by calls to Edward, "Come on down, we're recording at Larrabee Studios in Hollywood and we got a new song, we need a guitar solo. Come on down."

I was always very fiercely protective of what we were doing as a group, as a clan, 'cause there's always going to be pirates, there's always going to be carpetbaggers, like Simmons. And I would show up with Ed at the studio. Simmons would look at me with horror. *Horror*. 'Cause I was on to his game way early.

There were scenes like: "Oh, all of you guys are invited to the big KISS show down at the Forum," and I would show up and there would be no tickets for me. The Van Halens would be inside, comfortably ensconced in the back room with Gene and his pals. Of course I knew what was up, and I was super protective of the band at the time, or people like that would have picked us apart right away. In line with that kind of thinking, when we made our first album for Warner Brothers, Ted Templeman, the producer, approached Ed Van Halen and said, "I'd like you to play on the Nicolette Larson album." I got right between them, I said, "No way! You're not going to run off with bits and pieces of the scenery before the play starts." Ed wanted to play on it. I said, "Great. But you got to put a question mark where your name goes. Got to keep it in one camp." A theory that has stood Van Halen well to this day.

The Green Hornets

I went to work after junior college. I was with Van Halen, playing clubs and dives anywhere you can spell and some you're still working on. I was night janitor, the nuclear janitor, the custodian, a porter in surgery, asepsis tech. I went through a couple of seminars in asepsis, sterilization, bedside manner, people skills, these kinds of things. How to clean the spaceship. Without me, you got no spaceship.

The nurses were hard-bit, wizened old gals, mostly chain-smokers, who had been, done, gone and seen everything. Many had done military service time, had returned for that camaraderie. You are a very, very important human being when you work in surgery, especially night shift, trauma care. Trauma meant you were not only important, but you were important right the fuck now. There's no "fix it in the mix tomorrow." We were called "green hornets" because we wore surgical greens, like a shower cap to keep your hair in, green shirt, green pants, green paper booties over your sneakers, and then a backwards green smock down to your ankles.

We struck fear into the patients. We were not allowed to walk through the normal corridors of the hospital. We were seen as angels of death and pain. In the mind of somebody who's about to go under an exploratory laparotomy, or he's going to get his neck opened up and find out if that tumor is benign or got a mind of its own. Last thing you wanted to see was the mechanic walk into your living room, "Hey, I'm not supposed to deliver the car till tomorrow morning at eight sharp. Now back the fuck up."

So there was a feared respect and that super-hyper responsibility—this was not shoveling horseshit. This was mechanic-ing human beings.

Untouched By Human Hands

In 1979, I broke my foot jumping off the drum riser and landing on cement. The doctor said to me, "This is not going to heal. You're never going to dance the same way again," all those jump-spinning back kicks, and all that aerial work, and so forth.

So I spent the better part of a year standing in the doorway of my bathroom. I would put my arms against the door, and I would practice moving everything but my feet. I would test it by putting a glass on my head, with some water, so I could walk and do my hip-swivel without spilling the water. Because I figured, "Well, if I'm never leaving the ground again, okay. God gave me lemons; lemonade for sale."

Back in Swampscott, Massachusetts, seven or eight years old, I built myself a little lemonade stand. Five cents. Just like in the cartoon "Peanuts."

Things were not selling well at all.

My pop said, "You know what you ought to do?"

I said, "What's that?"

He said, "You ought to put a hood over your head, with two eye slits, and big rubber gloves up to your armpits, and write 'Lemonade, five cents, Untouched by Human Hands.' "

I got it. Right away.

Big Ed

Come late '78, Van Halen sold, what, five, six million records. I'm the only one out in the streets. Everybody else is very domestic, and sometimes I wonder if that might not be a great comfort. I'm the eternal wanderer, except now I'm noticed. So I got to get a baby-sitter.

In Los Angeles, we interview a lot of different guys

for security. Last guy walks in is "Big" Ed Anderson, right out of the mountains, by way of *Goodfellas,* Bensonhurst, Brooklyn. The scene in *Goodfellas* where they hijack a truck and suddenly everybody in the neighborhood is wearing a yellow sweater? That's Ed. He had the sweater. I'm feeling surly and sarcastic. I figure I'm going to fool with him, I say, "I got three questions for you. What do you think of people partyin', you know, carrying on, gettin' high, doin' whatever on stage, under the stage, backstage, in front of the stage?"

He says, "I got no problem with that."

So, "Okay, what about underage girls on stage, under the stage, backstage, in front of the stage?"

He says, "I could adjust."

So okay, tough guy, "You know how to roller-skate?"

He said, "No, but I could learn."

I said, "You got a job."

Ed said, "Great. What's our schedule?"

I told him, "Six weeks on the road, ten days off; the band goes home, you and I go to the tropics. You got a bathing suit? Cool, let's go buy you some skates."

And we did. Drove to a skate shop in Venice, got him some roller skates.

Went right to the beach, commenced to roller-skate, and of course I'm Mr. Flamboyant with the hair flying and the shorts, you know, the whole thing. This is Ed's first hour on the job. Somebody yells, "You fag!" Well, of course I have to step off into the sand, raise a little gorilla dust—you know, when you hit your chest, that's gorilla dust that comes off. Welcome to our tiny little island, Ed.

M&M's

More frequently than not, things are not what they seem. You may have heard of the brown M&M's story of Van Halen. And it read like this in the contract: "There will be no brown M&M's anywhere in the backstage area or immediate vicinity, upon pain of forfeiture of the show with full compensation."

I would come in backstage, and if I saw brown M&M's, I'd trash the dressing room and threaten to cancel the show, and the promoter would come backstage, all consternated. We pitched it as "Caruso forbade whistling backstage," that it was bad luck. It's a luck thing. It's a charm. I made it seem like it was a complete act of self-indulgent extravagance—which I've always found very attractive as a performance. Or even a lifestyle. Hey, sign me up. Can she come too? Great.

I already mentioned Van Halen was the first band to take huge productions into tertiary, third-level markets. We'd pull up with nine eighteen-wheeler trucks, full of gear, where the standard was three trucks, max. And there were many, many technical errors—whether it was the girders couldn't support the weight, or the flooring would sink in, or the doors weren't big enough to move the gear through.

The contract rider read like a version of the Chinese Yellow Pages because there was so much equipment, and so many human beings to make it function. So just as a little test, in the technical aspect of the rider, it would say "Article 148: There will be fifteen amperage voltage sockets at twenty-foot spaces, evenly, providing nineteen amperes . . ." This kind of thing. And article number 126, in the middle of nowhere, was: "There will be no brown M&M's in the backstage area, upon pain of forfeiture of the show, with full compensation."

So, when I would walk backstage, if I saw a brown M&M in that bowl . . . well, line-check the entire production. Guaranteed you're going to arrive at a technical error. They didn't read the contract. Guaranteed you'd run into a problem. Sometimes it would threaten to just destroy the whole show. Something like, literally, life-threatening. And I'll give you an example.

The folks in Pueblo, Colorado, at the university, took the contract rather kinda casual. They had one of these new rubberized bouncy basketball floorings in their arena. They hadn't read the contract, and weren't sure, really, about the *weight* of this production; this thing weighed like the business end of a 747.

I came backstage. I found some brown M&M's, I went into full Shakespearean "*What* is this before me?" . . . you know, with the skull in one hand . . . and promptly trashed the dressing room. Dumped the buffet, kicked a hole in the door, twelve hundred dollars' worth of fun.

The *staging* sank through their floor. They didn't bother to look at the weight requirements or anything, and this sank through their new flooring and did eighty thousand dollars' worth of damage to the arena floor. The whole thing had to be replaced. It came out in the press that I discovered brown M&M's and did eighty-five thousand dollars' worth of damage to the backstage area.

Well, who am I to get in the way of a good rumor?

"Tonight! On 'History—for All the Wrong Reasons,' my special guest . . . David Lee!"

Let me invoke the P. T. Barnum prayer. It's right up there with "Hallowed Be Thy Name," and "Havah Negilah." I, being a card-carrying member of the great unwashed public, can testify. We love nothing more than to be duped. Except, perhaps, to be duped *well.* I'll pay for that, every time. And I want the T-shirt.

Personal Best

My personal record is five chicks at once, in Nashville. They were all doing each other on the bed, and everybody was arrayed around the bed. We were making video, and the promoter was there, and the agent was there, and the band was there, and I was directing. It was so beyond the pale that all I could think of to do was play like volleyball and go, "Okay, change!" And all the girls would shift. And in a moment of inspiration, I ran off to my room with two of them, and said, "I wanna be with both of you," and they sat bolt upright, and said, "But we're sisters."

Herbal

Now, I'm a pot smoker, and what happens when I don't smoke pot, it's like one of those photographs. My life is like one of those photographs where somebody opens the shutter for a long duration, and all of the headlights and belt buckle reflections make one long beam of light that runs for eight city blocks. So when I sit down to write a list, it will be three items long, maybe five. Need to do this, check up on that. When I smoke pot, everything's cut by two-thirds speed and I can see in between every car, I can see the pedestrians and their haircuts, I can read the sign in the barbershop window, and my list will be forty things long. Keep these things in mind and confide in Big Ed. Ask Ed in confidence, "What's the difference between a pot list and a non-pot list?" And he'll tell you something in a Little Italy–Bensonhurst kind of way, like, "Well, a non-pot list will take me till eleven in the morning. A pot list will take me till Thursday."

54

Studio 54 actually happened for, maybe, three years. I think it was less. I headed right for it after the first Japanese tour, late '78.

The doorman, who was quite famous, Mark Benecke,

stood on a fire hydrant and said who could come in and who couldn't, and there'd be a gi-normous line of people waiting. I was Tarzan of the Apes meets Marilyn Monroe, with hair down to my tush, and a Japanese T-shirt with "Ichiban #1" printed on the front, in my jeans. I didn't get in the first time.

I was so pissed. I said, "Just like all spiritual injuries, I'll treat it with alcohol. From the inside."

Same thing happened to my friend Nile Rodgers, the guitar player, producer, and writer for Chic. The Led Zeppelin of dance music. He was pissed too.

Eight and half million singles later, within a fiscal year, both of us were comfortably ensconced in the ladies' room. Which was the ultimate place to hang because the music was so belligerent and pounding.

The cognoscenti, the glitterati, could get into the ladies' room waiting area and hang there. You would tell your favorite tennis stars, and other musicians, and colleagues in the print industry, "Okay, I'll meet you in the ladies' room, about two A.M." That's how you knew that you was up and surfing, big time.

Well, it became so glutted with people in the waiting area, that we began to just sort of ooze into the actual bathroom. And the Era of the Bathroom came into play.

We all know where to hang out at a house party; it's either the kitchen or the bathroom. But, at a club, this was a first. And I would be there, with John McEnroe and Vitas Gerulitus and you would run into movie stars, and the *cool* models, those in the know.

So, Lauren Hutton would be in there, Baryshnikov, the Playboy Playmate of the Year, Halston, Liza Minnelli. It was the coolest place to ever hang from a branch. And people would say, "Excuse me," walk three steps into a stall, use it for its proper purpose, and just rejoin the clan.

This spread to all the other clubs. And they began to build their ladies' rooms bigger to accommodate the guest list. And this was a very sexual time. It was not unusual to see the backs of three pairs of women's shoes underneath the door of the stall. And it was totally accepted. It was beyond accepted. It was par for the course.

So later, within spitting distance, you had clubs like Area, and Xenon. They all had magnificent ladies' rooms. This is how I would conjure my social schedule: "Okay, I'll meet you in the ladies' room at Area, about three o'clock this morning." Cool.

Studio 54 summed up an era. The conceptual leap from going to lesbian bars to Studio 54 was a simple one. You had this giant crescent moon that would lower down from the ceiling, with a cocaine spoon, with little sparkles going up its nose, while everybody was dancing with their arms in the air. This crescent moon had to be a good twelve feet tall, and it would lower, hydraulically, from the ceiling against the wall, with this big spoon that went up and down, up and down, like a fulcrum, with this big pile of sparkles which would go up its nose.

Gay people were completely integrated into the fabric of this, too. Guys dancing with their shirts off, in their jeans, next to royalty. You had Margaret Trudeau dancing next to a bondage freaky-deak who was dancing next to a performance artist, who was dancing next to a movie star, who was dancing next to a rock star, who was dancing next to a magazine publisher, who was dancing next to a fashion designer, who was dancing next to a fashion model.

And it was very polite company. It was dignified debauchery.

HUCK

I've read *Huckleberry Finn* two hundred times. First time I'd gone on tour with Van Halen, a friend of mine who writes scripts for television sitcoms showed up in my room. I asked him, many years later, "Jerry, what do you remember from that time period?"

He says, "I remember walking into your room, on the road, big time rock 'n' roll, stadium gigs for the first time ever, and seeing a copy of *Huckleberry Finn* with a pair of handcuffs sitting on it."

What was I doing with the handcuffs?

I was doing the Elvis. I was doing everything that I read was okay to do from Hugh Hefner. I was doing everything I'd read in *The Carpetbaggers* late at night, under the covers, with a flashlight.

Don't get me wrong. I've always seen it as a sharing experience. It's like the psychiatrist always said to me, "You gotta wanna help yourself."

My favorite form of humor is co-conspiratorial. I confide in you. If we really make the connection, I don't even have to utter a syllable, all I have to do is kind of raise my eyebrows.

Rothing Your Room

Despite all the festivities, there were a lot of times you had to bow out and sleep, try and catch up. The work and discipline ethic that surrounded Van Halen was *severe.* You had four Captain Ahabs. Well, surely, when the boat puts to port it's gonna be wild, because when we were sailing and working, it was severe.

And I followed a few philosophies and codes throughout. Starting with our first top-bill shows in '79 and continuing up to now, what I do is the night before the first performance, I'll show up extra late when everybody's gone after a rehearsal, nobody there but a couple of crew and some night watchman. I get a big bath towel, and I get on my hands and knees, and I wash every square centimeter of that stage. Sometimes it takes me quite a while, but it reevaluates for me that if I'm willing to do that—if you're willing to get on your hands and knees, like a wash-woman, and scrub every centimeter of that deck—then there's nothing else left to do. There's no further commitment that you can make. And I still do it. There's your contrast to those rest-and-relaxation stories that continue to this day. It's always been a contrast with me.

"Rothing your room" became an expression. When I went to record with Bob Rock, the producer related to me early on in rehearsal that this was a special pride of his to do this project, that it was a completion of a circle for him because he was once in a traveling band and was known for "Rothing" his room, which meant exploding suitcases, and your room becomes an art project.

The contrast to that was that I would train every day in my room, and before I'd do that, I'd get down on my hands and knees with a wet bath towel and I'd scrub every inch of the floor, then organize the room completely, then train. I did that this morning. This room hasn't had a maid in it in four days, but at 7:15 this morning I was under the bed on my belly, scrubbin' the floors. Therein is the balance.

That's why the music—or at least my contribution—sounded like it did and does. That's why it looks like it does. It's a big part of me. But it's not the exciting part; it's not something the media is going to grasp onto. But the balance is critical. Freewheeling is easy; being able to execute it and make it happen is a whole 'nother story. Or conversely, you're capable physically of doing anything, artistically, athletically, but it takes you forever to think of what to do. Once you wash-woman the floor a few thousand times, your focus on how to think and get something done develops geometrically—making it happen, taking care of business.

Hellfire

Late '78, '79, Studio 54, *Interview* magazine, the Warhol gang, Bianca, Calvin, you name it, and I made friends with the music journalist Lisa Robinson. She said, "Dave, I gotta show you something special." And we went down into the meat packing district and there's this underground bondage club called Hellfire, very famous. I'll never forget, right in front of us was a very demure-looking little gal, early thirties, bobbed haircut, very school teacherish looking. Red dress. We paid our way in and it's very cavernous and dark. And as my eyes are adjusting, I look over to the side and I noticed that she has taken off all of her clothing and put it in a nice, neat little folded librarian pile on a little bench, and was wearing full-bondage gear; stockings, merry widow corset, panties, garters, gloves, the whole thing.

And as my eyes adjusted I see that half the people in the place are naked, guys crawling on their hands and knees in leather jockstraps. One big guy, big dock-worker guy, leather jockstrap, got leather gloves on, he's holding—maybe fourteen little pieces of fishing line, a foot and a half long with fish hooks on the end of it. People were chained and gettin' whipped.

I had to go to the bathroom, it's pitch black. In the men's room there's a bathtub to urinate in. I positioned my legs against the edge of the bathtub, I'm starting to take a leak, and I hear a little voice that says, "A little more to the left." So I kind of flare my elbows a little bit; I can't feel anybody next to me. There was somebody in the bathtub. First thing I thought was, "Do I tip this guy?"

Well, the Hellfire went the way of all flogged flesh. About three summers ago I was at a Halloween party sitting with a group of people and Elle MacPherson, the fashion model, shows up. And she's wearing a Catwoman suit, you know, Batwoman, vacuum-packed PVC, with the heels and the mask and the whole thing. She's with her boyfriend. Everybody says, "Where should we go? Let's go somewhere."

"I know a great place for Halloween. Let's go to The Vault."

We walked into this place, it's packed. All kinds—you had people in tuxedos, people in leather jockstraps, everything in between. Some guy throws himself at Elle MacPherson's feet. She says, "Oh my God, what's he doing?"

"Well, honey, have some fun, he loves it, be abusive."

She says, "I couldn't do that."

I said, "You're a woman, you come by it naturally. Tell him he's a jerk."

She goes, "You jerk." He loves it.

She goes, "You asshole." He's coming unglued.

A little light comes from underneath that Catwoman mask. Pretty soon she's got three, four guys on all fours kissing her boots, whatever, and she's posin' for them and saying, "Worthless bum," this kind of thing. The only one who wasn't enjoying it was her boyfriend.

Grandma Roth

My Grandma Roth came to shows whenever I would play in Miami, up until she was about ninety-six, ninety-seven years old. It was funny because she would wear these big, oversized Converse tennis shoes that cousin Jimmy had given her. My aunts and uncles would walk her in and I'd see her backstage, before the show. We would give her earplugs and everything, and they would go into this massive, glutted crowd. It was animal seating, on the floor. It was really wild, really hysterical in there.

They'd be walkin' her in slow, and the security guys with the gorillas in front, to clear a space, to get her to her seat—they'd be shouting, "Get out of the way! We got Dave Roth's grandmother here!"

It would be like the Red Sea parting.

She would sit down, and people would come from all over the arena to give her five, and salute her, and say "Right on!" She would sit, and she'd make it through three songs, 'cause she was afraid that the sound was gonna break her bones apart. She expressed this directly. She felt that the vibration of the music would shake her to pieces, so she could only make it through about three songs. Then they would take her home. But she never missed a show.

What Made Classic Van Halen Tick

What made Van Halen tick, more than anything else, was this primal approach to the social contract. I don't even know if social contract's an actual term. I use it. It's like a contract that's between us. It's tacit. It's unstated.

There was always that taunting and competing and chasing each other, and then running back up our tree and saying: "I never heard you play better." Or cracking a joke and going, "Hey, kid, what'd melody ever do to you?"

This was mutual and it was furious and it was constant. There was conflict from day one—massive egos. Egos big enough to fill entire football stadiums. And it wasn't because we got along so communally and lived in a tepee and all shared the same religious, quasi-spiritual basis. We weren't all Presbyterian, we weren't all followers of the new Zen, we were not all jocks, we were not all intellectuals. There was a lot of overlap. There was a lot of resentment coming from opposite ends of the sphere, you know, I was "have gun will travel," they were family-oriented, God bless. I wonder frequently what that would be like. I never experienced it. How do you describe the big aquarium until you've seen it? True love, relationships with long-time commitment, domestic bliss—I'd never experienced this, so I was coming from a whole different versification. Musically, same thing. Worlds collide. Right off the bat, two entirely separate record collections and everything.

But out of this, out of the ashes and the foment shall rise a great bird, the Phoenix. The most beautiful orchids grow in shit. We're only at our best when we're ascending toward something. And when you're ascending, you're furious, you're focused; you have to be, or you'll fall off. So of course there's going to be conflict. There's going to be plenty of times when you're tying a knot and somebody starts tapping your shoulder, going "Hey, dude . . ." "Hey, man, *not fucking now.*" And that's all it is, that kind of conflict.

Van Halen had that. Everybody was ascending. We were not afraid of change. We were not afraid of defying convention, breaking the rules. If you think back to the way that we looked in the late seventies, this was the age of the deep sabbath, black purples, whatever it was:

"I've been up since the late sixties, and I eat once a week whether I need it or not," school of thought. We showed up with our cool little designer pants that we'd bought in Paris on the Champs-Elysees, in our high-heeled shoes and with our hair styled and everything. Oh, man. We defied all convention. The media, the rock critics squealed like wieners on a barbecue. Wholly unacceptable. *Wholly* unacceptable. We weren't afraid to try anything.

We weren't afraid, and there was constant conflict on which way to defy. It was healthy. To me it was the equivalent of smacking each other on our helmets before the kickoff in a football game. It's a version of support. It's how you show love.

This was the basis for our relationship, and there are entire families that are based on this. I understood it intrinsically. I think they did too.

If that conflict gnawed away at all of us constantly, out of it came earthshaking, culture-changing music. We sold hope and faith and a jubilation right on par with a lot of your favorite religions. Right on par with a lot of your favorite politicians. We sold the idea of imagination—*extreme* imagination, *forced* to the breaking point.

The Van Halens are very technically oriented. Their father was a trained musician. They were classically trained, always looking for the perfect. Well, my favorite jeans got a lot of holes in them. My favorite boots do not look new. Why would I be any different? And we were at each others' throats constantly. But out of learning all these different kinds of music to play in the clubs and the bars, came a signature sound, nothing else like it.

I had to learn to "Stop dancing," which means, "Don't get up there and disco dance; communicate.

Look people in the eye and really tell the story." If you have something physically that you're going to do, use it as a means of communication. How many times have you gone and seen the latest pop diva or whomever, doing choreographed steps? There's a limit to how many of those you can do in a two-hour show without running out of gas, because at some point you're keeping up instead of leading the way. At that point, do they drop their heads, look at the floor and act like they're dancing at the local saloon? That's *just dancing*. It communicates nothing.

"Stop dancing" means that when you close your eyes, are you truly lost in the moment? Or is that just a cool look for this part of the song? Little red light pops on the video camera and you close your eyes, you look up toward eleven o'clock. Hey, there's a balance. I'm a very imbalanced individual. I know that. And that's all I know.

"Progress report, sir?"

"Well, the good, sir, is we know exactly the extent of the damage. The bad, well, we haven't the vaguest idea how to remedy it. But at least we know."

Edward as well as Alex was so adept at music, it was a whole new alphabet. Starting with the sound, he had called it "the brown sound." I call it "girl-friendly sound." Which essentially means when you take an electric guitar you can make it squeal and lunch it and dive bomb it and angst and strain and all those great words. But the tone has to be there, rich with depth, with character. So even in the super-high registers you're not putting your hands over your ears, and the first people who will do that are women. So you got to get it so it's girl-friendly, to where you can really pitch and squeal and make points and edges, but at the same time, it is "Now I am strong! Now I have full power!"

Tone is a direct result of your personal character, I think. And that tone will come out of your guitar regardless of the equipment that you use. You will fiddle about with the electronics until you have the perfect representation in your mind of who you are, whether you know it or not, especially if you know it not.

Edward's not a very complex human being so that sound is not very complex. But there's substance in terms of all the basic emotions; he doesn't have a lot distracting him. Some say simplicity is ultimate: I do. Just like sex, who you really are will come out when the lights go down, or up. The sound that you build for yourself through your choice of amplifiers and guitars and so forth, is a demonstration of that.

Regardless of how a song was written though, the key to the Van Halen sound is that it was live in the studio, even the echo effects and such on the guitar were Ed operating a foot switch on his amplifier. In the nineties, if you went to do that, most producers would just flip. "No, no, play it dry, we'll put echo and reverb and so forth on later." Because you have a million variations of that in these huge 48-track consoles, plus you have digital consoles now that are 150 tracks, you can compile the tracks and what-not. But it's not life; it's after the fact. It becomes something other than a live group playing together, ensemble. It becomes kind of a cut and paste and think about it later, and certainly not tested in front of human beings.

It was a great thing to be able to test your music and see if the message you were transmitting was being received, to see if people were responding the way that you responded to it when you heard it, 'cause if they weren't, there might be a difficulty in the lyric, there might be a problem in the format of the song. If you're trying to impart extreme hilarity or complete erotic something or other, and you're getting confused looks, it's probably in the transmission. It's great to be able to play that in front of people. And of course in front of people, it's all in the saddle. You have to be able to do it all right there. You know, hit the switch, throw on the echo, hit the switch, turn it off. Be able to hit that high note as opposed to going and resting for an hour and then coming in and trying that high note thirty times in a row and picking the best one. You can't do that live.

But the very finest Van Halen material was performed absolutely live in the studio, all of those first albums. And the best material on the later albums was completely live, including the solo, including the echo that was on the individual instruments. And we played each song three or four times. We would pick the best version, but almost inevitably the very first version would be the best because we weren't thinking about it. You can fool yourself with this we're-just-warming-up rationale, you'd be absolutely distraction-free, fear-free, and it would land every time. Once you start thinking, "Okay, I got a little trouble spot right around this chorus right here, I'm going to have to be careful of that, I'll watch for that," that's on your mind. Suddenly you have a distraction. It's a hindrance.

It was very pure because there was very little done later except to rearrange the volumes of the individual instruments; let's turn up the guitar, let's turn it down. We can't quite hear the voice here so let's turn it up, let's turn it down, whatever. That was the extent of it.

Go back and listen to these songs with that in mind. Most of the vocals were recorded at the same time that the band played the music. I went into a vocal booth and we would look at each other through glass windows, and I would sing the song, directly. It would take an hour to go back and fix a little piece here and there, something that was awful; a hole in your jeans that threatened to lose the leg. Yeah, you'd have to fix that up a little bit. But otherwise, left as were.

It was a complete slap in the face to what was popular in terms of recording. Either you took the Bee-Gee approach and really refined it and polished it and went over it and over it and over it and did it piece by piece and stacked it up, or you took the punk rock approach, which was no polish, no effort toward sophistication or finesse, just kind of hammer away. And we used a beautiful combination of the two. It was recorded on very simple equipment, 24-track at the max. Sometimes 16-track.

We spent most of the time in the studio attempting to re-create the actual sound of the band out of the speakers that were in the studio. You think, well, you just set up a microphone, right, and it comes out sounding like it normally does. Wrong. You have a choice of five thousand different kinds of microphones, five thousand different kinds of coaxial cable, five thousand different filters, noise filters, five thousand different kinds of channeling systems. Soon as you introduce even one of those into the formula, you've altered the sound. It doesn't sound like when you're sitting right in front of it.

The natural sound was searched out to such an extent that, for example, when it was time to sing "Jamie's Cryin'," I had taken special good care of myself. I'd watched what I was eating, watched what I was exercising, didn't smoke any cigarettes, nothing. Walked in, started singing, and Ted Templeman the producer said, "Dave, it doesn't sound the same. It sounds like . . . it's not you, it's not real, it's like it's been worked on or something. Did you do something different?"

I said, "Yeah, well, you know, I didn't smoke any cigarettes and really made sure of what I had for breakfast."

He said, "Well, go outside and smoke a joint. Somebody order up a cheeseburger."

I went out and sat in the little basketball court area outside of Studio A, I think it was, at Sunset Sound recording on Sunset Boulevard. And I ate half a cheeseburger and drained a soda pop and smoked half a joint. Walked in, knocked out "Jamie's Cryin' " in forty minutes.

In a number of Van Halen tunes there's places where the lyrics don't make exact sense or you can't quite decipher what's being said. And that comes from trying to imitate old blues records where you couldn't get anything but the end of the sentence, that's how you speak blues, you go "Bopedy bop blah, baby, all night long." You couldn't quite make it out. And also if you forget the words, you don't stop singing, you just kind of approximate syllables or a syllable that you can remember, or a consonant. So even though you may have well memorized the lyrics, when you go in to sing, when you get to a certain part of a phrase, you might forget something, so you just kind of mush-mouth it, and press on. Nowadays you would go back and fix that. Everybody would go back and fix that.

That was not to be fixed. So, you hear a lyric like,

"Yuh-duh lodda people that are looking for a moonbeam," I'm not even sure what the original lyric was. It makes perfect sense to *me.* Something about people and a moonbeam. Depending on what you had for breakfast, you're going to come up with a different interpretation of it.

Some of this is meant to be rhythmic, sometimes it was attitude, which revved up so hard that it just defies lyrics, no certain string of words can approximate those single syllables. There are certain things that shouldn't have too much meaning, like Saturday night. Don't overload it, you know. If your message is that important, use Western Union. God forbid you're singing to somebody who doesn't speak your English, the King's English.

In the song "Everybody Wants Some," I think the original lyric was, "I've seen a lot of people just lookin' for a moonbeam." That doesn't sizzle and snap, crackle pop for you like going, "Sheepa latta peepah dabba looka foh a moonbeam," and it means so much more, and you're adding a little editorial. You're throwing in an opinion—so critically important in the first verse. Even more so in the second.

On stage, out of fifteen, twenty songs, whatever it is you're playing, you're bound to lose a lyric here and there. I've lost entire verses. Sometimes you get right up to the chorus and the bridge is out, and we's caught in the current! Sometimes one of the biggest noises responded to is when I'm just lost, bein' dragged out to sea and I go, "I forgot the words." That's all I could come up with. People cheer, "Yeah, Dave, if I was you I'd forget the whole song!" That's so cool.

If you'll notice, all Van Halen songs, the really good ones, end up faster than they started. That's how you'd know if Alex was knocking at your door in the hotel. Things became more furious right around the end of the guitar solo. So, you know, we might cut a version—version one with version three halfway through, because sometimes the horses would pick up serious steam. Things weren't just exactly right. We're not looking for perfect, we're looking for right. The great intangible.

The band played all the songs all together in the studio, including the guitar solo, which means it was exactly live. Go back and listen and you'll hear that when the guitar solo came up, that's all you heard was a solo and a bass guitar and a drummer. There's no overdub of another guitar except for twice on that first album. One was in "Jamie's Cryin'," where Ed went back and put down a rhythm track, and another was in "Feel Your Love Tonight." Same thing for the solo, he added a rhythm part. But other than that, it was a very, very airy sound. You could really distinguish each instrument perfectly.

Finally, don't forget that 1978—the year Van Halen released its first album—was the year of the Sex Pistols and *Saturday Night Fever.*

So right up the middle of this channel sails Van Halen, 'cause contained in this band are components of both sides of this coin. I love dance music, I was raised on it. I love *Saturday Night Fever.* I have bought that album—easily one-third of the 20 million ultimately sold. You know, one for the car, one for the house.

The Van Halens understood the heavy rock approach and were proponents of that which begat punk rock, that crash and burn approach. But also there's overlap there because our first base always was to take our music and make it sophisticated without losing any emotional content, and polished without making it seem contrived as possible. That's Bee Gees, man, that's Bee Gees. And I stress the name of the artists, *not* the producers. Most of you reading this right now, upon pain of most grievous torture, could not tell me the name of one of the two producers of those great albums of the Bee Gees. Can you?

So Van Halen contained all of those elements. We were storm and thunder and belligerent and complaining, but gleefully so because we were—well, "You can tell by the way I walk, I'm a woman's man. No time to talk." That was a celebrative element; you had the combination. Isn't it curious that those three elements, those three entities, are perhaps more popular today than they were at that given time. Because ultimately, the great Sex Pistols' album, *Never Mind the Bollocks, Here's the Sex Pistols* at the time sold only three hundred thousand records. You can't even pay your cigarette bill for that much money. That's not even shortstop money, especially for the millions that Warner Brothers poured into it in all of the ensuing hype and hysteria and media attention.

Van Halen was roundly dismissed as qualifying for neither the Confederacy nor the Union. They were turning the other cheek before we could even belt them the first time. The Bee Gees sold, what, 30 million records within a couple of years just on *Saturday Night Fever*? Most people are not aware, they have sold way more than the Beatles. There's only one other band in history who has been covered by more artists than the Bee Gees—and that's ABBA.

And out of all that has passed since 1978 when all three of us convened, all three of our art forms, our approaches and who we are or direct imitations of us, are more popular than ever. There is no functioning club, disco, beer bar, boite or hangout that does not have an old-school seventies disco dance night. There is no city on the face of the earth that does not play—*religiously*—classic old-school Van Halen, and have at least one band whose entire approach is to imitate that, right down to the clothing and the haircuts. They had an old classic Van Halen night and there were some fifteen bands, all of whom are tribute bands, who played in Fort Lauderdale on a Wednesday night. Every city on earth has this. Everywhere I go I see it in the papers. The most popular one in L.A. is called Atomic Punk, and wherever they play it's sold out. I checked. I wanted to go see. Evidently it's hysteria. They start having tailgate parties in front of a beer bar before sundown. In Laramie, Wyoming, they play classic Van Halen over the PA system between innings, it fires the team up. Evidently it fires the coach up too, 'cause he gets thrown out of more games than not. Glad to have been of assistance.

Personal Interaction

Now when people think about groupies they usually think of one of two things. They either think of something they've been told about or vaguely heard about from the sixties, where the girls were almost professionals. There were a couple of girls named the Plaster Casters, who had a little bit of a twist to their game. The way they got backstage was to make plaster molds of guys' dicks. I think they had a collection of some twenty or thirty of them, including Hendrix's and Morrison's dick. Those gals must be in their fifties now or somewheres near it.

They were professionals, they would call ahead, they would come around to the hotels. Sweet Connie was fairly well known as well. Of course she was great looking back then, in the early to late seventies. She would hang around with the Stoneses and the Zeppelinses and whoever. There were a handful of girls like that.

The reason they were really popular is because you didn't have to go through that whole "getting to know you" phase. You didn't have to be concerned with having somebody kicking the bed at 5:30 in the morning, standing there naked with a Kool filter extra-long saying, "What do you mean you don't want pizza?"

Now, none of these girls made any money off of this. In fact, some of of them were school teachers and such; this was their fling. But by and large, there were very few of them to go around, there were probably three or four at any given time. That's why they got such a big name. They were specialists.

The other kind of gal that you might meet backstage was quite literally "the girl next door"—the prom queen, the homecoming queen, Ms. Popcorn Festival of Marion, Iowa, a couple of the girls from the water ski demo team for the wet suit company who happened to be in town doing a demo at the local waterpark. But these were girls next door, and that was halfway in between.

We really didn't pay attention to a whole lot of the opposite ends of the extreme. These goings-on were fairly innocent in that everybody knew the rules. This was not "Oh, I tricked somebody upstairs." Never had to lie. Everybody knew what was going on. It was part of the show. It was part of the fantasy. And for the first time, the public got to participate in a big kind of way, even if all you did was read about it. Van Halen started up in the same years that the Bay City Rollers were hiding their cigarettes till after a press conference. If you leapt ahead, bands like Journey and what have you, were not much different. Everybody wanted to go mainstream.

When Van Halen started out in '78, we looked mainstream. If you look at old pictures of Van Halen, it's really hard to tell what kind of music we really played. You look on the album cover, except for a pair of leather pants, everybody is wearing rip-stop nylon, very clean. It was not Sid Vicious at all. That was part of the appeal. I talked very freely about what was going on backstage on the radio, in interviews or what-not. Otherwise you wouldn't have anybody showing up *to be* backstage. Or you would wind up with professional groupies, which were kind of old hat.

When you talk about what's happened—about what went down backstage, a lot of the way people perceive what was, has been conditioned by imitators over the years. We now live in the age of the adult video. Everywhere you go is an adult video store. Everywhere you go is an adult video section. These girls are known by name.

We're back to the era of the pro. When Van Halen was happening, there wasn't even cable television. Cable television was something like public access, Channel 3. Something where you would watch your neighbor's gardening show.

Well, had there been anywhere to buy those videos back in 1978, I'm sure some of those girls might have wound up on our bus. Most bands would sail through and do the Hank Williams thing and wind up with the lady from behind the counter at the hotel—living in sin at the Holiday Inn. Or "the wife of the promoter's best friend would love to meet y'all, especially you. No, you really should meet her. She's really bright and she's a great water-skier. And since you boys are going to be here over the weekend I understand, I just thought . . ." That tells the story right there.

I was discussing this with one of the fellas, Steve Martin, who's been working with me some seventeen years.

"Dave," he said, "I was talking with a couple of the other guys, you know, that worked on the teams. You realize I didn't ask for a date for seven years? I didn't have to. Even if I was going to, if I told them I was working for Van Halen, they would beat me to it. I even wound up with some great gals that I spent a long time with."

"How do you do, my name's Ordelle and I'm from around here, born and raised. And I hear that you're just—you're going to be spending the night here."

"Well, not really, we have to leave at 4:30."

"Oh, okay, because I just thought . . ." that's how it would start. Not, "Let's go upstairs and fuck." That I would shy away from. That meant you had a specialist. Somebody was collecting scalps. Why fool around? Medically, it made a lot more sense.

So it became a mutual fantasy for a lot of people. It was a way to participate in everything you read about in a magazine. Nobody had any visions of marriage, nobody had any visions: "Will you still love me tomorrow . . .?" There was not supposed to be a tomorrow.

I kept up with most of these girls over the years; some are married. We still stay in touch. I guess they ain't *that* happily married.

When I visualize those carryings on, what reflects in front of my eyes is like the back pages of *Vanity Fair* or one of these Ocean Drive kind of fashion society magazines where a number of parties have taken place and they make a collage of a thousand little pictures cut apart and put back together again till it's a big collage like you used to do on your wall in junior high school. And in it everybody's smiling.

Super-8 film happened, mid to late seventies. You had a film camera and you had to have a film projector for it. And that's what we would use to make films back in the hotel or backstage. We would film everything. We would document everything.

These were the girls who were going to go home and call up the team quarterback in downtown Greensboro the next morning and explain why she didn't call him the night before. Can you dig it? These were girls who were going to go watch their daddy in the club golf tournament that Sunday afternoon, get all fixed up the next morning and kiss you good-bye and say, "Oh, my daddy is in the amateur tournament. He's a dentist, he's a lawyer, he's the biggest stock broker in Greensboro. And my momma's in charge of the reception, you know, and I gotta go, honey. Can I borrow that shirt?"

" 'Course, baby."

Now, you tell me, is that not a fantasy?

And when we started to make video rather than Super-8, it was right out of Belushi and Ackroyd. There was a huge packing case that was just for the video equipment, 'cause we had a tape deck the size of a suitcase. It weighed one hundred pounds, took two guys to carry it—*just* the tape deck. The camera and the lights and the tripod and the cords and the cable and the junction box and the transformer and everything, that was in a whole 'nother case.

So that right there lent a complete ambiance of hilarity, just getting the shit out of the bus and getting it up to the seventh floor. Of course everybody had had a little drink—you'd been working like crazy. And I had a case made just to contain all of the props, because what's a movie without props?

We had costumes in one trunk. We had a schoolteacher costume, a Catholic girl's school outfit, you know, the plaid with the socks and the saddle shoes, and we had a scuba-diving wet suit, kind of we-met-on-vacation kind of thing.

I would be on my bicycle in every city. I'd see these outfits in all kinds of different department store windows and I'd tell Big Ed, "Oh, we got to get that—that would be a great schoolteacher outfit!" Ed would lock up his bike and I'd wait outside and Ed would come out and say, "Okay, you want the shoes too, we have to get the shoes in another store." "Oh, yeah, saddle shoes, of course." There were a couple of riding outfits with britches and boots and spurs and what-not. But you're talking about the lower end of the acting scale here. We're not talking about DeNiro and Streep. We're talking about Mutt and Jeff and Delores and Tina.

We got a catalog somewhere on the East Coast, one of these warehouses that advertises in the back of comic books for monster makeup and fake gunshot wounds that you put under your shirt and fake scar tissue, everything for the monster movie thing.

The nuns' outfits were for the roadies to wear when they were holding the lights. Now, if this little dissertation was being carried on by Quentin Tarantino, you'd think, "This is an amazing script. He's going to have more cameos than *The Player.* Everybody's going to want to be in this one." Right out of Monty Python—which was the truest blueprint for all of this—if not Lil' Abner comics. Throw in a little Kickapoo Joy Juice, enter Marrying Sam. Marrying Sam the preacher man, with the hat and the frock.

We would stage complete scenarios and we would rehearse and shoot. But next we started making "the makings ofs," because that was even more screwball than anything. Again, we were either shooting Super-8 film on a hand-held camera—and this is like when you got ahold of Mom and Dad's, and you first started off with stop motion. "All right, take another step. All right," then you shoot two frames. "Now take another step," 'cause it looked funny to you; it looked like Charlie Chaplin.

I played director, you know, in a kind of accelerated fashion. We got a lot of mileage out of the school girl and the teacher outfits. But the really bizarre stuff, the monster stuff and the preacher collar with the nuns' outfits and everything, were pretty much worn by the crew guys running the lights or the tape deck, or some of the completely dysfunctional crew guys who acted out a part in the movie. The girls were pretty . . . come on, they were the girls next door. Have a little respect.

Close as I got to disrespect—and this was *not* a home movie—was somewhere in the Midwest. I had a knock on my hotel room door. A rather demure-looking girl, no spandex, no PVC, said, "Dave, I hope I didn't wake you up."

"No, I've been up since the late sixties . . . how are you tonight?"

"Well, I was just thinking . . ."

"Well, bless your little heart. Come on in this little room here, it will be easier to think. There's so much distraction in this big scary hallway."

She comes in, we sit and we talk and everything. She says, "Look, I hope—I hope you don't think that I'm weird or something, you know, but I was just thinkin' . . ."

"Yes?"

"I know what goes on around here and that's why I fought my way up here. I want to tell you that I'm very glad I did . . . but would you mind spanking me?"

"Well, right off, I think we should talk. Right for starters, darling, I think we should at least do lunch. Wait a minute, I don't have time for lunch. Golly, look at the time." And of course you can always answer a question kind of with a question, like a lawyer: "Do you have a brush?"

She says, "Oh, yes." Goes into her purse, comes out with a hairbrush. Now, it's not the Annihilator, okay? But it's got some weight to it, it's got some swing.

I said, "I'm not sure, you know, how we approach this—I have some ideas that I'd love to explore . . . with *you.*"

Things begin like a normal ballgame, the ball is kicked, there's some running, some passing, each team makes a few downs, jockeying for position, it's a pretty even match. In fact, it's a good day for football. And then here comes that famous Statue of Liberty play. "There's Roth. He's going for the brush!"

What she wants is to get on all fours, and she wants her little tush spanked.

In fact, I don't like violence unless there's a referee and we have gloves on. Or if Sly is doing it for me on a forty-foot screen.

But, hey, there's an eighth time for everything, huh? And who's countin'? So I commence, and I'm—like tentative—but I begin to spank this little gal's bottom. Actually, she ain't so little, she's like in her mid to late twenties. Looks like a legal secretary. And she's lovin' it and she's requesting a little more arm, you know, I'm paraphrasing, "Put your body into it, kid. Throw from the legs."

I am *very* slow to do it, because I don't want to leave welts on the girl, and I don't want to "go too far." I can play-act, but it's something I got to work at. Things continue for a while, they finish up with a great resolve—big finish, a lot of talk about a sequel. She gets dressed, we kiss each other good-bye and she disappears off into the night, big smile.

We got on the buses the next morning. Things had been somewhat calm backstage at the local armory or wherever it was we were playing because the police station was built in as part of the arena. The offices were like, "upstairs" and in the back part of the same building.

About an hour down the highway, eight highway patrol cars surround the bus, sixty miles an hour, slow us down, pull us over. They talk to the driver, "You're going to have to follow us to the station." The bus turns around—this is two-lane blacktop, we drive for thirty minutes. Everybody saying, "Jesus Christ, what's going on?" We pull up to the Highway Patrol. We're escorted into the compound, everybody's walked off the bus, all identification is collected, and everybody is forced to sit like POWs in the dirt, with our backs to the brick wall in a parking area surrounded by barbed wire fence. The buses are impounded elsewhere. We sat there for hours. Nobody told us what was going on.

I thought to myself, "Oh my God—I killed her." I mean, not only did I not mean to kill anybody, there weren't any marks. It was all just play-acting, just a little tap and a lot of great talk; I'm good at talk. These would qualify as love taps . . . but I don't know, 'cause now I'm sitting in a blowin' dirt, dry-summer wind, blowing through an empty brick-wall parking lot with barbed wire and being impounded and sitting like in every Japanese internment camp during the war. I'm thinking, "Oh, my God, maybe she had some unusual skin condition, and I activated it with just one tiny fragment of an ounce too much pressure, and a pore opened up and a deadly spore from the pore got in her bloodstream and made like a blood clot from sitting on her little butt in her car on the way home, and on account of how far away she lived, the blood clot got a chance to travel, and it went straight up into her head and killed her right there in the driver's seat!"

Second thought: "Where's the brush? Did the brush get packed? Was it found in the smoking wreckage of her car when she died from the brain clot from the skin condition at the wheel in excess of ninety miles an hour and careened off the interstate into a school bus full of blind kids? Oh man, I'm in for it now. I knew God was saving me up for something special, at least that's what I say to myself every morning but, wow, looks like I'm the next Christmas window."

It was like tequila, you know, when you get so uproariously blotto and you're doing the technicolor yawn, and you're kind of externalizing the way Courtney Love sounds. And you're making all kinds of promises to every saint what you can remember. You got a fourth mortgage on your soul by the time you get to God himself. God's kid, selling a fifth mortgage, with liens.

It turns out that some kids had gotten through some windows at the cop shop, and started a garbage can fire. Actually, not even in the station itself but somewhere adjacent, but of course everywhere in that armory was adjacent to the police station. So they pulled us over, thinking, oh, maybe this was one of our wild carefree parties that their kids had been reading about. No, had not. In fact, most of us were tired from playing roller hockey most of the afternoon on the floor of the armory. Nevertheless, I couldn't look at a hairbrush for the next two months without a note of terror, and I never heard from her again.

Nobody was ever duped into doing something they didn't want to do. Everybody got carried away in the moment—that's the whole reason that we create moments, so you can stop thinking like an adult and get carried away like a kid again, whether that's at a square dance or backstage.

Over the years other bands attempted to imitate this, making videos on a Cecil B. DeMille kind of a level, as opposed to "We're going to make some dirty movies." What I did came from the fun. It didn't even require any strategic thinking. Half the time we never even got up to the sex part, 'cause everybody would be carrying on, having a great time. You'd pair off or triple off and wander off into your own little room . . . and get off. Who knew how to make pornography? Who cared? I never could understand how you could get it up in front of a room full of people, or with the camera running. I have a lot of respect for that. That singlemindedness, that kind of focus—I'm impressed with that.

We talk about sex a lot in this book, but I don't think it takes the form that most people expect: "Then I fucked her this way, then I fucked her that way, then I fucked her friend." How droll, how boring. You already know I did that. It's sort of like when I got busted for ten dollars' worth of reefer, you think anybody said, "Whoa, tell me it ain't so, Ma. Who woulda thunk." Do I have to describe to you how to roll a joint?

My whole perception of sex is through the eyes of a super-enthusiastic kid, it's full of smiles, it's full of playing, and there's mutual fascination. There's a mutual celebration there, that's what I look for. So my stories always seem to take a left turn when it comes to sex. Okay, did we round the bases? Uh, did we get to third base? Of course. You know that.

Far as naming names, I could name names, ruin somebody's week. They're not names that most would recognize and would be instantly forgotten, so why wreak havoc? Believe me, without naming names and trying to tiptoe around—I have tiptoed around none of the incidents or the particulars—I revel in them. Believe me, there is going to be havoc at the dinner table in more than one domicile, even without names and birth dates. So, there's no home addresses here. Everybody's guilty. Just fill in your favorite name.

As I currently reside, I look forward to great company, good sharing, and out of that, hopefully, will come some kind of love or affiliation, a relationship. But that's a tough quantity to fill because I occupy a unique niche. It's very hard for most people to relate to my experiences, and the greater number of them add up to "take me to your leader."

What about the women in my life? What I regret most is that I have so many great stories and memories and visions based on those things, and not one singular human being that I can share that with and refer back to regularly.

The girl I went to New Guinea with wanted to get married and have children. I said that's not me right now. We went our separate ways. Six, eight months later, there's an article in *Rolling Stone.*

"Supermodels Discuss Their Love Affairs" whatever, she took off after me. So I'm very careful, I'm very hesitant.

I had been in a true blue relationship, no fooling around for the better part of a year and a half. And I knew that as per her upbringing and her family it was about having kids and setting up shop. And she said to me, "I have to go back to New York to work unless I have more of a commitment." And I said, "I don't think I can make that commitment to you right now." This was like '85—there was a *lot* going on in my life.

But it wasn't having the child that she wanted, so much as it was getting married. I think I knew even then I'll make a great dad, but I got to work on bein' a husband.

I love kids. It is the kid inside adults that's the most

attractive to me. You wouldn't even expect that from David Lee Roth initially.

I 'spect I have not wound up with a significant other 'cause I'm not happy with me. Always something new to prove. Always something new to challenge. Always a new treasure mountain to climb. So my whole battle is based on defeating that impulse; quit competing, quit trying so hard, go smooth. But I am no monk, by any stretch. I'm a pretty happy guy, but I'm not content at all.

The Engine Room

Being Jewish has always been a real hard jacket for me to wear because we all want to be accepted. I had learned at a *very* early age—brief, but impacting—from wearing little braces on my feet for a few years, that I was different, I was *not* part of the clan. At the same time, I didn't have an Orthodox Jewish upbringing. I went to Sunday school. I went to some Jewish summer camp for a few weeks. I had a bar mitzvah.

But now I live in this age of political correctness, which means silence. Doesn't mean that we've legislated human behavior out of existence; it merely silenced people, and now they operate in the dark. The best you can hope for as a Jew is to be tolerated. You'll never be accepted. You'll never be just one of the gang. You'll always be "that Jew," or "a Jew," or "the Jew."

Even a surgically mutated Michael Jackson can go on record with "Kike me," and say, "Well, it was poetry." He will issue a little edict saying he didn't really mean it. Maybe he used it as a publicity premise—it got the publicity. But had not a Jew raised their hand and said, "Hey, you! Shut the fuck up," nobody would have said anything.

Every now and then, if I go to temple on a high holiday, they ask me to lecture the kids. Talk to the kids in the kids' services. They've stopped that because I would tell the kids: "Stop thinking of yourself as a white; nobody else does."

Once again, the great barometer—let's go to jail, man, where you've got nothing else, no material goods, no rights, no privileges, no nothing—but you're honoring your opinion. If you think of yourself as white, well, let's just see what the Aryan Brotherhood thinks of that when you check in. Okay?

In the late fifties and the sixties, it was not quiet. It was not unusual to walk off to temple, find swastikas painted on the door—literally six blocks from where John F. Kennedy was born. The standard op.

What we saw on film, from the time we could walk into the assembly hall, was emaciated bodies being thrown into big pits and burned to death by German supermen. If it wasn't them, it was Russian supermen; and if it wasn't them, it was the Spanish Inquisition, and on and on and on.

I grew up with people who had numbers tattooed on their forearms, and they weren't that old. I could go over to the DiLido Hotel in Miami Beach right now and talk to a few. They're in the swimming pool doing aquatic exercises.

The Six Day War brought back the whole idea of the Maccabees and the fight for Masada—and these were thousands-of-years-old conflicts—the Jews didn't even win. Everybody got whacked, the entire crew. The victory was they held off ten thousand men for *X* amount of days. Well, we give them an A for enthusiasm and effort, but in fact, the whole crew died at the end of a spear.

It wasn't until 1967 that we saw the first real Jewish physical heros, like in the movie show. We saw Moshe Dayan, with his eye patch. I was a thirteen-year-old. It was the first time I'd ever heard of that. Otherwise it was turn the other cheek, accept whatever; the Chosen People. Well, chosen for what? Because if most people had their way—let's just take a poll here and if everybody here told the truth, I wouldn't be here.

My full name happens to be David Lee Roth. It sounds southern. It's definitely Indiana. It's my real, full-blast name. But I'm sure the "Lee" throws a lot of people off. This almost sounds like I'm in the Allman Brothers. Made it much more palatable for people. Were I just David Roth, I think things would have been different.

My speech at my bar mitzvah was about "It's really difficult being Jewish and I don't like it." It shocked everybody. They were stunned. Fourteen pages of "I'm not proud to be Jewish. Everybody hates me." Everybody was silent, like an E. F. Hutton commercial, because they all knew I was right.

I've done so many interviews—American, European. I remember one interview, the height of the Van Halen era, some German magazine (I forget which), a German equivalent of *Life* magazine. First question out of the guy's mouth is, "So, you are a Jew?" I said, "I very much am. But as opposed to beginning the interview with that question and providing the readership with some tinted color of glasses through which they will look at all the rest of what I say, what if we put this at the end of the interview?"

"Okay, we'll do this."

We finished the interview. Then I said: "You racist piece of human fuckin' garbage. You don't deserve to be in my court. Fuck you and everything you stand for." I picked up his tape recorder and smashed it to pieces against the wall, called my security guy, Eddie. I told him, "Eddie, pick a window. He is leaving. And I hope he doesn't hurt his right leg on the way out." He was stunned. He had never seen a Jew react like that.

I come from a generation where there was a slight turnover in attitude, where we shifted from turn-the-other-cheek to a different kind of mind-set. If you say, "Oh, Dave, New York is full of Jews. Jewish people are accepted all over the world now," somebody has conned you. You're in fucking dreamland. If you believe that, you live where Tinker Bell lives.

Here come the Syrians and the Iraquis armed with Chinese weaponry, roaring across the border for that little crescent of land. The only reason Israel exists is it's just another little parcel that landed on our doorstep that the British gave us with the Balfour Declaration. "Let's find a nice little slice of geography that's non-productive, non-fertile, unplantable, non-livestock-usable land.

It's pretty rare to find that. They found it. They said, "This is yours." It was only when the Israelis cultivated it and made it alive and valuable that everybody else started lobbing grenades over the fence. Still continues.

I didn't study at the hand of a Talmudic scholar. I did learn that learning is sacred, and reading is great. I appeared on a television station, Much Music, the MTV of Canada. This fellow in his mid-twenties showed up. You could tell from his smug attitude that he thought he was dealing with the guy from Motley Crüe. He said, "So Dave, we're going to talk about some things, if you don't mind, in this interview, that you might not be familiar with." Okay, so we're not only smug, we're inept.

"Sure, man, talk about anything."

He said, "Now, you're probably not aware, but Thorn EMI—"

I said, "I am."

He said, "What was I going to ask you, Dave?"

I said, "You were going to tell me that Thorn EMI is a subsidiary division of the Ellises Corporation out of Italy, and that the Ellises Corporation manufactures land mines. And because of all the problems in Afghanistan since the Russian withdrawal, kids are getting blown up out in the fields and that we should boycott Thorn EMI records in an effort to get the Ellises Corporation to quit doing what they are doing and go out of business."

I said to him, "You're about to dispense a kind of a broad-based, hippie-dip generalization, one big simple cure; we're just gonna put the land-mine company out of business and everything's going to be fine." He said, "Do you have another idea?" I said, "Yeah. There's no such thing as broad-based, simple, generalized rules and policies that just solve everything."

I said, "You strike me as a crybaby who's only seen

bloodletting on a screen that's eighteen inches wide. For two and a half years I worked in a surgery clinic as a night-shift porter. I've walked in and had my union break, smoked a cigarette, covered with blood up to my armpits. You're talking about little kids blowing their leg off? I was the one who took the leg down to the freezer. Don't talk to me about your MTV generation perceptions." The guy said, "Well, what's the reason for having a land mine? Can't we just all get along together?" Sure, Rod. Sure.

I said, "See that guy standing off camera over there?" I'm pointing to Big Ed—Ed's two hundred-plus, he's a fireplug. I said, "Just imagine that he wants to kill you. In fact, if he kills everybody in your family, he goes to heaven. It's now the '73, Syrian battle, Golan Heights: Just imagine there were nine of him in this studio right now, and they all get to go to heaven if they can kill you before this interview is over, because that's what the Syrian conflict was." I said, "Now, I'd sure hate to see the Jews disappear off the face of the earth, because if the Syrians or the Iraqis or the Iranians or the Lebanese or the Egyptians or the Palestinians have their way, that's what's going to happen. I'd hate to see the Buddhists disappear off the face of the earth in Tibet because that's the way the communists would have it. Okay? We can continue this. I'd hate to see the Karen tribesmen disappear off the face of the earth in Burma because that's what the Burmese government would have." I said, "So I think maybe there is a time to take up arms, or blow someone's off." And he was silent. He was astonished.

"Okay, I understand that," he said, "But hey, man, my father works with UNICEF. He's seen all of that. He knows what's going on. That's where I learned it from."

I told him, "Well, you go back to your da-da, you tell him that neither of you exist without somebody with a gun standing at the gate."

He said, "Good idea, gun control. A lot of people carrying guns to school, a lot of people getting killed, and the death rate's climbing. Aren't you for gun control, David?"

I said, "Absolutely. But we gotta analyze something first here. I just need help with a little something. Because about five, six years ago my father was in his doctor's office, a fellow walks in with a briefcase and says, 'I have some court documents that need to be signed, legal case.' Pop says, 'Not unusual, let's go back in my office, sign whatever you want.' " Went back in his office, closed the door and the guy pulls out a loaded .357, puts it up to his head, okay?

Says, "Surprise. I'm not really from the court system. I'm going to tie you up, put you in the trunk of your car, we're going to go call your kid and make a few dollars. Leave you in the car, tell him where you are, and everything will be cool. Anything goes wrong, I'm going to shoot you."

Pop talks, is cool for a half an hour, "Hey, put the gun down, please. I'll do whatever you want. Just relax." After about a half an hour, the guy lowered his weapon. Pop smacked him in the head, stunned him just long enough to make a beeline out the back door and ran three blocks down the street.

So now my house is like the Berlin Wall because the guy got away. Rottweilers, strangers with loaded shotguns coming up and down the driveway—it was like that for a couple of weeks. Lo and behold, they catch this puke, he's a skell, okay? They put him in the Pasadena lockup and they leave him in the drunk tank, transitory—the Parker Center, Central Division down in Chinatown is overbooked four to one. This guy stays in the drunk tank for ten months, and the whole time he's in there, he's telling guys who are passing through on a nightly basis, "Yeah, man, David Lee Roth stole my helicopter, man, he ripped off my girlfriend Cathy Lee Crosby; he owes me a quarter of a million dollars on a drug deal," and on and on. Space age, this is a *cadet.* Okay? Ten months passes by; they're going to transport him from the lockup to a car to take him down to Chinatown when two of his buddies jump out of low-riders and bust him free, like the Old West. They beat up the two cops, steal their weapons and disappear into the sunset.

Ten days later, he gets in a shoot-out with the SWAT team and they kill him under a Toyota. This guy took on the whole L.A.P.D. twenty blocks from my house.

Now, you look me right in my eye, and tell me that I shouldn't sleep with a gun.

He said, "Well, Dave, this all leads up to a greater issue."

I said, "What's that?"

He said, "Death. Death is on the minds of a lot of young people these days. It's represented in the lyrics, in the music, you know, the alternative nation."

I said, "You don't know shit about death. You read about it on page twenty-six. You turn the TV set off when you're tired of death." I said, "I cleaned up after it."

He was silent. And I said to him, "I know you're going to edit this to make me sound like G. I. Joe, so I'd just like to say ahead of time, 'Go fuck yourself.' " And that was the end of the interview.

You throw a little Jewish on top of that, you got trouble. You got a bunch of wild, crazy energy.

Sorry that doesn't sound hippie. Sorry that doesn't sound like communal jubilant fun. Sorry I'm not a Pepper. Sorry I didn't pop out of a soda-pop ad, and life is just one big fucking cabaret, because a lot of what propelled Van Halen, what compels me and propels me is precisely this element. It's *fury.* If you approach me with anti-Semitic preconceptions, I'm not here to re-educate. I come from a whole different school of thought. If you don't get it on the first try, fuck you.

I once heard somebody say to the Van Halens, "You guys play the music; the Jew sells it." Well, you're fucking right. And now that I'm gone, Van Halen stinks. Okay?

Want to know why some of my contributions to Van Halen sound like they do? Didn't come from a smiling place in my soul. Not at all.

Nobody ever said to Mick Jagger, "So, Mick, you're Episcopalian, aren't you?" Nobody ever took Jimi Hendrix aside and said, "So, Jimi, you're a Baptist, aren't you?" Much less start off the interview that way.

Every step I took on that stage was smashing some Jew-hating, lousy punk ever deeper into the deck. *Every step.* I jumped higher 'cause I knew there was going to be more impact when I hit those boards. And if you were even vaguely anti-Semitic, you were under my wheels, motherfucker. That's where the lyrics came from, that's where the body language came from, that's where the humor came from, and where the fuck you came from. All equally as important. You want to know the ingredients? Don't ask if you don't want to know.

What you get from repression and what you get

from hatred is fury, and fury was one of the main trigger points for the great Van Halen. What you see now is a bunch of buffoons waddling around at the family barbecue, and their wives admonishing the children saying, "Don't worry, Daddy's just had a few too many Coors Lights and he's imitating what he used to do for a living when he played music, honey."

What's missing is the testosterone. What's missing is the fury. What's missing is the passionate convicted commitment. And I got a lot of mine from my religious background. So y'all best stop imagining the way Dr. Zorba looked, or some defenseless Hasidic Jew with a little yarmulke on his head, 'cause that ain't here for you.

Roadwork

It became imperative toward the end of '78 that we get our own barricade. Something a little closer to armed cavalry than "Please stay off the towers." Something closer to Berlin '61, than "don't take the brown acid." Okay? It took up a third of the truck; w*e had* to have it. And we started to stabilize the security environment, because every concert was one hell of a powwow, and the barricade was routinely smashed to trinkets.

We had what was called an "ego ramp," which means you have the flat stage going from three o'clock to nine o'clock, and then jutting out is a tongue of staging.

It's ten feet across, between five and twenty-five feet long; it juts out into the audience. It was the "ego ramp" for obvious reasons. People were launching themselves onto it, and were crawling up onto the stage.

We were one of the first to institute headset security, where you see thug guys in yellow shirts down in the pit behind the barricade, some wearing headgear. When there was some trouble, or somebody was starting to throw something, or something was getting smushed against the barricade, the guy on the side of the stage would radio over the mike down into the pit, and the situation would be adjusted.

If you could see the inside of our barricade, it was numbered from one to ten, red numbers on the right, and one to ten, white numbers on the left. So say E. V. would go for a guitar solo and I would dance casually over to the security guy on the side of the stage and yell, "Gorgeous blonde, red T-shirt, pink earrings, pink lipstick, about six feet back, red right, three and a half. Think she's got a boyfriend." I'd then dance right back out on stage and do my shimmy-shimmy coco-pop. He would radio down into the pit, and a gorilla would crawl over the barricade, into the audience, give her a backstage pass.

One night I had an idea. Starting around '79 when we really started top billing—we took gi-normous productions into third-level markets—Tuna Fish, Wisconsin, and Park Bench, Utah. It would take forever to get five, six semis, eighteen-wheeler trucks' worth of gear through the doors. Sometimes you'd have to disassemble because the doors were too small, move it through the doors, reassemble. Teardown time was twice as long, 'cause then everybody's tired, it's the end of the night, you gotta make an eight-hour hop for a show tomorrow and then tomorrow and tomorrow and tomorrow.

So I came up with the incentive program. Okay. All crew members will receive five backstage passes, they initial them. And whichever one of these girls that I wind up with at the end of the night, if it's got your initials—you get one hundred dollars. Now, in 1979, this is the equivalent of like three hundred fifty dollars. Which, for guys who were making three hundred and fifty a week, is an incentive. I know full well that I'm in charge of desperate men in search of desperate fortune. I know that they're taking at least half of those backstage passes, giving them out to pretty girls after the show, and telling them, "Look, meet me out at the crew bus at such and such a time." Within three days, teardown time was cut in half. Everybody had to get back to the bus and nobody knew *why* . . . 'cept me. The other band members had a vague idea of what was happening. But what happened with the Van Halens was not that freewheelin' sprawl that happened for me.

Every night, after a show, everybody who didn't wind up on a crew bus was instructed to go to the side bleachers in the arena. Everybody had backstage passes; a hundred and fifty people sitting in the bleachers, thirty wide and going up.

A security guy would give what we called "The Speech," which went like this: "Ladies and gentlemen, welcome. You're invited to hang out backstage with the band and the crew. This is purely social. Please, no autographs, no photos. We have music and food and drink for one and all." He would drag out the speech as long as necessary because coming in from behind, up in the bleachers, you have four three-hundred-pounders, separating the boyfriends from the girlfriends, saying, "Um, excuse me, but we're a little short on space. The young lady is invited but that's all the room that we really have and, you know, you should really make a decision now."

Nobody would notice because everybody is looking forward, listening to the speech. Meanwhile, they're working in from behind and thinning the herd. Until we were down to about seventy-two likely suspects, most of them girls, women of all types, of all ages. Everybody would file into the backstage area. Since the backstage area was basically my design—well, we fixed it up with a stereo that was created out of two bass speakers that had been on stage during the first tour. "Your little legs get bumps when the bass man thumps." And mid-range speakers, and horns and a control center that was five feet tall. Six hundred people was our record for backstage—in L.A. at the Forum. We took up like four different rooms. Had the stereo humping, we would get gels from the lighting crew and gel the lights even though it was a locker room. Turn it into Club Dave.

We would finish dinner in another room—this was basically myself and the road crew—then wander in. Not unusual to see forty girls dancing with each other to the latest tunes in the gelled red light. And we would hang out. I might wind up with somebody, I might not. Didn't matter.

It didn't matter because teardown time was cut in half, and the ritual the next day was way better than any ritual I could have fantasized the night before. Big Ed and I would show up backstage, hours before sound check, during crew meal. Well over one hundred human beings eating red meat and potatoes and soda pops and what-not on paper plates.

I'd walk in and I'd go, "Ladies and gentlemen. Ladies and gentlemen, we have a winna! He's young, he's hot, he's good-looking, and it's his first tour. He works on the lighting crew and he's got the Eye. Her name was Otisha and I wisha she was here in the city with us even as I speak, but even as I do speak she's in the rearview mirror, but this guy's right in front of us, his name is Danny, and he gets one hundred fucking dollars!"

Within a matter of weeks, these guys were pros. Different members of the crew start forming teams—"Look, if we pool our expertise, we can win this three nights a week easy. We'll split the money and over a period of *X* amount of weeks we're so far ahead of the wave . . ." And they became competitive about, well, who found who, because you'd wind up with a backstage pass where the initials had been crossed off, and somebody else's had been put in place of. "Well, hey, I saw her from the stage first. You guys waited until after electric check, ran into her out in the atrium. I'm not even sure what an atrium is, but I do know I seen her from the deck during drum check."

Setup and teardown time dwindled away to nothing, and the legend began to expand. I talked about it very freely in the press. Years later, the very austere columnist Cindy Adams, who deals with the glitterati, the political, the high-end movie folks for the *New York Post,* interviews me. She says, "David, I understand that you gave your crew members backstage passes so that they'd go out and get girls for you." I said, "Cindy, hold it. Hold it right there. Don't get your pants in a bunch. I gave the crew members with *taste* backstage passes."

She says, "Dave, now there was just a girl who was on *Geraldo Rivera,* a Mistress Constance or Connie, Sweet Connie. Groupie, she'd been with all of the rock stars. Claimed that you were with her and a girlfriend in front of a room full of people backstage in Little Rock, Arkansas, and carried on."

I said, "Wait, Cindy, when did this supposedly occur?"

She said, "1980, 1981."

I said, "Thirteen years ago?"

She says, "Yes."

I said, "I'd like to think so."

I would routinely make bizarre comments. I received the key to the city in Boston when we played there for a couple of shows. I stood up and I said, "Thank you very much. Receiving this key is sort of like becoming a member of a family. And I am very family-oriented, in fact, I think I may have started one last night."

In a very short period of time, things got way out of hand—better than we had ever planned. People were waiting to get near that barricade. Girls would show up during lunchtime, before sound check, to get a back-stage pass and come back later. The most repressed cities provided us with this best element. Salt Lake City. Pittsburgh. Oh, it was *great.* Not unusual to have fifty different gals show up at lunchtime sound check *demanding* to give a blow job.

One day in a legal meeting I said to this team of lawyers—everybody's sitting in a circle—"You know, a piano player can insure his fingers like a surgeon, and a ballet dancer, a ballerina, can insure their feet and their legs. Sooner or later I'm going to start getting more and more of these letters that say, 'Dear Dave, do you remember me? I'm Ordelle Johnson from Dental Floss, Iowa. We shared a wonderful moment and now you have two wonderful little children, both of whom need individual bicycles.' "

Well, we would get some of those in the mail. And I said, "Is it possible to insure my dick?" Like paternity insurance. Because 99.9 percent of this stuff is all just nonsense. I was always taking precautions, even way back when. Very unlikely somebody's going to get pregnant from me. Nevertheless, you got to settle out of court. Somebody shows up with an attorney or what have you, and Diamond Dave is guilty till proven innocent. I'm the product of carefully wielded, self-generated bad publicity for many summers. Well, the word got around that I had bought paternity insurance. And of course, who am I to get in the way of a good rumor?

Couple more stories from our days as an opening act:

There was no one particular show, but the best tour was our first one with the band Journey. We were third billing, go on at 7:30, thirty people in the audience. But we were bent on victory—whatever that meant. Journey had some backstage passes, but they were all married, it was very domestic, so we printed up our own backstage passes and handed them out. Our backstage would be packed with people. Ultimately, we started handing out backstage passes to everybody, throwing them into the audience, big clouds of pastel colors. There'd be thousands of people backstage and Journey could never figure out where this was all coming from. And of course we would routinely be threatened with being fired, kicked off the tour. During sound check their singer came on stage once, he had a scarf around his neck, and I said to him, "Why do you have a scarf around your neck?"

He said, "It was a rough night last night, strained myself a bit."

Next day at sound check—I had sent a crew member around—and everybody showed up on stage with scarves wrapped around our dicks.

Pretty soon, we were opening for bigger and bigger bands. In early '79, we were playing at the Los Angeles Coliseum, some ninety thousand people, Aerosmith was top bill. And I had an idea of a way to make an entrance, having gone down to the stadium to see the lay of the land some weeks earlier. There's a stairway comes from the great arches down to a landing—it's a big landing, visible to everybody in the stands—and then another three hundred steps down to the football field where the stage was.

The idea was to park a Volkswagen on that landing, and since we knew the people who were running the PA system, we would have them make announcements all throughout the afternoon and into the evening that whoever it was from the Aerosmith team that owns the yellow Volkswagen, could you please move it? This is where they were stacking some equipment, whatever, it was visible to all ninety thousand people. It's like up and behind the actual stage.

We rented an actual Sherman tank—in Hollywood, you can rent anything you want. The theory being that after all of these announcements throughout the day and the night, the lights would go down, they'd go, "Ladies and gentlemen . . . da-da-da . . . Van Halen," the spotlights would hit us and the tank would come out from under a cover on that landing, run right over the Volkswagen and we'd pop out of the tank and run down the stairs to the stage.

We bought two old used Volkswagens so we could test one on a Sunday afternoon. We went down to the stadium, the band got in the tank. The driver, little southern guy, with a Rawlings football helmet on, he's telling us all the movies this tank had been in, "Oh, yeah, *The Longest Day, Kelly's Heroes*."

We had taken the engines and the glass out of the VWs, but otherwise they were completely intact. You would never know the difference from two feet away. We all got in the tank and ran over the Volkswagen. This was before monster truckism graced our popular culture—monster trucks, bog racing, tractor pulls, I call these "turbo-pop entertainment." This was pre-turbo-pop entertainment.

That Volkswagen smashed flat like a bad textbook, lug nuts shot off of those wheels in excess of two hundred miles an hour, everybody was ducking and jumping out of the way. I still have the door from that Volkswagen at my house, one of the souvenirs that I saved. The door burst off, flew like twenty feet, everything just exploded outward. We figured we were on to something good. And of course we would then play our show and Aerosmith would have to make an entrance.

We discovered several days before the show that Aerosmith had been put wise to our little scheme and had found some stock footage of airplanes blowing up tanks, and that's what they were going to show when they came on after us. So here we are with a gutted Volkswagen sitting up on the dais and a Sherman tank under a tarp with gorillas standing around making sure nobody looks underneath.

We decided that because Aerosmith had a little trump card that we weren't going to do the tank trick, so we never ran over the Volkswagen, we just ran down the stairs. We didn't want to be one-upped on our one-upmanship, you know. I haven't spoken with the boys in Aerosmith since then.

You set up for a tour and you've got eighty people and six tour buses. They all pull into port, usually in front of the "Riot House," the Hyatt House on Sunset Boulevard. Everybody shows up just like at the docks, kiss their significant others good-bye, there's tears, there's waving. Then there's those of us who are streaming out of the bars, or waking up next to Juanita Somebody and going, "Jesus, it's first bell."

The ultimate guys show up with barely a belly pack, wearing a pair of shorts, some tennis shoes and a T-shirt. In the pack is a jacket and a pair of long jeans. That's about it. Some cigarette lighters, a toothbrush. You'll get your hair conditioner and shampoo at the hotel, those little bottles in every bathroom. Ultimately everybody is wearing free promotional merchandise.

In the late seventies, up until the mid-eighties, there was a lot more throwaway cash before Reaganomics—that's a quickie way to say it. It means that we all ran out of money. But up until then, Jesus, we'd all come walkin' in wearing a merchandising hat with the name of the band. Pair of sunglasses that had been supplied by the guy from Hawaiian Tropic because he got free tickets. A T-shirt that came from the record company. You got a tour jacket on. Pair of shorts featuring the last promoter's logo.

Every band would have a Nike or a Converse representative show up, a fan, and say, "Hey, I'm coming to the show in St. Louis. Do any of you guys need tennis shoes?"

"Oh, you bet." And he would show up literally with seventy pairs of tennis shoes.

Want to throw a little salt in the rice? You send a runner out to the local Harley-Davidson shop, which exists in every major city of the free earth, and invite the whole staff to the show, and you start your collection of Harley-Davidson shirts from city to city. 'Cause every Harley shop has their own variation, you know, the "Ride to Live," "Live to Ride," or whatever. And if you go through an entire tour like this, you're going to have three hundred Harley-Davidson shirts in infinite variety, all of them on black material.

This is how we all looked. It was something like from a Terry Gilliam movie. It was the wildest ragtag army, as all great armies are. Think of the great American Indian warriors and how they would dress. Traditional Indian breastplate with a top hat, a colonel's wool jacket and a loincloth and buckskin. The spoils of war.

So it's off to war. Everyone on the bus!

Low end of the bus spectrum was the first time Van Halen went to tour Europe and we opened for Black Sabbath. Literally twenty-two cities in twenty-eight days. I never knew there *were* that many cities in England. England, three television channels in 1978, two of them BBC. A lot of documentaries.

We got a "tour bus," which was for tourists; windows all the way down, two seats and an aisleway and two seats.

But wasn't meant for sleeping. The armrests were bolted into the floor, and the way that you would go to sleep—'cause you would travel all night after the show to the next city—you put your head down on your shoulder, slid your bottom leg under the armrests, across the aisleway, onto the other seat under the armrest. You're on your side, you put your upper leg on top of the armrests across the aisleway, and lay there on your side, like so. You're done, right? Wrong. 'Cause your right arm's hanging off the edge of the seat. So we all started wearing suspenders so that you could gaffer-tape your arm to the suspenders and keep it from hanging down off of the seat. And every set of seats had a body sleeping like this, all the way down.

Sometimes when we'd go into a bigger city from Peoria to Paris, a number of the road crew would get on our bus, the band bus, because we would leave sooner, and they wanted to get there earlier and shop. They would sleep head-to-toe on the floorboards underneath, all the legs going across the seating. It was like climbing into an Apollo module. Took a while to get in position. First you would arrange the little net piece that sits on the back of a bus seat, you know, to put your map or your cigarettes, your water, your sunglasses. I remember somebody saying, "Look, there's Edinburgh Castle," and it was too much trouble to get out of the capsule. I opened one eye and there it was reflected upside down in my mirror sunglasses.

If you had to use the toilet in the back, you had to monkey down on top of the seats over all the bodies. And if the bus hit a bump or took a weird turn—and Britain is not known for its straight-line construction—you'd crash down and if somebody was sleeping on the floor, there would be a five-guy pileup.

High end of the bus world is what I call Dolly Parton's bathroom. You'd get these huge Eagle buses that travel America and, you know, the country western crew spend so much of their time out there, they really do the insides of their buses. They can sleep fourteen comfortably in bunks, with a video, microwave, refrigerator, freezer, grill stove, hot and cold water, bathroom, shower, back room in the back with its own stereo and TV video system. Hanging plants, pink tile on the floors, this kind of thing. Dolly Parton's bathroom.

But nevertheless you're in a forty-foot aluminum tube, eighteen feet wide, with all these other guys. On this last tour I looked down the gangway from the back of the bus. It had the appearance of being round, cylindrical, because of the doorways. You'd see various arms hanging out of bunks and off of couches and one little bulb, red, hanging in the ceiling up front. It was right out of *Das Boot.*

Touring is intensely difficult work, and you will always bus it until you're playing nothing but stadiums. And even then all your road crew and front office and so forth are going to be on disco submarines. It becomes your home. It's like living on a yacht. Your own time zones, you wake up and go to sleep according to your own schedule.

German U-boats had no space for storing food or gear. Everything had to be stuck in and around the equipment, the engines and the men. Tour bus, same thing. Here you have the mighty Van Halen touring behind twenty million record sales already, halfway through the career, you're still finding nooks and crannies to stuff your paperback or your cigarette lighter, you're still finding little corners to tuck your extra shoe.

Take your bags onto the bus, spend the first couple of hours coordinating all your shit, set your space up and everything, because that's going to be your home for probably the next year. If things go really well, you'll be out for two years. And you get road burn within two weeks, terminal fatigue, but you're used to it. Everybody talks in a slower cadence. Lots of body language suffices. Everybody gets worn down and simplifies.

The only people who didn't simplify were the security teams. We would have maybe eight guys working security for the hall, the band, the hotel, merchandise, et cetera, and they traveled with us. They all had walkie-talkies, and they'd have call names. At the beginning of every tour it would be "Doctor to Lawyer, this is Indian Chief. Over." Within four weeks, "Butcher to Hacker, this is Paladin. Over." And Hacker was a little Woody Allen–type guy.

Just like on a boat, during the summer you'd stop wearing a shirt. And because you traveled self-contained, it's not like you're going to airports every day. People think, oh, you fly from gig to gig. You do if you're foolish. Sabbath did on that first tour in America. Jesus, you got to get up an hour and a half early, you get into some rent-a-cars, you get lost, you find the airport, you wait, the plane's delayed, you're in the public, you land, you get rent-a-cars, you get lost on the way to the hotel.

Or you walk out of the hotel wrapped in a bedsheet, get on your boat, and you're there. After a few weeks you see guys who haven't worn a shirt in a week. They eat all their meals backstage. Half the time the road crew doesn't even stay in a hotel. They drive right to the next gig. They're going to finish tearing down at six in the morning, drive six hours and begin to set up again.

Get used to sleeping in your clothes. You come up with little tricks because always during the summer they fire up the air-conditioning, it goes hog wild, you're sweaty and overheated and tired, maybe just ate late. Your body temperature's up, two hours later your body temperature drops a few degrees, and you wake up coughing and snotting and hacking like a stripper on a Sunday morning. So I learned: sleep in your clothes, always wear a ski hat, stabilize your temperature. Just like my sherpa Wong Chu told me at twenty-some thousand feet in the Khumbu Icefall. "Wong Chu, how will I know when I'm dressed right for up here?" He said, "Dave, when you can lay down anywhere on the glacier at any time and fall asleep, comfortable and warm and dry, you're there."

Same thing on a tour bus. And this doesn't matter if you're brand new to the groove or if you're Madonna's backup band on the way to a stadium. Sleep in your clothes, socks included. Pull a hat over your eyes so you can lose all the light. Earplugs block out ambient noise. You can go to sleep anywhere, at any time.

After twenty years of this, I still basically sleep in my clothes. I think nothing of it. My girlfriends have thought something of it. It's like decompression shock. Hard to let go, you know, it's part of my routine. I don't even think about it till somebody asks. My last girlfriend, I'd come back from biz or work or from downstairs, she would have made the bed and put my little ski hat on the pillow. That was so cool, to me. She realized I had a series of experiences that were way different. You just don't get it out of your system.

* * *

Trashing hotels was an art form that you learned about. It wasn't like you invented it. It was something that you had to read about. You read about the drummer from The Who driving a Cadillac into the hotel swimming pool. He went on to recite about how he was lucky—that he had heard somewhere that if you ever drove your car into a lake that you have to open the window and let the car fill up with water, otherwise you won't be able to open the door. These were great lessons in life.

We in Van Halen took it to a new level. On the second album it says, "Special thanks to the seventh floor—" I think it was Sheraton Inn in Madison, Wisconsin. Something amazing happened . . . well, maybe nothing happened. There were festivities, room to room, carryings on and it's a college town so there's a lot of carrying-onners to be found. You've got to understand, rock 'n' roll is a lot like God took the map of the United States and tilted it, and everybody loose and unscrewed down rolled into my business.

Well, we've heard about throwing a television out of a window. How about getting enough extension cords out of one of the trucks parked in back of the hotel so that the television can remain plugged in all the way down to the ground floor? I don't know, it's just kind of abstract. But that's what made it aesthetic.

Or taking everything that you could possibly find in the given hotel room and jamming it in the closet and the bathroom. That includes the bed frame, the television set, the stand, the dressers. Those colorful armoires and easy chairs are going to have to be disassembled.

Then wait outside the door once your victim comes

back. You can even make it a little more poetic if you take the door off the hinges. That way you can hear the response that much better from down the hall.

The science of hydraulics is taught in agricultural seminars in every major university in the world; it's part of engineering, it's part of bridge building, heavy construction, and it's a very important part of rock 'n' roll on the road. What happens when you jump on a toilet? What can we expect when you disassemble a sink? What happens if we do both at the same time in the same bathroom? Is it twice as much hydraulic force or is it exponential? Is it geometric? Is it four times, eight times as much? Well, I can tell you. These things all come into play!

We'd play a game called "Maybe it's in here." And you'd get way into somebody's room and go, "Damn it, I knew Bobby had that new *Playboy* issue in here somewhere. Maybe it's in here. No, it's not on the roof. Maybe it's in here. Nope, not behind the wallpaper. I know, he's clever, he knows I'm on to his game. Maybe it's under the sink. Nope, nothing under here but a bunch of nuts and bolts and . . . a lot of water," and on and on.

We would play "Maybe it's in here" in cars. You'd get into a limousine and maybe the driver had an attitude. In the late seventies, you know, truck drivers were just switching over to the long-hair mode. Now every other truck driver out on the interstate's got long hair and a beard and speaks fluent jive. Not in the late seventies necessarily. So you might run into a hard case in the limousine. Wouldn't be unusual at all to lose your backstage pass in transit and you'd have to switch right over to "maybe it's in here" mode. "It's not behind the door jamb, it's not behind the door frame. Maybe he sewed it into the cushion. Maybe when we made that stop at the Burger King he found my backstage pass and sewed it into the backseat cushion. Easy enough to find. No, it's not there either." And you would pull up to the gig in something out of *Paint Your Wagon.*

You would fish somebody. A lot of times you would go down in the market areas of towns, get yourself a big frozen fish, like a cod. And you would pick somebody—preferably someone who had registered the most dramatic negative reaction to any invasion of their space, they'd go right on top of the list.

What you do is get into his room while he's downstairs working or at the gig or whatever, and he's got to come back after sound check and change his clothes. He goes to pull open a sock drawer and he's been fished. You hear the screams. Threats of belligerence are issued in all four points of the compass, doors slam, fish is retired down the hall into the ice-maker, for further fishing.

Guy receives a call, urgent, it's from the road manager, "We got a little problem with per diem. Can I see you for a minute?" Makes the critical error of leaving his door unlocked. Runs down the hall, finds out things are reconcilable, comes back, pulls the curtain, steps into the shower, looks down . . . he's been fished. Now the fish can fly. It goes out the window.

Of course getting fished was actually a matter of honor, it's running the gauntlet at Annapolis or whatever they do. It's an honor, knowing that all eyes are upon you, watching your reaction, to see if you're suitably passionate and dramatic—not placid and accepting, that's unacceptable.

Getting fished is no time for meditational acceptance.

It's a time for fury! We went out of our way to fish you, now let's have some reaction. And of course the optimal—being an offensive player—is being able to solicit retribution, to know that you fished so well that there's going to be some payback, and that gives you something to look forward to. Now you got something to think about on the bus, knowing that the hunter is now the hunted. Hey, I read that. That's in the Bible, isn't it? Goddamn!

The mayhem would expand. There was a scenario where one of our clothing ladies had a little teddy bear that she always had with her, and she gave it some awful name like Puffy or Fluffy. She always would be clutching it to her breast and stuff, and this is in the midst of the White Lotus Fleet. It just wasn't fittin'. It was unseemly. Everybody would say, "Oh, would you put that thing away?"

I mean, she would talk baby cootchie-cootchie talk to it and make *you* talk to it. You'd come in and say, "Honey, my shirt got itself torn up. My shirt tore itself on that stripper's hand, and I need it to be sewed up for the show."

"No problem, Dave, no problem. Say hello to Fluffy."

"Fuck you, Fluffy."

"No, no, you're going to upset Fluffy."

"I ain't saying hello to no stuffed bear."

"You know, now that I think about it, it's going to take a little longer to sew up that shirt than I was thinking."

"Hi, Fluffy. How you been?"

"Now that I'm thinking of it even more, it's going to take half the time, Double D, Diamond Dave! Would you hold Fluffy?"

"N— yeah."

So we kidnapped Fluffy. Yep. We took a photo of Fluffy, cut off his ear, and sent it to her room with a ransom note, making a list of demands. "The word Fluffy will never be uttered onboard bus ever again. No working man amongst the entire team will be forced to even view Fluffy if he so chooses, and we so choose. And just in case you're wondering if we mean business, here's his ear. Don't fool with us." And we sent a picture of Fluffy with a bandage on his head. The result? It was like the New York City sanitation strike in the seventies; all laundry stopped.

Super Glue happened at some point in the seventies, okay? It's like the glue that they use to put the bumps on the yellow line in the highway. Those aren't bolted in; they're glued to the asphalt with a super-high-density acrylic adhesive.

One of our truck drivers knew somebody who was in construction workin' highways, so we got a bucket of it sent out. What you would do is call somebody down for an important meeting, and you'd need at least four to six guys to go into his room, and you'd take everything exactly as it's sitting, the beds, the chairs, the television, settee, and everything, and glue it upside down to the ceiling, reverse the room. And you would have to have three guys standing under an easy chair on top of another chair holding it to the ceiling, until the glue set, and it would. The victim would come in and find everything but the mattress glued upside down to the ceiling, in exact reverse of how he left it.

Well, you know, once you've seen one, you've seen them all. It was not unusual, if somebody would come back blistering drunk from the bar, realize he'd been reversed and possibly fished. You couldn't glue the mattress but that was it. The victim wouldn't wake up in the morning, had disconnected their phone or whatever; you'd have to get the key from the bell guy, open up the door, and there would be somebody sleeping naked on a mattress with all the furniture, including their suitcases, glued to the ceiling. Everything. Magazines. If something was on the floor, you'd glue it to the ceiling exactly where you found it on the floor. It was art. Salvador Dali would have been proud.

Fireworks are particularly exciting, but only if you light them *all* off at one time. So it would not be unusual to stop at a place called South of the Border in the Carolinas, which is open twenty-four hours. It's just like this little Mexican-themed village and all the shops sell fireworks. It would not be unusual at all to stop and buy eleven hundred dollars' worth of fireworks, boxes and boxes and boxes. You'd get these wheels of firecrackers that held six hundred rounds.

What you would do is buy a plastic trash can—and the police would be in on it every time, 'cause who loves firepower more? You'd take this big trash can out to the parking lot behind the arena and fill it up with eleven hundred bucks' worth of fireworks. Take all the bottle rockets out of the boxes, take all of the flame throwers, all the M-80s, *everything,* and just pile them into this thing and then dump gasoline all over it.

Everybody would duck down, like in the trenches. And you'd run a little trail of gasoline across the pavement, about half a block, over to behind a limousine, and torch it. Those things would go off for forty-five minutes. It sounded like the 1812 Overture. Everybody's duckin' for cover and it smells like cordite. The trash can would melt and bottle rockets be going everywhere. You'd be crawling under the car and shit, trying to get out of the way of the bottle rockets—not noticing that two of the men had separated from the group and were at the hotel, fishin' ya. Your night was just beginning.

Getting caked was another honor. Your birthday being the most outstanding time. And you would get caked on stage during a show. A huge cake, the size of the engine lid from a Volkswagen would be ordered up well in advance. Alex or somebody would go, "Ladies and gentlemen, we have a very special occasion tonight." Before you could make a move, there's that carpentry crew, blocking every avenue of escape, and the cake would be walked out and you'd be sacrificed to the general merriment of all who were there.

The highest point of the action being residual—you'd be covered with cake, you'd look like the Toxic Avenger and so would everybody else within baseball throwing distance, but the residual effect was like land mines for the entire rest of the show; all the butter in the icing would get tromped into that flooring, deeper and deeper, till it was like ice. And one by one we'd take falls, you'd be slipping, you spent half the rest of the show on your ass. Or taking running starts and sliding on your knees right into the barricade, off the edge, and security would see you coming and they'd hold up their arms and stop you.

"And Roth slides home!"

The whole rest of the evening would be about stealing bases.

Then, of course, it's time for payback. This is what we lived for. This is what filled in the spaces between the hard work; writing, rehearsing, performing. This is how you relieve the stress.

Also keep in mind that all of these activities were acted out or committed or perpetrated *not* in silence. What's the opposite of silence? Twelve rooms, each with their own stereo system *blaring*. Every kind of music you can possibly imagine out into the hallways, backstage, in the cars, you name it. It was constant fire and brimstone, din, bedlam. The only thing missing was the goddamn Muir High School drum corps.

Guests would come to visit and they would fly in to a little city, you know, Delray Beach, Florida, and it was like they were helicoptered to the front. We'd send out a car, somebody to pick them up at the airport, they'd show up at the hotel and it was bedlam, noise, constant foment.

"Glad to have you aboard, sir—get down! We're about to be caked. Here—wear this, it's waterproof. I know, it looks just like a shower curtain, doesn't it?"

"Jesus, how long has this been going on?"

"I don't know, when did we leave, March? Glad you could make it. We're gonna have a great weekend. If you don't mind, I'd like to send in a team to your room, sweep for fish—I'll explain that later. Whatever you do, *don't leave your room*."

They'd check into the room and go, "What's this?"

"This is a fire extinguisher."

"How come it's in my room?"

"If it comes time that you need it, you'll know."

You'd have guys walking around James Bond-like with a can of Reddi Whip stashed in their belt under an extra, extra large Harley-Davidson T-shirt. It's not severe firepower, like an extinguisher, but it's enough to make good your getaway. Or if you had to go out in the hall, and there was a situation. At any given time, a situation might be in full flower. So if you step out of your door, carry your sidearm. For weeks I wouldn't leave my room without a can of Barbasol shaving cream in the back of my belt.

Things would disintegrate frequently, and people would resort to human wave approaches. The entire transport team, all of the truck drivers, would burst into the room and just destroy everything—a human-wave attack. I spent more than one night falling asleep in a puddle of beer on an empty mattress in the middle of total wreckage, with the front door to the room leaning against the wall about eighteen inches to the side of the door frame. I woke up like that somewhere in Worcester, Massachusetts. Manager had flown in, and I woke up as he was just trying to jockey the door a little more to the side so he could squeeze through and shake my hand, asked me how the tour was going. I told him I felt that we were winning.

Censorship

There's fourteen school systems, in the United States alone, who have outlawed *Huckleberry Finn.*

Well, I have a problem with that. I would rather have a little kid of *mine* learn the true meaning and the background of the word *nigger* from reading *Huck Finn,* who was anti-racist. Tom Sawyer was a racist. Tom treated Jim like a slave. Was ready to turn him in, drop a dime on him. It was Huck who broke him free, put him on the raft at the end of the story.

Censorship can become very dense and convoluted as quick as you can say "Bob's your uncle." Because if you read *Source* magazine, it's hip-hop, it's completely Dre and Snoopy and Coolio. In the magazine, if it's friendly and affirmative—every single one of these acts refers to "Yeah, I'm hangin' with me and my nigguz." "Uz" means it's cool. It's not okay for me to use it, or anybody but that crew, okay? *Nigger* is negative. That's old school. That'll get you shot.

Okay. So what happens is, we move into this censorship way of thinking, we give it a nice, friendly name, like "politically correct," and we start referring to things as "the *N* word." We won't even say the word anymore. As if, if we don't say it, it'll go away. Kind of like date rape. If we just don't talk about it, then it doesn't exist, right? A lot like wife beating, or child abuse.

Okay. So we're all tuned in to "Court TV," and they're referring to the *N* word. Now, I think I know what *N* word is, I'm just not sure which *version* it is. Is it *-uz* or *-er,* 'cause that makes a difference.

We know what the *F* word means. And we kinda know what the *S* word means . . . what about the *K* word? That sounds like three different insults for the price of one, for me—all of them spelled incorrectly. But anybody who uses one of those insults frequently probably can't spell. Now, where does that leave me? I'm a little fuzzy. 'Cause one of the *K* words might be *kiss my ass.* I have a lot of friends who would have alphabetized that under *K.* I would have alphabetized it under *A.*

But anybody who uses that insult in their daily diet, more often than not, is probably coming from the former school of thought.

Anybody who uses the word *cunt* on a daily basis

probably spells it with a *K.* So now I have to adjust to the *C* word *and* the *K* word.

You can see how things spin right out of control. The joystick breaks right off, and things get desperate in a hurry here.

That's censorship. Wait a minute . . . is that an *S* word or a *C* word?

Primary Colors

I've only won one award, one really good trophy, okay? The Cinematographer Award, from Kodak, in 1985. What had happened is, during *California Girls,* I was wearing these glacier goggles, you know, mirrored. They're round with leather sidepieces; they looked totally cool, and intimidated everybody. And I wore them twenty-four hours a day. I would tell people "It keeps the lighting the same," because I basically produced, and directed, the video.

I was going for my Keith Richards Merit Badge. We'd get into that high-tech shit . . . Telecine: Television Cinema. Now, with the Nirvana and the Stone Temple mind-set, you call it "transfer."

Telecine is when you go from 35mm footage to video stock. In between, you do what's called "color correction." You go through every shot, and make each color in the lighting the same, so it doesn't blurt at you. You re-correct the blues in the sky, in case the sun shifted, the reds, et cetera.

So I'm sitting in the back of the edit bay with my

glacier goggles on. I've been up for four days and nights. And they go to color correct the blues. They say, "What do you think, boss?"

I said, "I don't see any blue. Come on, you guys, give me somethin' a little more heterosexual."

Nobody says to me, "Take your glacier goggles off." By then, it's an expected part of the front of my head.

So they dial the blue right off the scale, like somebody nuked us: "Now, *that's* a blue."

Okay. Now let's do reds. They correct, get everything balanced, and say, "What do you think, Dave?"

I say, "Guys, you know how much this costs per hour, and I'll joke with you at the local cantina. But not here. Now let's do the fucking reds."

Nobody thinks to say, "Dave, take the goggles off." They redial everything.

We did the *entire* color spectrum like this. I did not see the video till a month later, when it shows up on MTV, and it looks like somebody nuked the set. It looks like Chernobyl meets Chuck Jones. It's electrifying. Colors are bleeding everywhere, so much so, that it's the norm, so it's not like I'm breakin' format.

Now I'm getting calls from all over the world, to the office: Japan, Germany, London, New York. "Uh, uh . . . David-san, where you find this old stock of film, inside Technicolor I'm thinking, so?"

"I beg your pardon, David, but how did you resolve the colour, when you . . . did you go from black and white, and re-colour? Because it looks like Doris Day."

And I got the Kodak Cinematographer Award.

I'm very proud of my work. Sat down, '85, I was up for fourteen video awards; *California Girls, Gigolo.* But

We Are the World was happening at the same time. The mighty James Brown is sitting in front of me at the MTV awards, and he turns around to me, and says, "Are you Dave Roth?"

I said, "Yes, sir, Mr. Brown."

He said, "You gonna sweep up tonight."

I thought, "Great."

After my seventh loss in a row, I leaned over, and I said, "Mr. Brown, do you mean, like, after the show?"

Night Moves

I always use some kind of sportin' approach to get out and see the world, as opposed to just seeing it through the window going by in a tour bus. A window that doesn't even open.

Most musicians will proclaim to you loudly their worldly experience, their worldly travels, how many countries they've been to and so forth. But by and large, what we do is the Elvis. We put tin foil in the windows or just simply exclude the windows entirely. You live at night, you live vampire hours. If you work nine to five, your peak is either right before or right after lunch.

My physical and emotional peak has to be right around 9:15 P.M. and that includes on a Tuesday night. So everything is shifted to accommodate that. You can't wake up when the sun comes up, stay up all day and expect to peak at 9:15 at night. There's no way to do it.

You only have so many calories to burn in a given day. You only have so much distance you can do in a given day. So everything you do is designed to accommodate that; what you eat or don't eat or how you sleep or don't sleep.

And that is also inclusive of wildly diverse approaches, à la the guy who's way hyped on aminos and Met-Rx and is doing split training and eating pure protein, and that's how he accommodates. Or the Keith Richards approach of "I try not to eat during the week, man." Hey, Keith has been showing up at 9:15 on the dot for thirty-five years, and it's still worth seventy-five bucks a pop, if you're askin' me. I'm not sure Keith knows what an amino acid is. I assure you that it's not in his medical bag. Vitamins to Keith Richards is purely slang.

But whatever it is, you accommodate. You arrive in the dark before the sun comes up, and you go to work when the sun goes down. Now, if you're just doing two shows a week, of course, you're going to the Prado Museum, you're going to the Louvre, you're learning how to spell it—but hardly anyone does. Even the biggest acts are doing back-to-back shows, four shows in a row, five shows in a row. Because to put on a spectacular program like that requires spectacular amounts of manpower. You take the day off; you're still paying for everybody, still got to feed and water the troops, still renting all those trucks and tires that roll around under them.

Stones do a fabulous sold-out show, sixty to seventy-five thousand people at Joe Robbie Football Stadium in Miami. You would think Miami weather is kinda nice, seventy-five thousand people, probably take the day off next day, right? Sleep in a little bit? Wrong.

On the plane that night through Gainesville to play the very next night and then again and again.

So you have to go to some extreme lengths sometimes in order to survey what you are living in. And you're living in it; you're not visiting it. Visiting it is eating at the hotel restaurant.

Most of the world is not L.A. or London or Paris or New York. Most of the world is Bradford, England; Manheim, Germany; Tuna Fish, Wisconsin. It is. Most of the world is not Rio de Janeiro, it's Belo Horizonte. You know what I'm saying? It's nuts and bolts. Because your schedule is altered you're eating what the working man eats, nine times out of ten, that's what's on your buffet when you walk backstage.

I speak fair Spanish. I ordered a turkey and the fixin's in Madrid, because we were playing on Thanksgiving, wound up with chicken and red Jell-O—at least their version of it. You eat what they eat. Nine times out of ten you're going to eat it when they eat it too. It's like the French. I'm convinced because of all that coffee and those cigarettes, you wouldn't want to eat dinner until 9:30 at night either. Even then you'll probably just pick. So you're living there. You can struggle with it, you can rail against it all you want, but you're living there; you're not just visiting.

I've tried drawing little cards, little pictures of food items. Because you'll be stopping in places—in Poperinge, Belgium, or somewhere outside of Karlskoga, Sweden. These are little places—little, little places—and you'll stop at a roadside something or other. If you're looking for a hamburger, *that* you can draw a picture of and it's fairly well understood. Pizza I've had good luck with. Various fruit stuffs, apple, pear, like this.

Cottage cheese, I almost got punched in the mouth. There's no way to draw cottage cheese without insulting somebody. And I defy anybody to draw me a picture of yogurt that won't lose your audience within thirty seconds. Show them a picture of either one and I don't care how good of an artist you are, they are going to hand you a bottle of Belgian Pepto-Bismol, at best.

For the uninitiated, trying to draw a picture of French bread and presenting it to somebody behind a counter can easily be translated into "I love you." Especially if it's followed by a picture of two apples.

I've seen most of the United States, at least 220 cities in the continental U.S., on my bicycle at night. On a day off, you won't like waking up at 9:00 A.M. to go to the museum. You're still on the schedule. Or for that matter, when you're in Europe and you're jet-lagging, you're completely flame on, ready to go at 2:30 in the morning.

By now, I've seen most of the *world* by night, by bicycle, when it's fairly well vacated from human beings. It's a special kind of an experience, because it's not cluttered with the noise of the day-to-day. It's not cluttered with the humanity. Leaves a lot more space for history. Leaves a lot more space for mystery, you know, when it's quiet and electrically lit. There's shadow. There's beauty in shadows. It's in the shadows where you find the history, where you find the legends and stories. You don't find that under a bright light. You don't find that during the light of day. You find a representation of it or even more importantly, a commemorative statue. But the real history, the real guys who marched on Mecklenburg, the real Indians, the real Blackfoot and Cree up in Canada, the real pilgrims and puritans, the real Cortéses and Balboas . . . they don't come out till night. Their spirits are absolutely there, but you'll only find them in the shadows.

Kayaking. Go out in the wintertime, leave from the South Street Seaport, N.Y.C., all the way across that booming channel, underneath the Verrazano Bridge, past the Statue of Liberty in the snow, be snowing about midnight, you know, black. You play your little radio and it sounds like you've gone back in time, you're in a time machine. And you know the way snow deadens sound, it encapsulates it. You have the impression that that sound is only within the space of that little boat and all you hear is the splish of the oar. You keep it kind of low, and just like right now you can't really make out the words, sounds like it's coming through a megaphone and sounds like it's coming through time. It's reaching through all the waves of time, you know. And it makes me feel timeless. Everything goes away. I'm part of history somehow.

You can go paddling a canoe across the biggest golfing water-trap lake that you've ever seen in Cypress Gardens, it's so big that that's where they do the water-ski demonstrations. Circling Manhattan by the full moon in the summertime. That's where you can touch the history.

Whenever I get something silver, like a belt buckle or something, I never ever ever polish it. Because the more that the grime and time build up on it, the more it's shadow. It is in that shadow that you find the nature of the thing itself. If nothing else, it causes you to use your imagination.

Don't go visit the Imperial Palace wall at one o'clock in the afternoon while all the tour buses are pulling up. Go at three o'clock in the morning, and everybody who ever stood guard on the palace wall is still there, I assure you. Indeed, if you're not mentally prepared for it, they will come after you first. It will not be a settling experience. I've been there.

If you want to go stand on the parapets of Edinburgh Castle with all the same guys who stood on those parapets from the day they declared the building finished, don't go for the lunch break. Go as the sun's going down. Ride your bike right up next to it just before the sun's coming up. Same thing for St. Andrew's Golf Course in Scotland. If you want to golf with the spirits, you go at dawn just before the light is full, 'cause they're all still there, every one of them.

There used to be a place called the Masquers Club, which was directly behind Grauman's Chinese Theater in Hollywood starting from maybe 1918 until they finally tore it down in the mid-eighties. It was downstairs and it was art deco, all these colorful, sexy Maxfield Parrish paintings. It was a men's club to the tune of comedians and adventurers, Errol Flynn and W. C. Fields, Charlie Chaplin and the Barrymores. They would all go there to toast and carry on in the twenties and the thirties, forties. And over the dais, where they would have roasts for each other and celebrations, was the slogan for the Masquers—I use it to live by myself now—it says, "To the Masquers, we laugh to win."

When I discovered it, it had been co-opted by the North Hollywood underground to some degree, had fallen into some disarray. And there would be poetry nights on Thursdays catering to the new wave gang, the alternative gang in the early eighties. A drinking establishment. I knew what it was all about, but most of the folks who frequented the place had no idea. They enjoyed the paintings on the wall, but had no idea who did them. It really didn't get hopping until about 10:30, eleven o'clock at night. So I made it a point to show up at eight o'clock, just after it got dark and it was totally empty, and there might be one guy mopping up the bar. And that's when the spirits come out.

I sat in the middle of the main ballroom on the QE 2 just before dawn, 5:30 in the morning, pulled a chair right into the middle of the dance floor. I had tipped the little guy who was sweeping up to get lost, come back last. "Look, Raul, I know you got a whole rest of a boat to do here, so go do it. By the time you hear birdsong, I'll be long gone. And I'll even put the chair back." And I did.

Let's say you ride your bicycle through Huntsville, Alabama, at 3:30 in the morning, where the first bank of the great crop South was built—it's still there. Huntsville was one of the keystones of the Confederacy. If you go through it by day, it looks like most semi-gentrified towns. If you wait until well after the sun goes down, and John Q. Public has headed for Dave Letterman, then the truth of that city, the age and the substance and the history of that city comes out.

You get a much better taste of Gettysburg if you walk or ride your bicycle through it after midnight. It talks to you. And I've been to all these places more than four times. It is part of my permanent itinerary, music or no music. So I think it bears description because you might think of it as a lonely promenade. It's supposed to be lonely. You won't have the same experience in the light of the smoggy day.

When you're on the road—and we really discovered this when we started in '78—your schedule really tosses and turns. You'll drive all night, you get off of a bus, it's a whole new hotel, whole new set of stimuli, visual and otherwise; you're not going to go to sleep, you don't just walk right into the hotel room and fall out. No, you're going to watch the TV for a little bit, you're going to read for a little bit, whatever, until you settle back down. You may not settle in until ten, eleven o'clock in the morning, so you're going to sleep the rest of the day. Not at all unusual to wake up at five, six o'clock in the early evening, and begin your preparations for the show, whatever that means to you. For some people it means taking a long walk, or a shower, or warming up your voice, whatever it is. You become very used to this.

You also become very used to drawing the shades, or not having windows, staying asleep on the bus, becoming one with the road. The bus pulls up in front of the hotel, you don't even get off the bus, you stay. The windows, the curtains, the shades, everything is drawn. You live in a world of dark. It's like being a mushroom farmer. You have climate-controlled environments, whether it's a tour bus or a studio or a rehearsal place.

A dollar for every time that I would accidentally wake up on a night off. Okay, you'd be in a hotel on a night off, and all the windows and shades are drawn, and you look at the clock and it says 5:30. Well, road burn is that terminal not-ever-going-away fatigue. After your second week out at sea, you have permanent fatigue, and you become very used to it. You learn not to let your body control your mind; you're always functioning at 20 percent less than if you were well fed, well rested, well anything. But you're not, you're out on the highways. So this groggy waking-up process sets in like you're fighting your way up through cubic meters of sludge, only to break free into the darkness somewhere way out at sea. This struggle for consciousness is a twice-daily ritual, if not three or four times. Because for all of those years I would describe it as "I have not slept in a decade." I've taken a lot of naps, sleep is like six hours or more. No, I've been napping for two to four hours, two and three times a day for the last eighteen years.

A dollar and a half for every time I would wake up, fight my way up from the sea, the bottom of the sea, through the sludge and blackstrap molasses that is oh-sweet-slumberland express, takin' me gone home, break my little coconut head free through the surface into the pitch black of a hotel room and the only thing that's shining at me is a clock that's screaming in off-green neon, "It's 5:30."

You jump out of bed and you start the shower and you play the tape, your wake-up tape, whatever it is—dance music, Beach Boys, whatever, something 120 beats a minute or better—and you start your process, your "ignition sequence." Step out of the shower, shave, fix up, get your pants on, you got your shirt on, you haven't buttoned it yet, you got your socks on, you're about to pull your shoes on, and you do the ceremonial opening of the curtains to witness the sun going down as you begin to ignite, only to realize that you're an hour and a half early for breakfast room service.

This would happen regularly to all of us. You would wake up at six o'clock in the morning, you know, you got a night off, you go to bed early—big mistake. You're not used to going anywhere early. You're going to wake up at five o'clock in the morning, raring to go. You're used to being up until five, and then trying to sleep. Five o'clock, "Jesus Christ, they must have changed daylight savings time and I didn't read about it. Won't be the first time. How come nobody woke me up?"

Well, there were a number of occasions when everybody would saddle up, climb on to one of the tour buses and head off for the show, or after a show all the buses would load up, take off down the highway, you stop at a truck stop an hour and a half later, at 3:30 in the morning. Half the bus is awake, they get off, eat a little something, pile back on. Two-thirds of the way through *Godfather,* Part 2, you got a funny feeling there aren't as many bodies on the bus as during *Godfather,* Part I. "Oh my God, we forgot Townsend back at the truck stop. Had a bad stomach, he was in the bathroom." We're members of a team who only have to count to four by and large—"one, two, three, four; one, two, three, four; hey, you're a star, you're gonna go far." You had to turn around, drive two hours back to somewhere north of Fargo, pick up some forlorn figure at daybreak. It happened very frequently. Good thing I never went scuba-diving with this bunch.

So it was not an unfounded fear to wake up, look out the window, see pitch black, it's five o'clock, and think, "Daylight savings time changed, nobody told me, and they left without me." It never occurs to the celebrity ego that you might be wrong. Certainly not this one. So you call a few people. Or better yet, march down the hall, pound on a few doors, demand to know who was responsible.

And it was not at all unusual to get onto a bus in the middle of an afternoon to head to a faraway gig, and somebody would get on, all bathed and shaved and what-not, but completely comatose. "What happened with you?"

"Oh man, I woke up at 4:30 this morning, thought I missed the gig, took a shower, shaved, got all dressed, and I couldn't go back to sleep for four hours. I was totally pissed that I had missed the show. Then when I realized my mistake, I was totally pissed at me. I was up till lunch."

If you were drinking, watch out, 'cause your sense of where you are, your situational awareness would change. There's no schedule. I always laugh when people say, "So what's a day in the life of Dave Roth like?" Which day? Which year? You're so disoriented; oh, you don't arrive every morning at a certain time and check in and check out at night the same time at all.

Go to sleep in a hotel room. You get up, have to go to the bathroom, walk right into a wall, thinking you were in the bathroom in the hotel from the last night. It's pitch black, you can't find the light switch, so you've got to do everything like Stevie Wonder, and you develop little rituals. Like you get into the bathroom and you can't find the toilet, especially if there's a bidet in there, and you can't find the light switch or it's broken, and you're in a—what in *Gray's Anatomy* is called a hurry—you try and find the side of the bathtub with your knees and your calves, and pee there. Three dollars for every time I forgot to pull the curtain.

When Van Halen got its first gold record, we were on tour with Black Sabbath all over England, Scotland, Ireland, many, many cities. And it was in Aberdeen, just a very small provincial little hotel where they didn't even really have a bar. They would serve drinks in the lobby. It was almost a bed-and-breakfast kind of a thing. That very night I was introduced by the Warner Brothers representative to one of the finest beverages. You know,

My OTHER BOAT IS A AIRCRAFT CARRIER
(MARCIA, THE WORLD'S ONLY LOW RIDER BOAT)
THE AMAZON '83

YES I GOT A MOTHERFUCKING WHISTLE.

ONSTAGE '81

– VAN HALEN'S CURRENT MANAGEMENT TEAM –
1997
(USED TO BE THE CAST OF (CALIFORNIA GIRLZ)
'85

THEN THE OLD GUY GOES, "NOW BOYS BEFORE I HAND OVER THE KEYS, YOU'VE GOT TO PROMISE ME THAT YOU'LL HANDLE THIS CAR RESPONSIBLY AND FOLLOW THESE 3 SIMPLE RULES. RULE NUMBER 1 – NO SEX IN THE CAR RULE NUMBER 2 – NO DRUGS IN THE CAR; AND RULE NUMBER 3 – NO ROCK AND ROLL IN THE CAR. CAN YOU BOYS PROMISE ME THAT?

AIR ROTH

OPENING ACT 1978

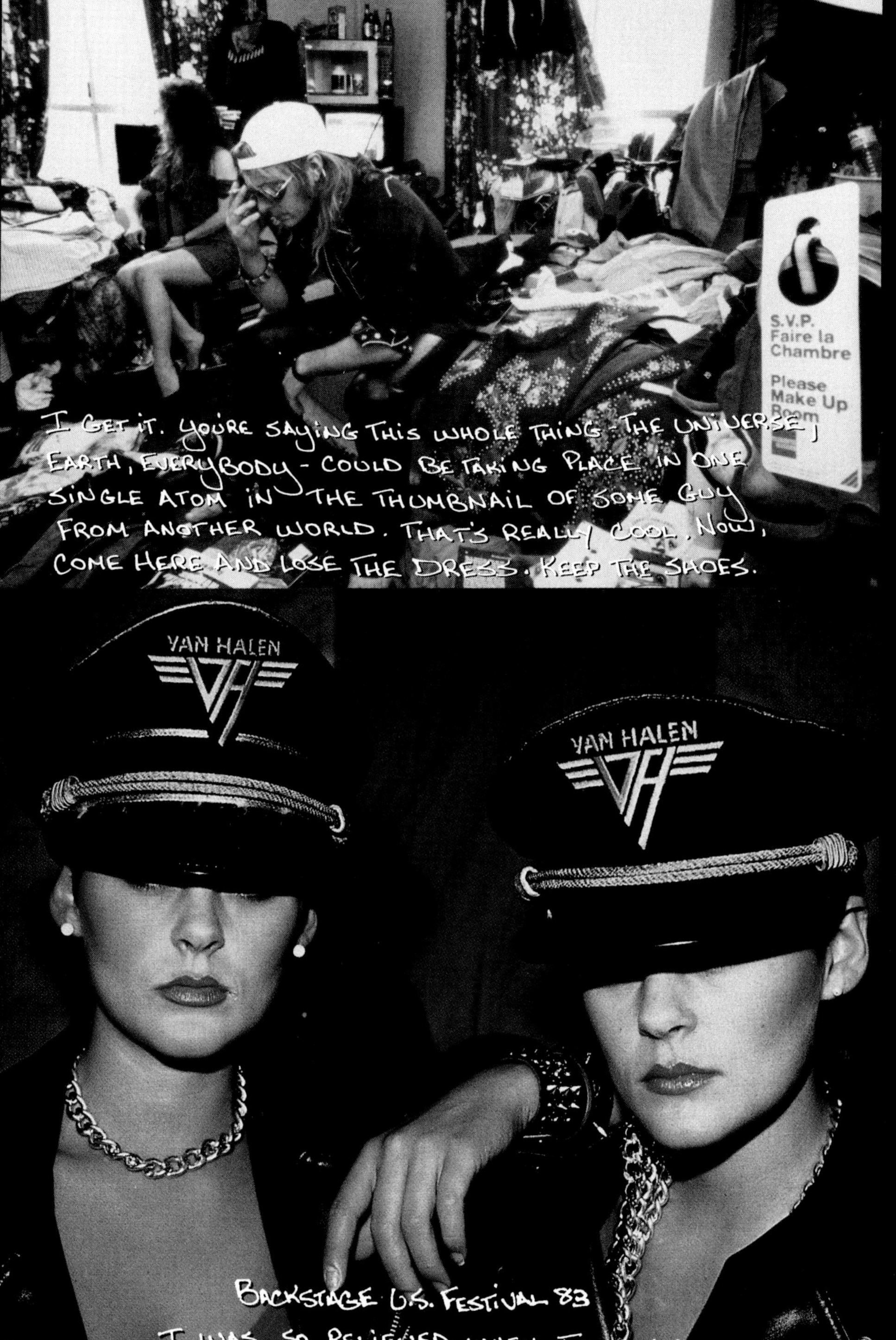

I GET IT. YOU'RE SAYING THIS WHOLE THING—THE UNIVERSE, EARTH, EVERYBODY—COULD BE TAKING PLACE IN ONE SINGLE ATOM IN THE THUMBNAIL OF SOME GUY FROM ANOTHER WORLD. THAT'S REALLY COOL. NOW, COME HERE AND LOSE THE DRESS. KEEP THE SHOES.

BACKSTAGE U.S. FESTIVAL 83

I WAS SO RELIEVED WHEN THEY SAID I'D BEEN A VERY BAD BOY...

Mrs Pitts

ALTADENA SCHOOL
Altadena, Calif
February 1964

Grade 4

THAT'S ME - JUST A LITTLE LEFT OF CENTER
ON A SLIGHTLY DIFFERENT AXIS
{ MY 4TH GRADE CLASS ALSO INCLUDED STEPHEN HAWKING, }
OLIVER STONE, TWO MEMBERS OF JOURNEY,
AND VICE PRESIDENT AL GORE.
CAN YOU PICK THEM OUT?

THIS IS THE GROWN UP VERSION OF THE LITTLE BOY
IN SCHOOL PICTURE VEGAS 96

... JUST LIKE THIS AND THEN I SPIN AROUND REALLY,
REALLY FAST LIKE A CYCLONE. NEXT THING I KNOW,
I'M OVER ON THE OTHER SIDE OF TOWN - JUST LIKE THAT,
SWEAR TO GOD - LIKE A FUCKING CARTOON.

OKAY, NUMBER B-27, WHO HAS B-27?

(ONSTAGE OAKLAND STADIUM, CALIF.)
DO I LOOK FLAMMABLE OR WHAT...

YOU'D EXPECT TO FIND HOWARD STERN HERE

WHAT'S GOING ON WITH THE GIRL ON THE STEPS
IN THE UPPER LEFT HAND CORNER;
ONE HAND'S MORE INCRIMINATING THAN THE NEXT.

"HOT FOR TEACHER" SET '84

HOLY SHIT, McDONALD'S COFFEE IS HOT...
{ "PRETTY WOMAN" VIDEO; ONE OF THE FIRST VIDEOS EVER BANNED ON MTV }
1980

"GOIN' CRAZY" VIDEO SHOOT
(I PLAYED THE PART OF BUCK, MY OWN 300 LB. MANAGER;)
WELL HUCK, I'M THE KING OF...
1988

THESE OTHER TWO GUYS LOOK SO GODDAMN FAMILIAR...

ONE SECOND LATER, HER BODY JUST SUCKED IN THE BIKINI AND IT DISAPPEARED!
{"CALIFORNIA GIRLS" VIDEO SHOOT}

" IT APPEARS TO BE SOME SORT OF SIGNAL, SIR."

I RUINED HER FOR OTHER MEN

NO STARBUCKS NEXT 700 MILES
RIVER REGION NEW GUINEA

PROOF THAT KIDS DO JUST FINE WITHOUT
BARNEY OR TICKLE ME ELMO

ANYBODY GOT A CIGARETTE?
(VENICE BEACH, CALIF.)
1985

HOWEVER, THE CLEAR AND PRESENT DANGER HERE IS THAT YOU REALLY CAN'T READ THE HOLSTERED GUN. DOES IT SHOOT OUT A FLAG THAT UNFURLS AND SAYS,
BANG-
OR WILL IT TEAR YOU A NEW ONE?
RADIO STATION VISIT
EARLY 80'S

NO ONE PACKS A CANOE LIKE MY MOM!
(TAHITI 1992)

LOBUCHE PEAK HIMALAYAS 1991 21,000 FEET

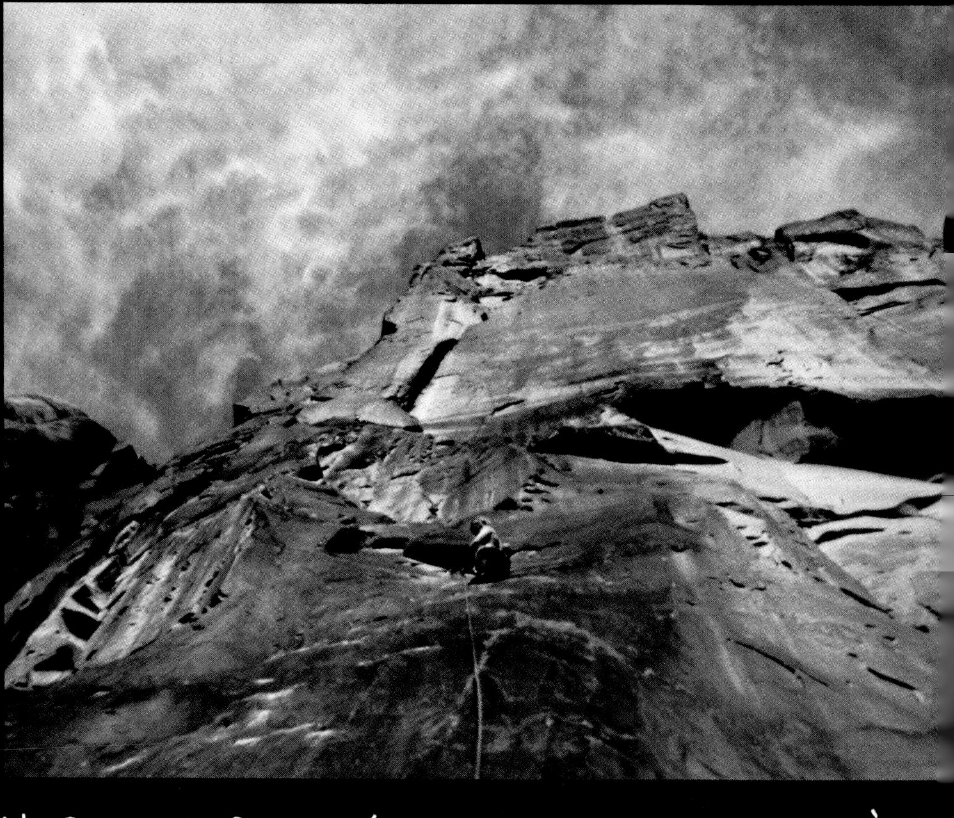

NO RISK, NO ROCK (CANYONLANDS UTAH DESERT '94

IT STARTS WITH TINY MULTI-COLORED CHASER LIGHTS AROUND YOUR REAR LICENSE PLATE. BUT EVENTUALLY YOU GRADUATE TO THIS SORT OF THING.

WORLD TOUR '88

LET'S PUT IT THIS WAY. I CERTAINLY HAVE NO SENSE OR MEMORY THAT I'VE LIVED BEFORE, BUT I IMAGINE THAT SOME OF THE ENERGY THAT COMPROMISES WHO I AM NOW MAY PERHAPS HAVE BEEN COMPONENT ENERGY IN SOMEONE ELSE BEFORE ME....

("PRETTY WOMAN" SHOOT '80)

NEW YEAR'S EVE? TRY A TYPICAL TUESDAY.

AND NOW FOR YOUR QUESTION: WHAT CONTRIBUTION TO WORLD PEACE WOULD YOU LIKE TO MAKE?

"A LITTLE AIN'T ENOUGH" VIDEO SHOOT '91

MANY WOMEN PREFER NOT EATING FROM THE MENU
LIKE THESE TWO WHO WISELY ORDERED
THE DAVE SANDWICH

IRV'S BURGERS
HOLLYWOOD CALIF.
1986

ALL I'M SAYING IS THE GUY RIGHT BEHIND ME IS WEARING BRUNO MAGLI SHOES.
(HIGHLAND JUNGLE PAPUA, NEW GUINEA).
SOMEWHERE NEAR THE OKTEDI MINES. 85

My OTHER VINE IS A PORSCHE.
MOOREA ISLAND

I DON'T THINK MOST PEOPLE FEEL PLEASURE ON A REGULAR BASIS. ON A SCALE THAT RANGES FROM DEEP DEPRESSION TO RIP-ROARING FUN, I'D GUESS MOST PEOPLE IDLE BETWEEN 'NOT UPSET' AND 'NOT TOO UPSET.'

CHRISTMAS-NEW YEAR CARD '96

THIS KID DOES MORE BY 9 AM THAN MOST
WHITE PEOPLE DO ALL DAY.
MANAUS, AMAZON RIVER 1983

Papua New Guinea, Sepik River '85

Haiti '84 Birthday of the Devil

PARIS, FRANCE 1992 (PREPARE TO RAM...)

SOME PEOPLE SEE A THERAPIST ABOUT THEIR FETISHES. I TURN MINE INTO 50-FOOT INFLATABLES. (HELLO CLEVELAND; ON TOUR '92)

WHEN WE WERE KINGS   FIRST TOUR 1978

WAIT. LET ME TURN MY RADIO DOWN.

WHOSE PANTS ARE WORSE?

WHO SAYS I DON'T PLAY AN INSTRUMENT?

ARE THOSE BUTTONS WELL PLACED OR WHAT?
- JUST A GIGOLO - SET, 1985

ARE YOU TALKIN' TO ME!?
(THIS POSTER MADE IT TO MORE CEILINGS THAN PAINT...)
BACKSTAGE HOUSTON TEXAS 1982

VAN HALEN
WORLD TOUR
1984

las Vegas
David Lee Roth
with the
Non Stop
Blues Bustin'
Mambo
Slammers
and the amazing
Edgar
Winter
Bally's
International
Hotel &
Casino
Oct 19-25
1995

I NEVER CONSCIOUSLY SAT DOWN AND DECIDED
"I'M GONNA START FRAMING MY CROTCH"
- NO ONE EVER GIVES ME CREDIT FOR SELENA'S LOOK. -

THE SPOT NEAR THE TOE ON THE SOLE OF THE SHOE WOULD LATER BECOME IMPORTANT BECAUSE OF DNA. (THE ICE CREAM BAND NYC 1995 NILE RODGERS, OMAR HAKIM, EDGAR WINTER, GREGG PHILLINGAINES: NOTHIN' BUT 'DA HITZ) AND MORE

PEOPLE OF EARTH

(TANGERINE BOWL WITH THE STONES '81)

LIFE VISITS VAN HALEN ON TOUR

ROCK'S ROWDIEST ROGUES

THE FANS STEAM UP THE STAGE

he name is mellifluous, deeptively gentle, but Van Halen ; the most ferocious rock band n the road in America today. torming 80 cities on its curent five-month, sold-out tour, : is filling the country's bigest arenas at a time when the ock music industry is in a deep ecession. Van Halen shows are yful rituals of excess. None f the four musicians enjoys xcess more than David Lee oth, 27, lead singer, loudouth and mucho-macho-man. n the band's recent three-day ampage in Detroit, Roth saluted a throng of 12,000 with a alf empty bottle of Jack Danel's and crowed, "We are gathred together in celebration of ex, drugs and rock and roll." 'e bumps, grinds and groans rough a two-hour assault of ar-splitting songs. Other band embers are only a little less olorful. Michael Anthony, 27, hews on his bass strings while lex Van Halen, also 27, rashes the drums and chugs eer. Little brother Eddie, 25, eigning prince of hard rock uitar (pop guru Frank Zappa ecently thanked him for "reventing" the instrument), raws gasps with his fierce cks. The group achieved its assive following in spite of ritical scorn ("This band is the istillation of every vulgar rend in over 20 years of rock nd roll history"). Six years ago e Pasadena rockers were laying bars in L.A. Now, five latinum albums later, they an afford the lavish producon—and life-style—of their ranked-to-the-max brand of ower rock." Frequently acused of promoting adolescent epravity, Roth maintains that ids need an escape. "They feel vincible after they leave a an Halen concert. It's like a eliverance. Some people go to urch for that feeling, some o to hockey games. The rest of m come to Van Halen."

oth clowns with a fan's ffering. After every show e stage is littered with ach tokens of affection.

hotography: heo Westenberger
ext: Nancy Griffin

THERE ARE CERTAIN MOMENTS THAT REMIND YOU WHY YOU GOT INTO THE ROCK AND ROLL BUISNESS TO BEGIN WITH

WE WERE LATER MARRIED IN A SMALL PRIVATE CEREMONY.

A woman hoists herself onstage in Detroit with a handhold inside David Lee Roth's Spandex lizard tights and gets a kiss as her reward (top). Above, she is whisked off by a security guard while Eddie Van Halen slams away. Says Roth, "I love to pull 'em up there with me. Everybody gets into the action."

A woman hoists herself onstage in Detroit with a handhold inside David Lee Roth's Spandex

ARENA SECURITY DID A GREAT JOB,
BUT THEY COULDN'T INTERCEPT EVERY
TONGUE...

VISIT TO A SMALL HOTEL ROOM

"We've built a career on misbehaving," admits David Lee Roth, who moved into room 2909 in Detroit's Westin Hotel with five metal suitcases containing among other domestic items a tape deck and cassettes, bikinis, leather chaps, a bottle of tropical oil, a wrench for unbolting sealed windows to let in fresh air and a copy of *The Adventures of Huckleberry Finn*. Three days later *(below)* the room had the lived-in look esteemed by Van Halen. The phone had been pulled from the wall. Lilac nylon stockings, left behind by a guest, floated from a lampshade. When the Van Halen traveling circus of 80—including security, lighting and sound crews, instrument tuners, roadies and wardrobe staff—invades a city, it takes over an entire floor or two of a hotel. Maids are forbidden to clean until the entertainers leave. Dwarf sentinels patrol the halls. After every night's performance, the party begun backstage relocates to the hotel, where "libation stations" offer exotic blender concoctions of fruit and vodka. To relieve the tension and monotony of the road, the revelers sometimes spray fire extinguishers, remove doors from hinges or launch "rockets" across the room by stuffing towel rods with firecrackers. Sleep does not have a high priority: "I always feel like I'm missing something," says Roth. "The sound of breaking glass and hysterical female laughter outside my hotel room door hooks me every time." Bills for damages trail the band around the country, but Roth shrugs them off with a disclaimer: "We don't set any fires and the maids have a ball going through the rubble." And because Van Halen pays for the destruction, most hotels say they would welcome the group back anytime. The band has also been known to trash backstage "hospitality rooms" not supplied by the promoter with the precise accoutrements stipulated in the contract, including food, liquor, colored filters on overhead lights, bowls of M&M's (with all the dark brown ones removed) and tubes of K-Y jelly. While Roth specializes in pranks, Alex Van Halen is the band's demolition expert, ripping knobs off doors, crumpling lampshades and punishing every surface with his drumsticks. "I just love beating the shit out of things," he explains. Michael Anthony thrives on food fights. That leaves Eddie, who mostly hides out in his room. Says Roth, "People always ask me if we behave this way at home. I tell them this is our home!"

166

167

wouldn't you?

ONLY THE SEA WILL TELL

"I AM THE GREAT AND POWERFUL OZ"
(SOMETIMES YOU HAVE TO KEEP THE BOTTLE AWAY FROM THESE GUYS ANYWAY YOU CAN!)

LOOK AT THAT ANKLE. SHE WANTS IT. DIRTY GIRL.
(BACKSTAGE PARTY FOR THE US FESTIVAL '83
HIGHEST PAID BAND IN THE HISTORY OF SHOW BIZ)
- ODDLY ENOUGH THIS IS HOW WE BANGED OUT
THE BRIDGE TO "PANAMA."

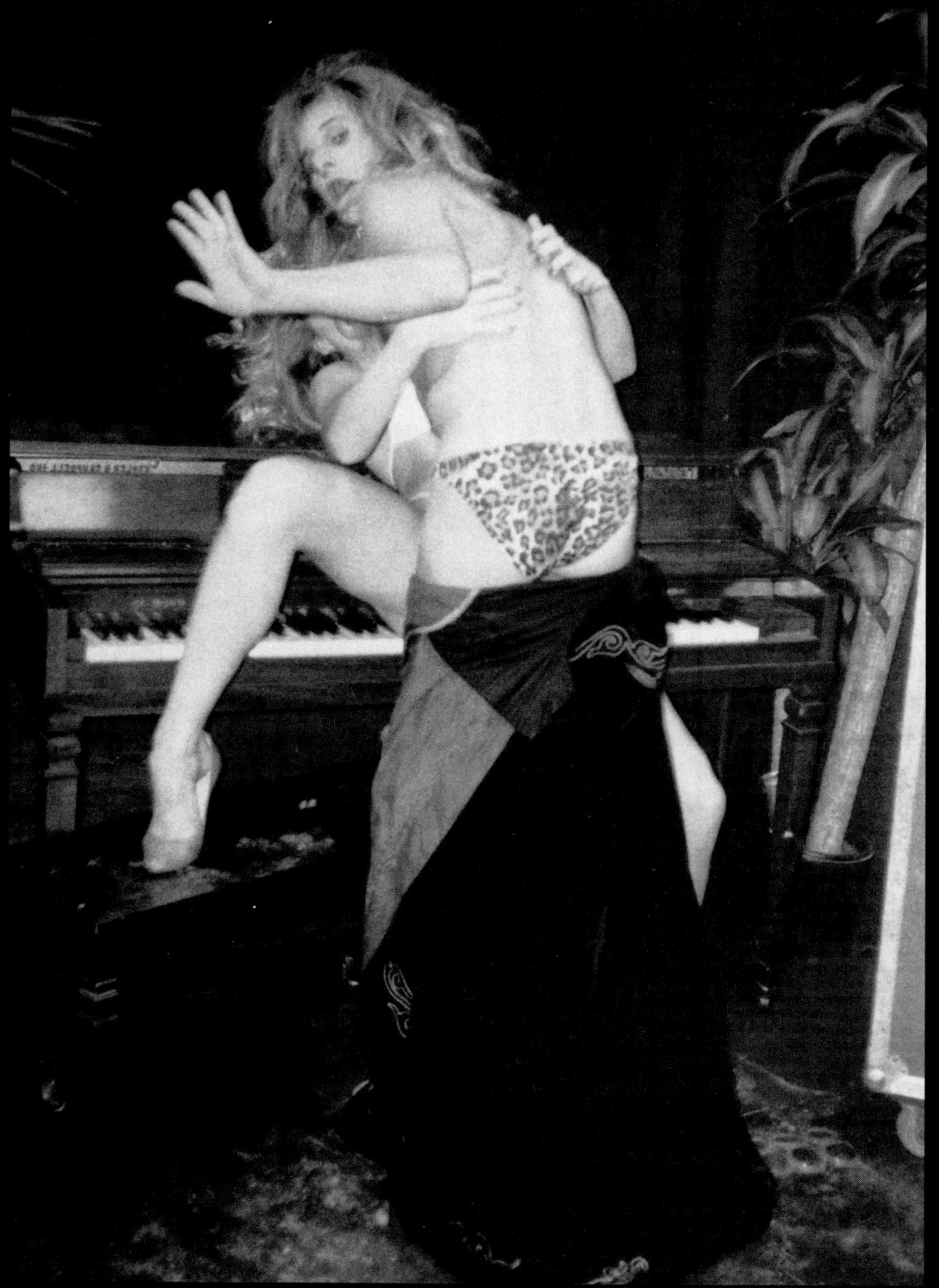

BEEN THERE..

the body absorbs cool liquids faster than warm ones, and this is the coolest liquid I had ever known. It was Glenmorangie Malt Whisky. I rewrote the song that night, "You take the high road and you take the low road, and I'll take the Glenmorangie." It was our first gold record. And we celebrated and drank and celebrated and drank a little bit more to pour on the celebration.

I went back to my hotel room and woke up in the middle of the night with an ungrateful stomach, and made a Flo Jo dash for where I thought the bathroom still was. "Still" being the operative word in the description, based on last night's hotel—not tonight's. I was a man on a mission. I jumped out of bed, slammed right into a wall, turned around, smashed right into the lamps, knocked a picture off the wall, thrashed around, destroyed my stereo, knocked the television over, barely made it to the bathroom. Got sick—like gloriously, gloriously sick—forgot to pull the curtain.

Business 101

If you read *Huckleberry Finn,* Huck and Jim arrive on their raft somewhere near these two British shyster clown-hustlers in striped suits and spats with bowlers being run out of town on a rail. And they connive their way onto the raft to escape from town—they've been busted for cheating at gambling—and Huck says, "Wow, who are you guys?" lookin' at the clothes.

And one of 'em says, "Well, I'm the King of England."

Huck says, "Well, who's he?"

He says, "Well, I'm the Duke of Canterbury."

These were my last managers.

First time we went platinum, on the first album, our manager at the time gave us all platinum necklaces with the VH logo on gold chains. Turns out we also paid for them.

You always hear about "So-and-so's a good business person." And "So-and-so's a great business woman," . . . horseshit! All that means is that either they've got a *great* representative, 99.9 percent of the time, who's either made them feel comfortable, whether they should be or not, or they have a really good front guy, 99.9 percent of the time, who's doing all the good stuff, and has *informed* them of what's really going on. Can you dig it?

There's so *very* few artists and musicians who *get it* at all who participate to *any* degree. This is just a fun thing to say, "*And* she's not just a great dancer and a singer, but she takes care of all of her own business arrangements."

Anytime somebody says to me, "This guy represents a *lot* of big entertainers," I shudder. In fact, so-and-so the entertainer probably has no *idea* on earth what's going on in their business.

Let's start with what I call basement costs—indirect overhead operating expenses which will be added to your check by the accountant, by the attorney, by the managers, by the agents, but it won't show up on a separate chit. It'll just be added to your bill. So you call them up and ask them, "What *is* this?"

Well, I called up *my* accountant. For the first time in five years, I saw a little card attached.

I said, "What is 'transport and courier'?"

He said, "To tell you the truth, Dave, I don't know. I'm gonna call downstairs, and I'll get right back to you."

He got right back to me two weeks later. He said, "You know, it's added into your bill. It's out-of-pocket expenses."

I said, "I *know* that. What, precisely, is 'courier and transport,' because now I've seen it's been added to my check. It's the first time in five years I've seen this. And by the way, I have my *own* courier and transport.

He said, "Well, this is always added to your bill."

I said, "I don't understand that."

He couldn't answer.

This went on. I said, "Find out the exact answer for me."

Five weeks after that, what I got was, "Well, this is out-of-pocket expenses. *Everybody* who works for you charges you these. I don't know why this just showed up on the check now. Usually, it's just added in."

I said, "Well, I don't think this is right."

He said, "It's the standard in the industry. *Everybody* does it."

I'm thinkin', "You remember that answer the first time your kid comes home from a seventh grade youth club dance smelling like Marlboros. And when you *ask* him why, and he tells you, 'Because, Daddy, *all* the other kids do it too.' Right before you smack him, just remember what you told *me.*"

So they're gonna slide around that cost. And what'll happen is, the same accountant will represent your manager, he deals with your attorney on twelve other acts, and the attorneys are sprawling little cities unto themselves.

I was involved in a firm that was pitched, "Oh, these guys represent all kinds of great people," and they *did.* It was me, it was Michael Jackson, it was the Rolling Stones and the T-shirt company who does the merchandising for everybody. At the end of the day, best as I can figure, the reason it would take two weeks to get a return phone call is because they represented, between basically four guys, over *two hundred separate accounts.*

So you got one guy who's in charge of *everybody's* money. You know the scene in the movie *Gentleman Jim*? It's bare knuckle days, John L. Sullivan vs. Jim Corbett, in a warehouse on the waterfront, surrounded by a lot of screaming, cigar smokin', bowler hat-wearin' guys, who eat a lot of prime rib and drink a lot of room temperature beer. They all—both sides—step up to the little Chinese guy, 'cause everybody knows he's, or at least thinks he's, the completely trustworthy guy, and both sides put the wager in his hands. Right?

That's your accountant. That little Chinese guy. Because everybody *knows* that since he represents *everybody*—hey, the only people who are gonna get burned are the fighters, at the end of the day, and they're disposable, they're done. What's the life span of a fighter? What's the life span of an average artist, or a musician? Three to six years? How long did The Doors last? Six years? Six and a half? How long did the Beatles last? Seven? Led Zeppelin? Seven years. Here today, gone later today.

So, this little Chinese guy's collecting everybody's cash in the warehouse on the waterfront, and nobody's really cutting deals, *per se.* Because it's not the "act of commission," where you went out and *did* something. It's I think what Catholics call "the sin of *omission,"* where you *leave out* information. Which to me is the same as lying.

So, the managers are probably represented by the same accountant—in fact, who do you think steered "the band" to this accountant? And to this lawyer? It was the managers, who discover "Ronnie and the Doo-dahs" playing the local cafeteria, somewhere in North Valley, and they go, "You guys could be big. Big. You just need somebody to point the way."

The manager says, "You can't be *big* unless you have a big army. You can't conquer, unless you got a real army; and an army requires an accountant, a business manager, an attorney-at-law, an agent, and they all gotta be *big, big, BIG TIME!* Otherwise people are gonna think you're little."

He takes them right over to the accountant, right over to the attorney, whatever, and comes back, he says, "Boys, I got us a five-hundred-thousand-dollar advance from Tookie Tunes Records. The *most* money that they've ever paid for a brand-new band."

And everybody says, "Yeah. *Big* time!"

Manager plucks his 15 or 20 percent right off the top . . . Pluck! The accountant isn't gonna tell that band, "Hey man, if you don't need it, don't take it. You been starvin' this long, starve another ten months while you make the record. Now you're millionaires, you're gonna start eating steak twice a day? Why fuck with your body chemistry, man? Remember Big Daddy Roth and the Road Agent, 1969: Little nitro, little methane. It's not broke. Quit touching the engine."

But your accountant, your business manager, isn't gonna say that. Because five hundred thousand dollars, of which he's going to neatly . . . Pluck! his 5 percent just landed in his backyard. That's *his* vacation to the Club Med. Two months from now, when it warms up a little bit.

Lawyer's not gonna say anything. Because *he's* working on retainer. And we always hear about all the two-hundred-dollar-an-hour men, the three-hundred-dollar-an-hour men are usually okay, but they're few and far between. They operate on a different kind of level; it's a different neighborhood. Nine-and-a-half out of ten times, you wind up with the retainer guy.

Well, how does he figure his retainer? They say it's based on workload. As in your band takes up *X* amount of time, *X* amount of energy. It's bullshit, it's based on how much money *you* have in your bank, at any given time. Because *every* contract concerning *every* single penny of exchange, passes through the legal office, as well as your accounting office. So they know every time. *They* argued for it. They *negotiated* it for you. They're the ones who pumped up the volume from two hundred and twenty grand to five hundred grand. You dig?

So that retainer's gonna be based on a percentage—working percentage—and it's anywhere from 5 to 10 percent of your *total* valued worth. At any time.

He's not gonna say anything. He doesn't want to upset the managers and the business accountant, 'cause they're takin' their share. And he's gonna slide his costs around. He's on a retainer; and he can adjust that retainer at any time. "Guys, you know, now that you're on tour, we're doin' a *lot* more work. We're doin' a *lot* more paperwork. I gotta put more people on your project and I'd like to increase the retainer."

Or, "I'd like a bonus for negotiating that big money deal for you."

Not unusual for them to pluck 10 percent and then tell you about it. "I negotiated a deal for you, and generally, you know, we get a bonus. Ten percent bonus." Unless you strong-arm 'em, they'll tell you about it *after* they have taken it out.

Well, if you're an apprentice, you're a rookie . . . *you* don't wanna make waves either, because the "big-time guys" might not want to deal with you. Therefore, you wouldn't be big time anymore.

So you let it go.

The artist is preoccupied. You should be working on your career, you should be concentrating on what you're doing as an artist right now. Don't get distracted . . . and on and on. I've changed accountants, business managers, half a dozen times since 1978.

Early on I caused real trouble, when it took me six, eight months to get 'em to finally just shut up, sit down, quit fussin' and let me sign my own checks.

It was a struggle. They would send me checks, and I would sign 'em, and had a *very* clear overview of where everything was going.

Oh, yes. And then I ran *smack* into a brick wall. Pow!

After about three, four weeks, the checks stopped coming. Because I'm sure they're used to the heavy metal bassoon player just getting tired of signing the checks; he wants to play a little denial, a little avoidance, and he doesn't want to say, "Hey, you know what? You're right. Fuck this. I don't wanna sign a hundred and twenty checks, twice a week." But if the checks never actually arrived to your hotel room, "Well, maybe something happened, let me just jam my head into the sand, and it will just sorta all go away." I didn't really quit. But we did manage to stop signing the checks. Or even more importantly, the business concern manages to get you to stop signing the checks. Okay?

If you're Van Halen, one day the manager's gonna show up saying, "I got you guys a twenty-five-million-dollar advance on your merchandising."

You're only gonna sell 5 million. He knows that. But he's being paid percentage on 25 million. And *you're* gonna pay it all back. If you go to him and say, "Hey, I didn't sell anything this year. I gotta *pay back* twenty-five million dollars, where's your piece of the action?"

You'll hear: "Hey man, operating costs. Gotta pay for typewriter tape, gotta pay for stationery. You know how much a logo on stationery costs?"

Your accountant's not gonna say anything about it, because 25 million dollars' worth of 5 percent, to him, just landed in his backyard. Attorney's not gonna say anything, because his basement is shifting into *overdrive*—they're celebrating. They're breakin' open champagne down there.

Oh, by the way, *every penny* that you *don't* pay back, there's an 8 percent interest attached to the figure. So if you were fronted ten dollars, and you only sold off five, you owe 8 percent interest on the remaining five. When you get up into the millions of dollars, you're not just gonna pay that back right away. You spent that cash on rehearsal and all this kind of rigmarole . . . It could take you two years to pay back that 5 million—at 8 percent interest.

So let's add this up, class. We're gonna go low key

here, say 15 percent for the manager; 5 percent for the business manager, that's 20; 5 percent for the accountant, that's 25 percent. Plus 8 percent interest is how much . . . 33 percent—a 33 percent loan.

That's racketeering. If I walk into your barber shop, and I loan you money at 33 percent on the dollar, *and* work you over when you're late on the vig, that's racketeering. People laugh. How much is a bank loan? Nine percent?

Most artists haven't the vaguest idea that this is going on. Somebody else is signing their checks. And, even if you *ask* about it, you get a song and dance that's university trained.

If things are going well, you'd rather not question. Why upset the boat? We're on a good track.

So how do bands like Fleetwood Mac, who sold 26, 30 million records, wind up living in little houses and pinching pennies, so to speak? Simple. Every year, 25 percent of their total value or more is subtracted by all of these various factions. Can you dig it?

So when I tell you that one time I paid out over a million, three hundred thousand dollars to just managers and agents, and not made a penny, now you can understand how simply that can happen. Because what business functions on over a 30 percent profit margin?

When I put on a show, you're gonna get your bang for the buck. The only responsibility I feel toward the audience is to *maximize* my inspirations and my imaginations 100 percent. Well, I got imagination the size of Texas. And that costs a *lot* of money. It starts right with the band. I'm not gonna bring you some ill-rehearsed horseshit, with sub-par musicians because I could pay them less. I'm gonna bring you one hundred days *slammin'* rehearsal where most people are gonna give you *ten.*

You know how much that costs? In terms of the staging, the lights and the whatever? Wow! So once that 33 percent is gone, all the rest I used up for the show. Yeah, I could have cut back. I could also have another name and be a different artist, too. I don't cut back. I'd rather *die* than be the last guy up the hill. I will never cut back. Period. Peri-fuckin'-id.

In 1978, Van Halen stayed out on tour for almost twelve months straight. We went to Europe twice, did complete international touring, sold, at that point in time, a solid two million, two-and-a-half million records. Within the next year, it'd be four million records. When we finished that tour we *owed* the record company over a *million* dollars in advances that they kept giving us to keep us out on the road. Advances against future record sales.

There was *no* profit, *none* of that went into our pockets. The only pockets that were lined belonged to the usual 33 percenters.

Van Halen was one of the most successful acts of its day. But nobody had taught us the map. At the time, the attorney who negotiated the original Van Halen deal was obviously playing buddy-buddy with the company. 'Cause we got the *worst* royalty rate in show business. And I think we got something like a twenty-five-thousand-dollar advance to sign.

The lawyer rolled us over. He didn't think that we were gonna become anything. So he played nice guy with the company, "I'll give you guys a break, 'cause I'm gonna be back with six other accounts, later, and you'll treat me nice."

Anyway, the way you wind up in league with all these various concerns is again, cut right out of a script. You'll meet with the main guy at the agency. You'll meet with the *main* attorney. You'll meet with the *main* accountant. They'll tell you how important you are, what a bold and bright future you have, and they're just simply fascinated. But unless you're already making big-league dollars, you'll be passed off to the guy who agents for Paul Revere and the Raiders. They won't tell you.

You'll call the main guy, and he'll have to get back to you with every answer to any question. 'Cause he's gonna have to call the Paul Revere guy to find out what's happening. Then he'll call you back and say, "Nothing's happening."

Well of course not. The guy wouldn't be working Paul Revere and the Raiders if he had anything going on. And you'll find this out months later, down the road. My last agent, I said to him directly, "So you're going to be the one to pick up the telephone and make all the phone calls on my behalf?"

He looked, gave me a lot of teeth, and said, "Yes, yes. I'll be the one to pick up the phone." And he picked up the phone and called the guy who handles Paul Revere and the Raiders.

I found this out six months after the fact. Before I was even out the front door, it was passed down the ladder to the lowest guy.

They're playing a game of numbers, as well. Since there's already too many artists to really focus on, to any great degree, why not add more artists? If you go join a company like ICM, there's a hundred and fifty *agents.* Not clients, agents. Each *agent* must have ten to twenty clients. So it's all filtered down to the lowest common denominator. What happens, by and large, with your execs and vice presidents and players in the record company, the agency, the lawyer, whatever, is what we call in rock climbing "falling your way up the wall." And falling your way up goes like this:

You're on a line already. Somebody who's a good climber went before you, and he's belaying you from the top. He's your safety measure. You go to make a move, and you hurl your body, in desperation, toward a hold. Completely out of control, you miss it by six inches, and as you fall, you catch one, and you just fell another three feet up. So you hang there, make sure your safety line's intact, and with a great determination and a lot of noise, you hurl yourself toward the next hold, three feet away. You miss it entirely, by overshooting it, whatever, and as you fall earthward, your hand accidentally catches another hold. And you just fell another two feet up.

Well, this by and large, is how people are promoted. Or, somebody dies, and you're the next guy in line. Or the Peter Principle: You will be adept and good at what you do, in your job, and you'll work your way up the hierarchy, the ladder, so to speak, until you reach the point where you're completely inadequate, and *that's* where you'll spend the rest of your working life. Comfortably in that office. Not because you're great at it, and you're accomplishing great things, but because you don't have the facility or the wherewithall to advance any further.

We can't exclude, of course, falling your way up the wall. That could happen at any point in your career. You *could* make a desperate lunge at an idea, miss it, overshoot it entirely, but catch another idea on your way down, and you will have fallen three more feet high.

Now, these birds—lawyers, accountants, record execs—are easily recognized. First you look for lawyer loafers. Record company people wear lawyer loafers, accountants, agents—they all wear lawyer loafers. They're these little shoes that are made out of either really soft goatskin, or even better, of velour. Always have tassels on the front of them, and just enough leather to cover the toes. Okay? To keep the shoe from falling off the front of your foot.

You'll see socks starting from right where your little toes connect to your foot all the way up to the pant leg. And they have a little crepe sole, which is perfectly useless for walking *anywhere* and this is precisely the message: It says, "I'm a man of leisure. I don't walk. When I do, it's not far, and it's always on a carpet." The socks are the exclamation point. You've got to have color-coordinated silk socks. It's best to shop on Rodeo Boulevard, where in Beverly Hills, silk on silk on silk is pro forma, okay? Italian surnames are cool. Brioni, Armani, whatever.

The first stages of this are your penny loafers, but they're too stiff. I remember back in junior high, a lot of us kids wore penny loafers, and your parents would give you a dime to put in the little slot, in case you had to make a phone call. My parents gave me sixty-five dollars in bail. It was only years later that I figured out what that was all about.

Keep an eye out for creases, because most of these fellas do not have any creases. Look for creases behind the armpit, at the elbow, at the waistline, in front of the pants, and behind the knee. 'Cause the guy who's really wrinkled and has a lot of creases is the guy doin' the work. He's at the desk, he's on the phone, and he's putting in his time.

Nine out of the ten of the fellas have no creases. They sort of waft around, from office to office. When they do sit down, their feet are up on the desk. A car won't make creases, so don't go for that nonsense of "I've been traveling on your behalf."

If you really want to test one of your team, make sure you show up just before lunch time. And see who's got creases. 'Cause if it's the guy who's got creases by lunchtime . . . that dog will hunt.

If you encounter silk on silk on silk—silk socks, pants and a shirt—what this may indicate to you, truthfully, is that this is a boss. This is a senior VP, or whatever, because those clothes cost a lot of money. It's nothing to pay six hundred dollars for a pair of silk pants in Versace, or whatever, a silk shirt is four hundred dollars at Dolce & Gabbana. But don't be fooled by the junior partner who's wearing workman-like khaki slacks and penny loafers, like you can get at Payless or Thom McAnn. You may think that this is somebody who is a true worker bee.

More than likely, he just can't afford the Dolce & Gabbana yet. Just because he can't wear the uniform doesn't mean he's not a hundred percent Annapolis. He's just a midshipman, that's all. He's still navy.

The dead giveaway, every time, will be eyewear. Oliver Peoples, those little glasses, or Cazals, whatever the trend is, at any given time, will be the *first* feather that you put in your hair, saying that you're going to be a chief, or that you're connected to the chiefs. Your first outward indication to the rest of the tribe will not be your achievement record but rather something that you wear on your head. It will be designer glasses.

Also, don't be deceived by the sport coat and blue jeans and penny loafers. This is a scout that was recruited from your side, so that he could lead the way to your tribe. This is what, in Vietnam, was called a "Kit Carson scout." He was recruited from the opposition 'cause he spoke the language and knew the mountains; looked *totally* like them, but completely worked for us.

Well, just reverse that. What you'll have is the ex-drummer for the such-and-such rock band, who's now a VP at a record company. He *still* wears his native clothing. It's a big part of the reason he's been hired. Look for creases.

Fans And The Cult Of The Spotlight

My first experience with the super fan was long before Van Halen made our first album. We played something called the Halloween Fabulous Freaks Ball out at The Proud Bird, which still exists on Aviation Boulevard near the L.A. airport. It's a big ballroom. Met a gal—how old was I? Maybe nineteen, twenty, same thing she was. Wound up back at her place, went into her room, didn't realize what was going on till I woke up in the morning or at dawn. My good pal Stan wound up at somebody else's house, gone with her in her car. I had my little car—my Opel Kadett station wagon.

When I woke up in the morning, every square inch of her wall and her ceiling and the facings of the bureau were covered with pictures of rock and roll singers. A collage that covered the entire surface of the room. That's when I kinda got it: that some were involved in a sport I was not familiar with. So I had to dwell on that for a while.

I got in the car, drove off. Lo and behold, there at the intersection where Lincoln joins the Santa Monica Freeway is Stan, hitchhiking. I picked him up and drove home. And I thought this could bear some further investigation. This is an interesting scenario.

Later on, down the line, I ran into the most ardent kind of fan, like the two girls who dressed as maids. They broke into a maid's closet or found a maid's closet that was unlocked, and put on uniforms as maids, got buckets and brushes and the whole thing, got up on our floor and had cleaned completely and fastidiously six different rooms before they got to mine. Hey, this is major effort. They got passes, they got tickets, the works.

On the other hand, they don't always turn out quite so charming. I've got a 180-pound white female, who's been haunting me for over a decade now. Let's call her "Mrs. Lance." She lives in her own little parallel universe. Claims that I wrote songs about her; alternately claims that I wrote the songs *with* her. I've never met this girl before in my life in any social setting.

We would have auditions for one of the videos, and she would show up in the line four times, in different clothes. Half of her looks like a bag lady, and the other half of her . . . she's got pretty good legs. So she gets through the door. She's got a good line. She's got a good rap. I think she's affiliated with a religious cult somewhere along the line. She's got a support group.

She would send me seventeen-page letters where the writing is so small you need those glasses that the dermatologist uses. Occasionally, when she can't make any real contact, she'll file a restraining order against me. Oh yeah.

When Pauly Shore was just starting to do his stand-up comic routine, he had yet to make a movie, yet to be part of MTV or anything. His mom, Mitzi, ran The Comedy Store. I had met him there. I knew Mitzi casually. Ran into him at a beer bar, English pub on Sunset Boulevard. Everybody's sitting outside, we're talking, "Pauly, pleasure to meet you." "Dave, Diamond Dave, wow, this is a trip." Suddenly I feel a punch between the shoulder blades, I turn around, it's Mrs. Lance. She stands back four paces and screams, freezes the whole patio, "You son of a bitch! That's the last time you run off with your midgets to Rio de Janeiro and leave me with four black guys. What am I supposed to do with the children?" Security had to remove her.

But her rap is smooth, see. When she cleans herself up, her rap is smooth. So what she had done around 1987 was go up and down Sunset Boulevard, walk in through any door. The sunglasses place, the burger place, whatever. She'd go boldly strolling in and say, "I'm David Lee Roth's fiancée. We're getting married and I'd like to make a purchase." She's the kind of person who goes through the garbage and comes up with all the right addresses and phone numbers, just enough information to keep you playin' dice, you follow? And she charged thousands of dollars' worth of goods—sunglasses, shoes, clothing. She charged a four-thousand-dollar wedding dress.

"Just send the bill to this address," she'd say. "You know Dave." Hollywood's a small town, the bills would arrive at our office. We'd have to call the people and say, "Oh, we have no knowledge of this."

She sent out wedding invitations all over the world, had them printed up in a kind of biblical script, that we're getting married in the football stadium in Rio de Janeiro that holds 150 thousand people. We're going to be doing a show together, we're going to be getting married on stage, and we're going to fly everybody in on special jets, and, hey, it sounded actually kinda cool. It's a great script, but I think we got the wrong actors here. We got to rethink this.

I'm getting calls from all over the world. "David-san, most graciously accepting invitation . . ."

"David, kind sir, the mind fairly reels, and so—"

From England, "A gossamer cloud of connubial bliss beckons."

Or, from New York, "Yo, what's up, Big D? Can't wait for the bachelor party. Have set aside a whole week. Keep posted. Love, Dwayne."

They're delivering the mail in gunnysacks, so I gotta go get a restraining order. I had to show up in court in Beverly Hills, "Your Honor," dah dah dah dah, okay, I'm telling this with some mirth, and levity here, some smiles. But this is about the time the actress Teresa Saldana answered the door and a stalking fan slashed her up.

So there's a little tension. They send her off for three months, for twenty-four-hour counseling, let's call it. She forges my name on a document, gains an early release. The next day she's back on the phone, she's got my number somehow, calling, thirteen times in one day.

Then she files her own restraining order, something to the tune of: David Lee Roth beat me and tortured me and chained me and left me in a closet, and then left me with Latin men who sexually abused me and sold my children to Arabs. This, of course, is all over the press, because whenever you file suit it becomes a public issue. The court reporters go, Well, this sure beats an insurance bust. Dig this now!

And people who've known me for years are sticking their little heads in the back compartment of the tour bus and going, "Hey, Dave, you got a minute? Can I talk to you?"

"Sure, Rock, sit down. What's up?"

"Say, boss, you wouldn't ever hit a girl, would ya?"

"No, Rock, I wouldn't even hit my last girlfriend."

"Whoa—you're strong, Dave. That's what I thought. Sorry to bother you. You're a tougher man than I am, boss. That's what I was hoping to hear."

But it's in print. So everybody's going wild, all the tribes on the other side of the hill are doing the dance. "Holy mackerel, see the smoke signals last night?" And I'm having to address all of this. She still exists. We got another restraining order, which is currently in effect, but she'll be back. She would leave things like self-made pornos, not good ones, gross ones, on the doorstep of the office. And these seventeen-, eighteen-page letters with photos of herself in the nude.

We called the mental health people and that's when we discovered a whole movie waiting to be made. At any given time there's like two guys and a gal in a van in orbit on the freeway system all around L.A. And when you get a call like this, they get a call in the truck, and they show up, these two big black guys with this little

Jewishy-Italian chick. They would show up and collect the evidence, get the story. It's like something out of *Cuckoo's Nest,* the update of *Cuckoo's Nest,* but now it's in a van.

They showed up so many times at the offices, we got to know each other. Big guy comes up, he has to be six-four, six-five, huge guy, ex-ball player, you could tell, in the white uniform, "Hey, Dave. Okay, we got a letter, we got here a couple photos, you ain't got no more videos, do you?"

"Not this week, Bob."

"Damn!"

On the lighter side: Then there was the fan who crawled up the vines on the outside balconies of a Marriott Hotel somewhere in the Deep South in an effort to find my room after a show. It was something ridiculous, like the sixth floor. Wound up climbing into the window of the wrong room. There were eight thugs there, all of them carrying pistols, counting out a few hundred thousand dollars of merchandise money, all of it in cash, piled up on the table. Stuck his head through the window and he's looking down the business end of everything available from your favorite gun dealer down the street. Before they could say anything, he down-climbed the whole thing. They were just going to pull him in and let him go. He got so freaked out, he down-climbed six floors. That's the height of the ceiling of your local hockey arena. They never caught him. I'd love to go climbing with him. That's the man I want on my rope. I would have hired the motherfucker if we could have caught him.

There are a number of people who went to thirty or more shows on a given tour. They would road trip it. I routinely hear stories from people who will collar me at the local McDonald's somewhere and say, "Man, during the '84 tour I would just say to my roommate, 'Man, we're kind of feeling down. Where's Van Halen playing?' 'They're in Boston,' or 'They're in Wisconsin.' We'd look at the map, and we'd say, 'Okay. Three days, goin' easy . . . road trip!' "

Guys who would follow the band from city to city. And we would get to know them. Guys who saw upwards of fifty, sixty shows in a given tour. We would let them in at the crew meal. Once you got to know them, they knew to show up backstage, ask for Big Ed, security, and so forth, they'd be taken care of with laminates and passes. If they didn't have enough money to make the laundry coin, give 'em a T-shirt.

There was one gal who was always hanging out with the transportation guys, the truck and bus drivers, and she would spend the night with different ones. Or she would spend five nights in a row with a given truck driver and drive with him, keep him company and stay in his room at the hotel. Everybody knew Tami, and word went out that she was to be respected as part of the team.

One night she got busted. She had some pot in her purse and the police busted her somewhere in Cincinnati. This happened during the show, they took her downtown, so to speak. I found out about it after the show and sent one of the runners from the promoter team to go bail her out. Everybody got on the bus, drove all the way to Cleveland. Lo and behold, who's standing out in front of the hotel, ten o'clock the next morning? There's our gal. She even beat us to the next city.

One of the upshots of fandom today is that we live in

the cult of the spotlight. The old Andy Warhol axiom, "Everybody will be famous for fifteen minutes in their life," has switched over to the way it was originally printed when they didn't use tape recorders in interviews, but they kept notes. When he first made that quote in the sixties, it came out in the press as, "In fifteen minutes everybody's going to be famous." Well, that's actually true now.

In the mid-nineties, everybody's got a video camera. Peter Gabriel's favorite charity buys video cameras for people. Everyone's going to be famous, whether it's a military dictator or a cop with a billy club, or whether it's an underground band making a video at home, or Tommy and Pamela's sex tapes.

It's a day and age when you see David Brenner eating a salami sandwich at a truck stop; this is front page news, you can't believe it, you'll never forget it for the rest of your life. In terms of most people concerned, "Jesus, I took a leak next to Ted Danson!"

I tell people, "Yes, I flew from New York to L.A. with Naomi Campbell last week. I mean, we weren't sitting together, she was on the plane."

That's a futile attempt at humor. But people don't get it. "Really? Like, what part of the plane was she sitting on?" It doesn't matter. The fact that we were in the same tri-state area is news, is worthy of a dissertation at the breakfast table for the next three weeks.

So no matter where you go, people say to me, "Oh, I know why you hang out in New York. People leave you alone. They aren't impressed with stars, celebs and whatnot. New York is very numb to that, we're above that."

No way. It's a constant review. People will pick you out of the crowd, walk all the way across the street, follow you into the men's room. That happens all over the world, and New York. You crack a *People* magazine or an *US* magazine these days, you don't even recognize the names until you read in the parentheses the name of the television show. All of this is printed and indexed. *Everywhere* you go. It's a constant parade, it's a constant peanut gallery.

It's played out that it's an obligation that you open up your entire life to the media, that the media be invited into your house. How many more shots of James Bond, or the latest James Bond, cooking eggs with his wife and two kids in a kitchen do we have to see? Why don't we just install a video camera in his kitchen and just have updates every month? With a still camera on one visit, you might miss something. You know, maybe there's a drinking problem in the family or some spousal abuse. You know how many magazines we can move if we can dig up some spousal abuse?

So if you refuse to do an interview or publicize yourself, you're considered a total dick. You're labeled as having a huge ego. "The nerve! He won't speak to my magazine? Who does he think he is?"

The media can't understand why when you watch the little blurb advertising *Eyewitness, Current Affair,* et cetera, here's a guy who's being indicted for something. Last I heard, you're innocent till proven guilty. And here comes some frustrated little dork in her work suit, you know, her little pants suit, some shrill, dry, sour, little character, clutching a microphone, running along, being chased by her film team. "Mr. Jones, Mr. Jones, why won't you talk to us?" He's trying to open his door with his key; she's trying to wedge her body literally between him and the door.

"Mr. Jones, why won't you talk to us? Why won't you talk to us?"

Well, for starters, any lawyer will tell you, "Don't talk to anybody, don't even talk to your veterinarian or even the press." Trial by the people's court on television insofar as "not stopping and answering immediately" indicates—especially after editing—that he's somehow guilty. No, no. The one who's being covert and feral is that reporter. She's got a shitty sex life at home, a little trouble with her old man, or her girlfriend. So she's gonna take it out on Mr. Jones. She feels she's wearing a robe and a crown. Nah. She's not even wearing attractive underwear. Fifty dollars says so.

This is par for the course. What she deserves is a belt in the mouth. Male, female, in between, doesn't matter. If I am putting the key in the lock of my front door and you jam yourself between me and my door with a film crew screaming, you're looking at a belt in the mouth. You're going to give an opinion? Be prepared for mine. I can't wait till you try and wedge yourself between me and my door. I'll French kiss you right there on international television.

I know a gal who worked for these kinds of shows for a while. She worked for "A Current Affair," the "Maury Povich Show." She's one of these clown show freaky deaks who contacted this cornball hose-bag named Tawny Kitaine. Remember the one who was always doing the splits on somebody's sportscar on MTV? Well, I remember Tawny when she was dating the Van Halen sound man, then worked her way up to the lighting director. Evidently she had some dalliances with O. J. Simpson somewhere along the line.

So they hooked up a little scenario where they were going to surprise her in a convenience store with the camera crew, like she didn't know they were gonna be there, and then ask her all kinds of questions about O. J., and she was going to drop the dime on the guy. Well, whatever you think of O. J. Simpson or the verdict, I see something wrong with cooking up theater with somebody who may have had an affair with O. J. Simpson. Great. But they contrived this "ambush": "Oh, we stumbled upon her, we surprised her, she was flustered," and she's going to do the dirt on this guy.

They shoot the episode. It turns out she doesn't have so much dirt to spill, they're unsatisfied. "Hey, we wheeled out the van with the sound crew, the video guy, what you're saying isn't dirty enough, it's not harmful enough, it's not negative enough." Got into a big thing about whether or not they were going to pay her, 'cause they had struck a deal; this was for pay.

I told my "pal" at the time, "Honey, you're getting off on a technicality."

She said, "What does that mean?"

"You make your living sticking your nose and your sticky little fingers into other people's business and creating trouble at the expense of somebody. That's your form of show business, and I think it's vile. Now, get lost and stay there. Go home, lose my phone number." Haven't spoken to her since.

A number of months later, she was lifting weights in a gymnasium out at the beach near Venice, forgot to put the pin in the weight, stuck her hand in under the weight machine. It fell, smashed out all her fingernails. Believe in metaphysics? Is there a spiritual circle that begins and completes itself? Is there a kind of spiritual justice that happens to us all? I recommend she stays away from the gym, while we ponder all the previous.

Rationalization

In the mid-seventies, I worked at a clothing store. And I learned the great rationalization that's gotten me through so many tough times in my life, so many tough times in other people's lives. I learned it from the general manager of the London Britches Clothing Store on Lake Boulevard. I said to him, one day, "Jim, how come we're not sellin' any pants?"

And he said, "Well, it's right before a holiday."

And another time, I asked him, "Jim, sales are off. How come we're not sellin' any pants?"

And he said, "Well, it's a holiday."

And another time, I asked him, "Jim, we're just not sellin' real well these days, how come?"

And he said, "Well, it's right after a holiday."

And I've found that this rationale works for just about everything. I heard somewhere that rationalizations are more important than sex. When's the last time you went three days without makin' an excuse? Me too.

Bomb

I've got a '51 Merc sitting in my garage. That's a Godfather car. That's a super bomb. But redone. It's got hydraulics so I can lower it all the way to the street, and you can't see the wheels. That's illegal. Regulation says the body of the car can't be any lower than the lowest point of the hubcap, the rim. So that's where it currently resides. When you sit in either of the seats, your elbow, when you put it out the window, will be higher than the top point of your ear. California law says your windshield can't be *less* than four and a half inches high. So I've got a regulation, four-and-a-half-inch windshield. The roof starts there, but because the seats are so low you can put a six-and-a-half-footer in there, and be totally comfortable. The windows on the driver's side door are only five inches tall. You can't get your head out the window when you're driving, and the windshield looks like a giant pair of sunglasses.

Crazy Horse

In 1978 I went, for the first time, to the quintessential striptease place. The Crazy Horse Saloon in Paris. It had been there since the war, same owner. He selected all the girls based on their appearance, of course, and he was a fan of the athletic, Swedish speed-skater body. Whoa. Can I get one in blue?

They did ensemble numbers. They would all show up on stage in bondage gear, wearing platform boots, but the platforms were adjusted to make them all the same height. And they would all wear the same wigs. Little Dutch boy bangs. Girl-girl scenes, all of it insinuated intimation.

Ultimately, striptease became the USO/Servicemen's Club for those of us on the road. I learned some of my best moves from those girls.

Elvis

Elvis Elvis, Elvis.

You know for a fact that Elvis is dead, because if he wasn't, Michael Jackson would be.

They gave me the Elvis dressing room the first time I played in Las Vegas; found a couple of half-eaten doughnuts under the bed, a few Percodan nut logs in the medicine cabinet.

I have a little tattoo on my ankle, a kind of Kabuki Elvis. It's a good thing I mixed a little coffee with all that rum I was drinking that night, or I might have had something like Roseanne tattooed across my ass. Who, come to think of it, *is* kind of a kabuki Elvis. . . .

Let's go to the Elvis buffet . . . you can fill in the rest of the joke. That's for people who go to Las Vegas and lose three hundred dollars, and figure they'll make it back by eating four hundred dollars' worth of the Elvis buffet. Let's not forget the Elvis All-Night Pharmacy. "Thank you v'ry much."

Though I did not relate to Elvis—I always figured him to belong to my parents—I knew all the movies. And we felt like the movies belonged to us, because they were so tacky. Okay, well that had to be youth culture, right? 'Cause we were all comin' from there.

Captain Blood

The tropics were really important to me as a kid, even though I had never really seen them. I had read *Moby Dick,* and Robert Lewis Stevenson—*Typee* and *Kidnapped, Treasure Island*, all these kinds of things.

Errol Flynn was always best when he was a pirate. I completely adopted his outfit from the movie *Captain Blood.* He's a prisoner, a brigand, you know. All of the prisoners escape, they steal a ship, as well as Olivia de Havilland, and put out to sea. They're pirates. And Errol Flynn crawls up the main mast to the crow's nest because he's going to read his edict, his constitution that he's drawn up, because they're going to join forces together, all these pirates from around the world.

As soon as he ascends the mast, Flynn pulls the rope ladder up behind him, and he reads the edict, which says, "We, men who sail under no flag, hereby design to sail under no flag together. Let it be the flag of blood: Desperate men in search of desperate fortune, all as one." Hey.

I wanna be a pirate. I wanna live by pirate rules. "Desperate men in search of desperate fortune?" You bet.

Jolson

In this day and age, Al Jolson would be considered racist. The whole thing of putting on black face, doing minstrelsy—I think that's the academic term—singing "Swanee River." I still know the words to all of those; I imitated him. That's what I lip-synched to: "Swanee, how I love ya, how I love ya, my dear old Swanee . . ." And singing in that black voice would be so politically incorrect now.

But the first records that I imitated were Al Jolson—getting down on one knee, you know, with the white gloves, singing, as well as dancing—the idea of entertaining. It was just something that was expected.

It was only later, in hippie years, that the idea of being an entertainer was somehow not cool. You had to be positively somnambulant, just sort of stand around, catatonic, and jam, the Grateful Dead approach. The idea that you could also be an entertainer was not hip, in the sixties, but I grew up with it being par for the course.

Most people don't know it, but Al Jolson was the first guy to take a real production on the road, do a road show. Had it not been for Al Jolson, there would be no Rolling Stones tour. Had it not been for Jolson, there would be no Grateful Dead show. There would not have been a Woodstock. Everybody would still be playing in little theaters, with the lights that go with the theater, and with the sound that comes with the theater. Jolson was the first one to really construct a whole show with wardrobe, dancers, his own lights, his own sound, his own orchestra, and take it on the road.

A Zen Poem

My music, personally, is best understood not by animals and small children, but by small animals and big children. You must have, however, something to talk about; you must have some life experience, some kind of mileage, either academically or otherwise.

You want to hear my poem about mileage? It's called "Maserati," and I call it a Zen poem, on account of it doesn't rhyme. It goes:

Get yourself a brand-new Maserati . . .
Open the door;
Smells like vinyl,
Corners like a brick, no bottom end,
no stereo to be found.
Now
You get yourself a Maserati
With a little distance under the tire,
A couple of good drinking stories
Packed into the rearview mirror,
Here, let me adjust that for you.
Open the door; smells like leather,
Corners like a dream shot through
the eye of a cloud,
Tipped right off of Babe Ruth's ghost
bat—Pow!
And your legs are gonna get bumps
Every time that bass man thumps.
The choice is yours . . .
That's what I thought; me too.

Meet Helmut Newton

In '79, we would have a break on tour, and I'd head right for Studio 54. There'd be Andy Warhol, the Guinness twins, with Steve Rubell and Ian Schrager, the two guys who architected the whole mise-en-scène, Bianca Jagger, Halston, Helmut Newton, the great photographer. Came time to do the second Van Halen record, and I said, "Helmut Newton should shoot a picture for the album."

Everybody said, "Who's that?"

I said, "He's the shit. He's legit."

Nobody knew. Told the record company, of course. The art department said "Oh, no way. This is a fifty-thousand-dollar-a-shoot guy. He doesn't deal with this kind of rigamarole . . ."

Lo and behold . . . (which sounds like a legal firm) . . . Helmut Newton is having a showing at the G. Ray Hawkins Gallery on Melrose. And I says to myself, "He can only be staying at one of four hotels, let's start calling."

I called the Beverly Hills Hotel, on Sunset Boulevard: "Excuse me, may I please speak to Mr. Newton?"

"Certainly, sir."

He picks up the phone, and I say, "Good afternoon, Mr. Newton, my name's David Lee Roth. I'm very aware of your talents and who you are. I'm sure you've never heard of me, but I'm in a rock band called Van Halen, and we're flavor of the week. I think we should shoot a photo."

He said, "This is very interesting. I've never had an approach like this. Did you call my agent?"

I said, “What do you mean?”

He said, “Precisely. I like your attitude. Come on down to the pool and let’s have a look at you.”

I said, “Great.” Put on leather everything—riding boots with the leather pants, chaps with the jacket, the belt, and I went down to the hotel. He was lounging by the pool.

I sat down, and we talked everything from politics to mathematics for about half an hour, then he leaned over and said, “Do you know what, David? You are my new favorite blond. I would love to shoot photos of you.”

I said, “Spectacular. When?”

And he said, “What are you doing for the rest of the day?”

I said, “Nothing.”

He said, “Great. Do you have a car?”

I said, “Oh, yes. I have a Mercedes-Benz that I just had painted black, with a big skull and crossbones on the hood of the car.”

He said, “Magnificent! Let me go to my room, get me my camera gear, my wife, Alice Springs, is a stellar photographer in her own right. Would it be okay if she comes along?”

“Absolutely.”

“Great. We’ll find her, we’ll get our gear together. Do you have a place to shoot?”

I said, “Well, I have a dog pound in my backyard, with a lot of fencing.”

“Excellent! I’ll meet you in the parking lot.”

The three of us got in the car and started driving. This is pre-cellular. We had to stop at a pay phone, call ahead to the Art Center College of Design, in Pasadena, and recruit a couple of assistants, school kids, to come down and assist. They met us at the house, and we shot all day. Dave chained up in the dog pound, Dave standing by the pool.

Next day, I got a stack of prints half as long as your forearm. And they were all magnificent. I called up Helmut and said, "Helmut, these are just spectacular, but I'm gonna put you wise, directly, here. I have no idea what we're actually going to use them for. Maybe a poster, or an album cover, a T-shirt, a magazine, something. How does a fella *pay* for something like this?"

And he said, "Well, the two boys worked very hard yesterday, and I think that you should give them forty-five dollars, to split. Okay?"

I said, "And?"

He said, "Well, there is no 'and.' You're my favorite blond. Use them for anything you want."

We made a poster: Me, chained up—it's a very famous poster—in the dog pound, and enclosed it in every album. It was sold from there on in. Forty-five dollars. The last remaining print I know of has been sitting in my sister's room folding up from humidity and the elements. And within the last two months, I had it framed and stabilized. This photo is easily worth ten thousand dollars. The photo of me, chained up in the dog pound, has been in every one of Helmut's annuals.

Body Language

I've always communicated the most thoroughly, physically. It's a big part of the reason that Van Halen defied the language barrier; it was truly Esperanto. And it is the same for me today.

The only way to really get it across is physically—the dance, the theater of it. It's in the way that you walk. It's in the way that you hold the microphone. It's in the way that you point to the other guy when it's their turn for the spotlight. Your tone of voice, which is another form of body language—not the melody, not the words, but your tone of voice—will tell anybody from somebody in Singapore to a Labrador retriever your state of mind about the subject at hand. Isn't that the whole point anyway?

I have an emotional reaction to something, and I would like to share that emotional reaction with you, not just so that you can analyze it but so that you may experience it at the same time. And for me, body language in its infinite forms has been the most direct straight line to that kind of a goal.

It doesn't mean acting, thinking ahead of time, "Okay, what does a person act like?" "What does a happy person act like?" It is about losing yourself into the song and actually becoming happy or miserable or horny or philosophical or what have you. When you can effectively lose yourself, stop thinking, lose all distraction, then you will truly walk it as you talk it.

My personal style of body language comes from being a people watcher. I love to watch people. I'm an expert at urban camouflage, I can dress like a building, you'll never even know I'm in the tree with you. And I always watch body language, how we communicate to each other with our hands, with our faces, our hips, our haircuts.

A great date, to my way of thinking, would be enough along in a relationship to go out to the local cantina, go dance, have a drink, have dinner, then we go back to the hotel or to the house and get in your underwear and imitate everybody that you saw that night. Take turns doing the walk, the hand language, the eyebrows. Least important is the occasional flat note—it's your intent and the body language.

Wars And Remembrance

Why did I get involved in the T-shirts and programs and such? 'Cause that's communication. No different than writing lyrics. It's no different than playing a guitar solo. It's no different than buying a pair of pants for that show, that program. It's communicating an idea, a thought or a state of mind. And rather than have somebody else's interpretation of it, get involved right from the start so that it all synchs up. You may hate it, but you will have understood it.

I got involved in the merchandising because I was tired of the same old boring, "Oh, here's a close-up shot of the vein." I call it "the vein." Which means piss-poor photographers getting a close-up lens and all you see is the side of somebody's face and that vein down their neck, and they're singing or they're playing that note really hard, and you can see the vein throbbing. "Yup, there's the vein shot." Obligatory. That will be fourteen bucks. Ugh!

Here's the guitar dude shot, with the legs spread and the dick stick pointed out, with a fake look of surprise. History for all the wrong reasons.

One of the reasons that Van Halen merchandise was so successful, as was the music, is because it was generated from the same source. I never considered it to be any different. It was a pure approach. Same as we created the songs. Pure.

VH music was not designed to sell. We went against the grain from beginning to end. It was designed to speak, to tell a story. And because of that, I'm convinced now, is why it's so massively popular. We're beseiged with people who are designing things for us to buy in our culture. When you find something that is truly pure in its origin and its source, you've got to salute the effort and the ambition, if nothing else—it's an inspiration. It's an inspiration to me when I see others do the same, in all art forms.

Right from the very start with Van Halen programs and T-shirts and such that went on the road, we hired out to other companies, but I presided over all of it, approved everything. Got involved in every level. Not just, "Oh, here we finished all the layout and it's done and here it is, what do you think?" But approving the layouts acetates, color tones, picking color patches, and on and on, right down to coming up with the original image.

Take *1984*, the album cover. I found that. And I

came up with the idea for the futuristic print type, and then told somebody where to find it. 'Cause those days, it was not Internet city. In order to come up with futuristic numbers, you had to go to a futuristic comic. Those numbers are from a Moebius comic by Jean Giraud, a famous cartoonist.

In terms of the money, well, if you're going to do all the work, then you should get the lion's share. It's a whole 'nother vocabulary you have to learn. We didn't just start out autonomous. I didn't just start out with, "Hey, I know everything." And most artists don't have the desire to learn that vocabulary or to invest time and effort in that direction. They are content to deal with a large company and pay the management to supposedly preside. God bless. You're missing out—come on in, the water's fine.

It is a huge responsibility, and you'll spend a lot of time in an office somewhere, as I did. And for those who don't care to get involved, I understand. Nothin' sounds so happy as horses whinnying once you take the packs off their backs. I understand that.

Most would assume that I personally got involved in merchandise in all of its facets or that the band would start our own merchandising factories, purely as a commercial maneuver. It wasn't at all. My sense of what was commercial was based on some movie scene out of the Prohibition era with sacks of green cash lining the walls of a hotel room with everybody with their pistols on the table counting the loot, with a lot of cigarette smoke in the room and bottles of Pearl beer, somewhere near Midland, Texas. And you would hear things about, "Hey, five dollars a person's worth tonight." "Hey, you sold seven dollars a person," "ten dollars"—whatever it was.

It was like the take from a card game. Like any good card shark, one day you figure you're going to buy a Mercedes, and the next day you may have to be sleeping in it.

Why would an artist like Prince get involved in producing his own records? So that he can save the 5 percent the producer gets? No. It's to more completely realize his vision. To have it come out on tape the way he dreamt it. To have you understand it more completely as he meant it to be understood. From there, it's your ballgame. You can dismiss, you can deify, you can become completely outraged and groove on that for a week if it's really good.

And if you see some of these old Van Halen programs, they look like no other programs or merchandise before or since. They are complete art projects from top to bottom. For one tour, the logo design was a lion wearing sunglasses with palm trees in the lenses. Just the logo for the tour delivers a message, delivers you a lifestyle, an attitude. You don't even have to crack the book. Right away, whether you're from Korea or Tijuana, you get it.

A number of times, my favorite approach to designing a program was to make it a chaotic family album, something between your college days and the summer you spent in Youth Authority, or the time that you went on a road trip and here's the napkin from the restaurant, and here's the hotel key that you found in your pocket later, and here's a picture of Doris just before she passed out. Right? That's the stuff I want to see.

Here's a cigarette pack, from that Greek island. You can't read it, but it's just cool. And here's a pair of sunglasses that we got in Taiwan—not made in Taiwan, we got them *in* Taiwan. And you can see it says on the side, it says "Ray Ban" in Chinese. Totally cool. Right? That's the stuff I want to see. Those are the goods.

Do you know the guys who stand out in front of the stadium about fifteen blocks away from the actual structure where you park your car, who are selling black T-shirts with these really gaudily colored band logos and photos, and the ink looks like it's been laid in four times? You can feel it's on the surface of the material. It's really thin, cheesy cotton something or other. They sell them for cheap, seven bucks, whatever. They've got thirty of them hanging over their forearms, and they walk in between the traffic. These are bootleggers. Bootleggers pay no percentage to the band or the artist or the copyright or the building or anything. Anybody can get a T-shirt printed up. Even if you do it with ill intent.

Well, jackals outnumber all other animals in the jungle nine to one. That's a fact. With the rhino comes the budgie bird. Bootlegging became a massive multimillion dollar industry right off the bat. Instead of Hanes heavy stock T-shirts, built to last, or Fruit of the Loom, bootleggers buy cheesy stock from Pakistan; black T-shirts that if you pulled it, stretched it and laid it on a printed page you could read through it. Print it up with the most gaudy, blistering colors and explosive graphics. Then you get homeboys of every background who will take *X* amount and go out and sell 'em. It was very organized, it was a cash cow.

As I described, we had started our own merchandising company—get a designer, print up the shirts, carry them around in the truck and sell them. That's gypsy, that's basic. It was massively successful, we had complete creative control. And the bootleggers were all over us like a cheap suit in August.

At the time only one other guy, Billy Joel, had taken up the sword against bootleggers, and we both had the same attorney. His name was Jules, New York trial lawyer, gung ho, marathon runner. It's copyright infringement, you know, trademark infringement, but every city has their own rules and ordinances on how to approach this. You can't just pull into town, collar all the bootleggers and deliver them to the police station. No, you gotta get a federal injunction in each separate city, *X* amount of weeks before the event, which expires at such and such a time, any kind of charges filed have to be done in such and such steps.

So initially we took the attorney out on the road. He rode on one of the buses. Every night he would conscript off-duty cops, and they would fan out around the arena of the stadium and chase down bootleggers, drive them away as best as possible. A lot of these guys are rough trade, you know, they didn't go away easy. Two little tiny gnats properly motivated can drive a water buffalo out of his mind. This was tax-free money to these characters.

A few mistakes were made. I believe it was Dallas, Texas, where a bunch of bikers were hired out of a bar. At the end of the night they'd not only chased off and beat up all the bootleggers, but also took all their T-shirts and all of their money and jewelry, marched into the middle of the arena during teardown, threw a half a ton of bootlegged material in the middle of the floor, said "You don't have to pay us. We've made enough tonight."

Ultimately we had a team that was the bootleg squad, and they were all ex-policemen, military, firemen. How many were there? Maybe six, all of them wearing camouflaged gear, you know, Marine Corps hats, soldier-of-fortune silhouettes. They came equipped with walkie-talkies. Tremendous amount of running and chasing and cornering.

But a lot of times, in a small town, you know, Tuna Fish, Alabama, the cops know these bootleggers, they're there every concert, things are quiet. This band's going to be out of town by birdsong. Why do we want to reenact the battle for Atlanta here? Shut the fuck up, play your fuckin' music and fuck off. Ran into that pretty frequently. Might be a little confrontation. Hey, everybody's got to take the walk now and then. Let's face it, we're total aliens from out of town.

One night, about '82—let's call him "Danny." Bootlegging the top bill act at a stadium run that we were doing. Keep in mind when you're running a stadium gig, everybody kind of houses together. It's like a bizarre version of the Olympic Village. You have five bands each with forty to eighty people, there's a circle of hotels or one giant hotel. Everybody dines together, everybody gets drunk together. The parking lot barbecues were like from Jupiter. You'd have seventy-five people there, all road rats. Greatest procession of giveaway merchandise that you ever saw. And about that time what we called the "bootleg wars" got serious.

At one point in the Olympic Village, I believe it was Houston, Danny and his crews were staying in the same hotels as the bands. They were guarded by jurisdictional rules, little municipal loopholes. But one night somebody hung Danny out of a fourth floor window by his ankles, told him, "Clear out. What part of 'fuck off' don't you understand?" Well, he not only stayed, but he brought in arm breakers. Pros in charge of merchandise from various arenas. They were obviously mobbed up. Guys in their mid-fifties with Italian surnames.

One night in my hotel in Odessa, Texas, a week later, fellow shows up, bootlegger, and he's got a fella, looks like Jimmy Hoffa, wheezing and chain-smoking Pall Malls. He's the union merchandise boss for the whole region. Said, "We'd like to talk to you." And I being Mr. King of the World said, "Sure, let's go up to my room." We sat and negotiated for a good couple of hours. They said: "Look, we need you to lay off, and we're prepared to make some kickback in an effort to show our good faith. 'Cause in this business, Diamond Dave, you got to have 'etics.' Etics and morals is ev'ryt'ing." It began to dawn on me that I should be very scared. I, of course, denied everything. I'm not in charge, I'm a jerk-off singer. I was the president of Pacific Manufacturing Corporation, at least on paper, and we were talking about playing stadium shows, sixty-five thousand average, and on a smokin' night, eight to twelve bucks a head for merchandise. This was the gold that was fought over every night.

Violence occurred regularly. We had to beef up the security team on the buses—it was very exciting. All that it takes for evil to transpire is for good men to remain in silence. We fought them off, cut their havoc by two-thirds at best. And when we vacated the fields of fire, they swarmed right back in.

So, here we are, *X* amount of summers later and every time you pull over to park, five, twelve, fifteen blocks from the arena, there they are. So I said, Let's take the Patton-Montgomery approach, "I hate you but I need you."

"Who's your artist?" I asked Danny, " 'cause they kick ass, and I'd like to hire him to design our T-shirts."

He flipped. We had geeked him at his own game.

Turns out Danny's factory was in the same fuckin' mini-mall that my factory was in. His warehouse was thirty meters away from our back door. I said, "Hey look, you know what? Those cheap-shit Pakistani low-stock T-shirts that you're buying for forty cents apiece? That strikes me as very pop, it's very disposable, it's very, kinda surface, very superficial, very cool, I like it. You gotta pile so much ink on it to hold in the weave of the fabric, it's really garish, and frankly, when the weekend kicks in around Tuesday, I feel garish. Turn me on to your supplier." And that's how it turned. We began to use elements of that bootlegging because it was very cool, it was underground, it was illegit. But the bootleg wars were a constant.

Then having contacted the bootleggers' suppliers, we took in stock of all this really cheap shit, almost cheesecloth kind of black T-shirts to print on. We issued a line of T-shirts with suitably bombastic designs in Day-Glo colors, and it looked really cheap and shitty and downtown. It was instantly popular.

I mentioned the kid climbing up the vines, the fan, to the sixth floor. What he ran into was not UN peacekeeping forces. What he ran into was an intervention. Everybody in that hotel room had a pistol.

Figure it out. What's the take? Nine bucks a pop times 65 thousand, in cash. Nothing bigger than a fifty. Has to be counted up, tabulated several times, once in the arena or the stadium, then again at the hotel, bagged up. Two guys have to be left behind by the tour buses so that they can take that cash to the bank first thing in the morning and then fly to the next city and rejoin. This is Butch Cassidy and Sundance Kid territory. Over half a million dollars a night, four nights a week, sometimes five.

For years we couldn't go to the bathroom without double escort. Threats were issued regularly, sabotage, to the trucks and buses, tires slashed. One of the bootleg team would get jumped by five guys and wind up in emergency.

Also, just to color in the miniseries that will never be made about this, there were so many rules and laws and, you know, tactical one-upmanship involved, yet there was still diplomacy. "Hey, there's nothing we can't solve." Not at all unusual to have had major violence two nights ago in the parking lot outside of the Checkerdome, three bootleggers hospitalized, one of my guys left behind for a week and a half. There you are in the hotel, Minneapolis, St. Paul, and a bottle of champagne arrives at your table. Look over and there's Danny with his crew. They're staying in the same hotel. Their trucks are parked next to ours. There was always that polite thing of, "Okay, when we're in the teahouse, tacit agreement that we won't burn the place down."

Everybody walked around with bodyguards times two. It was right out of *The Godfather.* Innumerable meetings backstage at dawn, you know, "Gentlemen, gentlemen, how did we let things get so far?"

Well, the Order of the Black Hand is not going to go away, so we had to strike a compromise, and that would be changed daily depending on who had advantage. In this city, we have allies. In the next city, you know the lay of the land better, and back and forth. All in the name of millions and millions of dollars. All of it in small denominations.

One day in Shreveport, Louisiana, one of the front office guys comes in and he says, "Dave, this is Valerie Bertinelli." I had no idea who she was. Had no interest at all, so she fixed her eye very seriously on the door to Ed's dressing room. Disappeared backstage with Ed, and they were an item from then on.

After that it was basically a bottle of Blue Nun to Ed and Valerie up in their hotel room. Alex and Mike, not sure where, really. Mike would usually socialize with the crew, likes a drink now and then. Alex always had a steady gal and was off on his own. So it was me and the midgets, and eighty other costumes, ranging from Sperry Topsider lawyer loafers to hobnail jack-bootin' box pushers. The little guys really summed it up; they were mascots.

I spent more days and evenings sitting in a hotel room somewhere and trying to create whatever the latest poster was going to be, whatever the latest video was going to be, or the latest backstage pass, or more importantly the lyrics, the vocals, the harmonies, the melodies. Heat expended cannot be replaced by simply walking back down the stairway.

I was lucky enough to enjoy a moment of inspiration together with some other people. There was a chemical reaction that can never be duplicated, can never be replaced. To have it simply stricken from the record is a bitter pill to swallow, which I think is Van Halen's entire designation now. Whatever anger you read in my words comes from that. But the reality is, it's only going to be one voice that's going to tell the story.

In most jobs, whatever you do, you'll get a license to do it and nobody can ever take it away from you unless you've really fucked up, unless you hurt somebody.

With Van Halen, all that hard work and all of that effort could be gone within ten summers. It might not be available; no film, no picture, no recording of you, nothing on the radio. If you think different, then you're only kidding yourself. You can't find all the records anymore, and you can only write Beethoven's Fifth Symphony once. You can only write "Love Me Tender" once. And it lasts forever, as long as you can buy it.

The horse will find its way to the water if the water exists. But if you dry out the pond intentionally, that's it, man, it's gone. All you'll have is a story.

The emotional impact for me is, once you've encountered hatred and ugliness like that, once you really become aware of just what human beings are capable of in that kind of sense, you're not so quick to rush back out onto the field with a sword in one hand and a torch in the other. I'll combat and contest anybody, but I'm not so quick anymore to form a team.

I did what I did with Van Halen in good faith and I left on good faith and I asked for no quarter. I asked for no settlement, nothing. And I guess that's precisely what I got. I should have led with my fist instead of my heart, but that would have put me right down in the bottom of the barrel with the kind of thinking that I'm railing against now.

I'm very proud of what *was* that band and what *was* that show and what it did mean to people. It disgusts me that it has turned into the complete opposite. That it now represents everything that I spoke against, that we supposedly represented the converse of. I don't want to have to remember that the team turned into that. Makes me question what the team was while I was a member. Was it all bullshit? If nothing else, it confirms in my mind that from my standpoint—yours truly, David Lee—not a fraction. If nothing else, this kind of morbid, wounded animal anger aimed my way has caused me to look deep into that bathroom mirror and come back to you with "my shit was legit." It *was* for real. And perhaps the test is time. Because here I am, a decade and a half later, haven't changed much. I look a little different, but not much. My sense of humor is about the same.

When I see the Van Halens dysfunctional with that kind of anger, it's like looking at a Hezbollah freedom fighter, those people who have nothing else to fight for. And I'm very hesitant to even continue 'cause my anger wells up. My emotional content is enough to stimulate a stadium full of people. My emotional content is enough to change what people see when they look in the bathroom mirror the next morning after my concert. I am not the master of self-control. I am not Mr. Peaceful. I don't own any peace symbols and we don't burn any incense in my little room. So I'm very hesitant to get up and move across the face of this wave because I become angry. It's not a place I want to live. Nevertheless, it still pains me deeply to know that all of that hard work is going to be completely demeaned and belittled the entire rest of the way. It's the work of misguided spirits.

This is music that could well feed and tuition my kids, down the line. That's not going to be the case. I'm lucky that I'm smart enough to have found other ways to take care of my Cuban cigars and Junior's football lessons some time down the freeway.

When I left Van Halen, it was not something that I was delighted to do. I was not celebrating. I was not relieved. It was one of the scariest moments in my life. I perceived that Van Halen was heading towards catastrophe. So do you ride that plane all the way into the sand? I said no, we'd already been through a year's worth of the Hatfields and the McCoys with the bottle of moonshine in between—and I'm *not* a prince. I am not Mr. Not Guilty at all, but the chemistry between us was becoming morbid, it was becoming threatening and nonproductive. You can hear it in the music, it started turning melancholy right after I left. That's great, there's plenty of room for melancholy music, but it's not my personal constitution.

Took me a long time to figure out what to do as far as staying in Van Halen. When I left, I had a screenplay that I had been working on with a couple of other fellas, but no movie deal. I did not have any movie company behind me. I didn't have any musicians. I had no equipment to rehearse with or anything.

It wasn't till some three, four months later that I had put together a band. It was some time after I left Van Halen, but I had nothing to leap to. I had nothing specific that was beckoning or that promised to be greater than. It was a question of watching a great bird augur in. And as time went by, there was more and more backbiting, more and more mudslinging, most of it coming from their vocalist and his management.

And here we currently reside thirteen years later, same mudslinging, same kind of thinking from their camp. So I guess the most critical decision I have to make is, do I really describe some of their carryings on, on the road? Or do I continue to be the quiet guy? Do I continue to be the nice guy? Ninety-nine percent of all the hijinks and carrying on was my contribution, but everybody had a proclivity. Everybody had a little sidebar to their story.

It's unfortunate that this feuding has to continue all the way up until the present, because what Van Halen meant to a lot of people and myself in particular, was very positive. What it meant in the early days—read: The time period that I was involved in the band—is hanging in there like an Indian summer. It's still all over the radio, still in the magazines, people still ask questions about the breakup.

I guess the best I can say is: Don't believe every syllable of everything that you read by everybody who wrote it. Go out and buy those records and see if you can hear the truth in the music. That's my recommendation. Some of those records you may have to buy twice—just in case you want your best pal to listen in too so you can discuss it some more. Dolemite, motherfucker!

Isn't it curious what we read about Gene Simmons now that he has put out his book? Gene Simmons chasing after Ed. How he had asked Ed if he wanted to join KISS by 1981, 1982. There you are. Dolemite, motherfucker!

At a Thanksgiving dinner, it must have been six years ago, we were talking about the band, and most of my family was at the table, in Pasadena. My father said, "You mean you guys haven't communicated at all?" I said, "No, Pop, not at all." Two days later my pop calls me up and says, "I hope you don't mind, but I took the liberty of calling Ed Van Halen." Well, this is a Roth kind of way of thinking. "I'm going to help you whether you want it or not. I'm going to help you—even if it kills you." I froze, because I knew what was coming. I said, "Pop, you shouldn't have done that." I said, "There's so much anger and hatred in the air coming out of those guys. Who knows how that's going to be translated?"

Lo and behold a week later there's a full page in *The Star* and in the *Enquirer.* Ed Van Halen saying, "Dave Roth is trying to weasel his way back in the band, he's destitute, even tries to have his father call me. Who does he think he is?" That kind of thing. I think the biggest victim of that page was my father; he was just trying to do what doctors do. He was being a dad.

But that was seized upon and turned into a daytime soap. So I'm very careful, as to how we approach each other. But I always felt, let's protect the story a little bit, let's protect the legend a little bit. Because it was very positive. And I stayed back from the backbiting and the screw you and you're a bad guy-ism and what-not for a number of years. And then about four years ago on Howard Stern I really laid into them. Said everything that I thought at the time. I didn't say it quite as nicely. Their new lineup to me is not of interest. And Ed Van Halen without a guitar in his hand is a crummy human being.

I'm not a junior psychiatrist. Why do people behave like they do? I think everybody was hurt. Everybody in the band felt let down. Everybody in the band felt abandoned. I felt the same thing that they were feeling. Two opposites become the exact same thing. "Well, Dave was working on something else." "No, that's what Ed was doing."

How far back are we going to go? Historically, how

far do we go here? Are we talking about this week only? It's just damned unfortunate that it's got to continue for this many years. I don't have a fantasy. I'm not waiting for the band to reconvene. I'm not waiting for the band to do a grand reunion. And I'm certainly not sitting here thinking about stepping on stage and how that's going to feel with them for four minutes come Rock 'n' Roll Hall of Fame time.

See, I don't know how far to go with the Van Halen story because everybody has domestic bliss, everybody has domestic rest, everybody's got kids, you know, forty acres and a mule. I got one smokin' passport, enough financial wherewithal to get me anywhere on the map, and then enough for a new suit to wear when I get there. And if you go with me, I'll buy all the drinks.

So how far do you go? Because I recollect Ed Van Halen at his . . . at *his* wife's wedding—now there's a slip! Last time I ran into them on the streets of New York was three, four years ago; I did not recognize them. Just out of the corner of my eye—you know how I walk with my ball cap down around my eyes, my sunglasses, walk very softly in mean streets.

I'm heading down Madison Avenue, it's nine in the morning, and somebody walks by and goes, "Hey, Dave." And I think, that sounds very familiar. I turn and I look and a full block away on the corner is a fat guy waving his arm, he goes, "It's Ed, Dave." I didn't recognize him, he's gained thirty pounds, you know, and a dozen years gone by. Thirty pounds. Or was that Valerie?

I walked up, I said, "Ed"—I remember I said the exact same sentence that my grandma said to me when I saw her at the hospital when she was eighty-eight years old. She said, "All my life in front of my eyes, look who's here now." It just popped out.

And I said, "All my life in front of my eyes, look who's here now. Ed, how are you?"

And Valerie said, "He's fine." Now you know the whole conversation. He says, "Oh, I hear you're playing with Terry," this was a mutual friend that we grew up with.

"Oh, yeah."

"How's it going?"

"It's going good. I hear that you're a dad, congratulations." I wanted desperately to ask who was the father but . . . it was not a time for levity.

Now, how am I going to write about Ed Van Halen whose white suit—that was my wedding present to him, his tailed white tuxedo, custom-made—is what he wore to his wedding. Cut to upstairs at the reception, the Beverly Hills Hotel, and Ed and I are doing blow and taking turns holding each other around the waist so we don't plunge head first into the toilet from dry heaving. You know, when you pack in a good Keith Richards–size thumbnail full, it drains right down the back, hits the old gag reflex, you sound like a Honda 125 on a cold morning: Hak, hak-hak, hak!

Anyway, I don't know that Ed was tuned in to the business and greed side of what was happening around him. And I, having watched every Blaxploitation movie ever made, knew every possible scam on earth.

I always felt that if you kept it in-house, it made it more special. Nevertheless, Ed pursued a number of outside projects: made-for-TV movies for his wife Valerie, a movie with Sean Penn's brother called *The Wild Life,* solo works with Allen Holdsworth and Brian May, a variety of interests.

The ultimate being when I came back from vacation at one point and I was in a parking lot on Santa Monica near Sweetzer, the 7-Eleven, there were a couple of butch Mexican gals with the doors open of their pickup truck and the new Michael Jackson song "Beat It" came on. I heard the guitar solo, and thought, now that sounds familiar. Somebody's ripping off Ed Van Halen's licks. It was Ed, turns out, and he had gone and done the project without discussing it with anybody, feeling as though I would stand in the way. Which actually, in that echelon of company, I wouldn't have at all. Quincy Jones is stellar company. Great, go play it. Don't waste it on Nicolette Larson or Gene Simmons. If you're going to do something, climb the big one.

But this was all done behind the scenes. It had become secretive at that point. And it was at that time I said to myself, hey, how many solo projects will he do while I stand guard at the gate of dreams worth dying for here? Saying, "No, no, I'm not going to act, I'm not going to write, I'm not going to be on television, I'm not going to be on anybody else's record, I'm not going to make any appearances or anything, I'll just be straight away with Van Halen."

It was at that point I said maybe I'll do something on the side as well. Certainly nothing that would conflict with what we were about as Van Halen, but I'll keep my eye open. It was some months later when I was in Mexico with my trusted assistant, Ed Anderson. We were sitting under a thatched roof, empty little bar out in Playa Blanca, looking out upon the sea, and the Beach Boys were on the stereo. Ed said to me, "You should do this song," it was "California Girls." I said, "Great, let's pursue it." I was very careful to keep the band posted every single step of the way as to what I was doing, so that I would not be operating in the shadows. Then I went ahead to do the *Crazy from the Heat* EP.

But ultimately what did happen in terms of the fracture of Van Halen came in '84, after sitting around for the better part of a year trying to make an album. When I talk about trying to make an album, I'm sitting with Ted Templeman outside of Ed's backyard studio for four and five days in a row, in the summer. We would sit on this little bench for hours waiting for Ed to pick up the phone in his bedroom, knowing he was in there but he wouldn't pick up. He had been up all night working on his own version of a mix for a song or working on a tune for one of Valerie's TV movies.

It was at that point that I determined if we're going to have so many gaps of time, hey, life is too short to drink bad wine. Maybe I get involved in something else during the interim. I never perceived that I was going to do something else and leave Van Halen. It was instead of, "Hey, I got a reason to get up every morning," there'd be weeks when there was no reason to get up—nobody's going to answer the phone, nobody's going to show up in the studio. If they are, they're going to be bleary-eyed, sullen and argumentative, which are group therapy words for acting like Spinal Tap. "Fuck you" being the operative word of every sentence. Fuck you—wow! That's the sound of one hand clapping for some people.

So I created my *Crazy from the Heat* EP in four days and went on vacation. We had struggled for a year to make the album *1984*. I mean struggled through the type of ludicrous behavior where I'm sitting with the producer in one studio in Hollywood, while Ed and the engineer are in another studio. Working all night, not getting up during the day, threatening to burn the master tapes if we don't desist, or if something's not returned it's going to get destroyed. Please, it's only music, it's only rock 'n' roll. But it turned into a lot of alcohol-fueled, wasted time. A lot of wasted calories. Third basic law of thermodynamics: Heat expended will not be replaced. Spent it going up the stairs, going down the stairs, you're not getting it back. Sorry, tracing your steps gets you nothing but more calories expended.

Got back from vacation, nothing's going on with the band. Things are delayed, as usual. Great. We'll make a video for *California Girls*, something I had not expected to do. I made the video, was ready to start with Van Halen come New Year's as per the plan. Nah, gonna be a couple of three-week delays, somebody's driving cross-country, somebody's getting married again, whatever. I said, "Great, but I'm not going to sit here with my dick in my hand, the other hand trying to retune the clock." I'm going to make a video for *Just a Gigolo.* I had not expected to do that. But let's not throw away more of my life.

A good barometer that I learned from working in surgery in a hospital is: What if you're dying? What if you have something that's gonna kill you in a determined length of time, and I throw that little ticket in front of you and say, "Just waste three weeks." *Uh-uh.* I don't think so. It's my barometer; every day that I wake up in bed feeling a little tired or a little cranky I think, what if I had AIDS? What if I had a tumor? Or Lou Gehrig's disease?

At the same time I said, "You know what, what if

we made a script for a movie?" Because MTV was wide open at the time, anything that was good or colorful or interesting, you got some kind of rotation on the channel. I started writing a movie script. Sat around in the Van Halen offices while everybody was involved in whatever personal issue they were struggling with.

It took some five weeks' preparation to do the *California Girls* video. When that was done, we finally started writing songs for the new Van Halen album. The music was turning morose. Probably because of individual personal habits more than anything else. And you can hear it on their succeeding albums. The arguments became more and more vehement, loud and venomous, with threats, hands balling into fists.

I said, "Okay, since there's so many breaks in time, so many times when there's no answered phone calls, I'll make another video, I'll wait until everybody does arrive back in Hollywood, to make the new album." And I started to create *Just a Gigolo.* Came time to release the video and I ran into a routine that a lot of drinkers practice. I call it "selective amnesia." Selective amnesia is where you select what you're going to forget. So here's Ed, crying at his baby grand piano in his little studio, 5150: "But you didn't tell me that you were going to release *California Girls.*"

"Well, yeah, I did, Ed. Why else would I spend that much money and recruit that much stellar talent?"

"Yeah, but I don't remember . . . ." This is on the heels of easily half a dozen private projects of his own.

I did not want to be guilty of any kind of subterfuge. I was always the protector of that band, so I made sure—goddamn sure—that everybody knew. And I also knew that memories were short when diluted, so I had repeated my plan, again and again. Nevertheless, when I released *California Girls/Just a Gigolo* on New Year's of 1985, the cry was, "Oh, my God, we didn't know about it. We don't remember you telling us about this."

All of this transpired in an interim. A *major* interim. But I figured, sooner or later this circus was going to reconvene.

We worked on what was to be the next Van Halen album early in '85. There were constant delays and screaming. It sounded like a sack of sick cats. And that's what rehearsal was like. That's what trying to write the songs was like.

Somewhere around March, it came to a head. I wanted to play live, they did not, particularly Alex. He wanted to play half a dozen stadium gigs, keep it very low key. I can't even begin to say hello in six shows. I'm the guy who always had the band rehearsing for two months before we'd go out on the road.

So we went our separate ways. My contingency being, well, I have a *script*—had not shopped it to a company yet. I certainly didn't have a band or any musicians to deal with. My design originally being, well, we'll do this movie and we'll have Van Halen do the music. Wow, what a one-two punch. This was not to be. So I had to scurry around, come up with a handful of musicians, created what we'll call the Yankee Rose band—players like Greg Bissonette, Bill Sheehan and Steve Vai.

My other choice was to commit poetic felonies, wind up doing melancholy power ballads. *No way.* The chemistry had turned rotten. So where do you go? Ed and I hugged each other and cried at my father's house.

I said, "Ed, your brother is up to two six-packs a day. Maybe if we get ourselves square, down the line we can reconvene, and I would love nothing more than that." I don't think he understood. We went our own ways.

I began to pursue the movie as well as putting together a new band, something that I frankly dreaded. Not for a second did I think that I could easily replace the signature sound of Van Halen. But I don't believe I had any real choice. If nothing else, this move was a jarring force that woke everybody up—especially the Van Halens. Suddenly it wasn't about playing six or eight stadium shows in a year. For them it became exactly what it was for me. Again, going out on the road and barnstorming, canvassing the place, taking the campaign to the people. There was silence and dignity as I went about my way, putting my band together, working on the movie.

Some six months later, perhaps less, somebody deposited a stack of magazines as long as your forearm on my desk, full of all the new Van Halen interviews. It had been easier for them to put a new album together because I had worked with Edward on half of that album already. Brought in a new singer, went right to all those old tapes and started with that as their go point, so it was much easier for them to reconstruct. It was going to take *me* a considerable while longer. So that first stack of magazines landed in front of me, and it was a Van Halen hatred campaign that was peddled belligerently and strongly as it is to this day. This had been a spectacular group, spectacular writing unit and a sensational show, and if you got anywheres near any element of it, it changed your life.

So at worst I'm sad that I have to deal with their whining, but you're only as big as what aggravates you.

So I took off and spent about three months really sellin' the idea of the movie. Let's finish up the script, and let me start looking around for some other musicians. Making a movie was a side bet. Beyond that I had no visions of being an actor or a director. My day job is music. Always has been. Everything else is a sidebar.

Started snoopin' around. Saw a videotape with Steve Vai in it, who had been working with Frank Zappa, and had a wealth of information in terms of the school of music approach, which is very different than my learning it at the local cantina and having to make a living with it. He looked pretty good on the video, so I made an effort to get in touch and I met him—actually after a police raid at the local Zero One Gallery, an after-hours spot where I was a partner. We got busted every three months; there's supposedly no after-hours in L.A. We ran into each other out on the sidewalk while the sun was coming up. We commenced writing songs.

Composed most of what became *Eat 'Em and Smile,* which had *nothing* to do with Van Halen. Okay, metaphysically it was a time of conflict. It is aggressive, okay, makes sense in the rearview mirror. But at the time, all it was to me was an idea from a book of old labels from old fruit crates from the twenties and the thirties. Eat 'Em and Smile was a label made for watermelons, and it pictured a little kid holding up a great big half of a watermelon with a big bite missing out of it. You could just laser copy that right onto my gravestone. "I ate it and smiled." Made perfect sense.

We wrote songs in my basement, took a few months to come up with a dozen tunes. Went to the studio, recorded it in fairly short order.

We plowed ahead to success. That first record went double platinum. The videos had an impact, *Yankee Rose, Goin' Crazy.* The tour was very successful, but with that frequently comes "I was actually the architect, and now I shall architect even further."

On the next album, *Skyscraper,* the keyboard player that we'd brought on the road, Brett Tuggle, started to contribute some songs. Was very much more oriented from the college of musical knowledge, five forty-five-minute sets a night, had played with all kinds of other artists around the world. Brett wrote "Just Like Paradise," which today is the theme song of the major radio station in Hawaii. It was also requested to be the theme song for "Beverly Hills 90210." The manager didn't feel that the money they were offering was worthy of a phone call to me, so I never heard about it until some seasons later. But the song had impact, and Steve just hated it. He didn't want to play it.

He was leaning farther and farther into that abstracted direction of unusual chord structures, unusual time signatures. He headed out into the territory and kept on going—God bless. But our frame of reference became less and less mutual.

After the *Skyscraper* tour, we went our separate ways.

We split because of two schools of thought, two completely different mindsets, two different patterns on conditioning. Steve had never played in bars before. He had never done the college of musical knowledge; hence his music is way abstracted. It exists in a parallel universe, and we went our own ways.

Well, trying to hire genius is like designing art by committee—damn near impossible. But I came so close you could feel the heat coming off of it, with a fellow named Jason Becker. Jason was maybe twenty, twenty-one years old. His parents had been like Haight-Ashbury hippies. So instead of growing up listening to Ed Van Halen records and duplicating that, he had grown up listening to all the old classics I had, as per his parents—Hendrix, Bob Dylan, Crosby, Stills and Nash. What a wealth of references in his playing. He was just finding his way. You could hear the influences and name them if you were sharp. And he was a season or two away from where you couldn't name the influences anymore. It would then be a signature sound. He would become Jason Becker *the* guitar player, as opposed to *a* guitar player.

We made the album *A Little Ain't Enough.* And as we were working on the songs, he was complaining of numbness in his leg. He was having a stiff leg, he was having trouble moving around.

He had such a full, substantial, articulate sound, played through the simplest equipment—one amp head, one set of speakers, a foot pedal or two, all of it Dennis-the-Menaced together with spit and chicken wire. That kid could move air, man. And the kindest, gentlest, most flexible, absorbing, want-to-learn spirit that I've ever really worked with.

Big hands, like six feet tall, just poised, poised. It turns out that that little leg problem was ALS; he had Lou Gehrig's disease. Today he's in a wheelchair and that's it. I cried when that verdict came in. The world was waiting to print his picture, man. And he got struck down way too fucking early in the game.

Soon as he realized that he was going to start stiffening up all the way around, instead of balling up in depression, Jason just went to work big time. As this whole voodoo situation increased, he learned to use computers and worked through other musicians and folks, developed a support system. And released a solo album.

Right around that point in time I started to lose my desperate passion for putting a band together and trying to maximize what I was doing in rock and roll, working ensemble. You run into so many wanna-bes, never ever gonna-bes. Spotlight junkies, folks who would play an Edward Van Halen riff and watch my face to see if I was impressed. Run into the likes of the studio drummer, who was brought in for fifteen hundred dollars a day to play on the last album, and couldn't play a whole song straight through. He could only play with a computerized click track keeping time like a metronome. Playing in the studio, I learned, most session drummers play the song all the way through, and then they go back in and fix all the slow parts. "Ain't a problem I can't fix, but I can fix it in the mix." So you will never know at the buying end when you walk into the local record store. All of a sudden Junior's playing with a live band, and he's out of control, he's speeding up, he's slowing down, he's missing parts.

Guitar players would do the same thing. Characters who would rehearse for two months, go on the road, and two weeks after you started come in and hit you up for a three-thousand-a-week raise, or they're gone. This is a carefully planned little missive to be delivered somewhere in the middle of nowhere, like northern Japan, so you're completely over a barrel.

Drummers who don't own a drum set, or show up at

an audition and explain how their drum set is still in Seattle. Guitar players who only own one guitar. Guitar players who don't own their own amplifiers, their own set of speakers, and on and on.

And I started to lose my passion for it. We could play "Happy Birthday" in Van Halen and it was a completely unique sound, full of soul power, sophisticated, musically adept, and here I'm playing with some stooge drummer who literally doesn't know how to end a song live.

Musicians who would get into an argument with the manager, and start crying because the big bad road manager screamed at them. I'd have to step into the middle of this, it was like something out of "The Honeymooners"; I felt like Norton.

I was spending more time than not putting Band-Aids on issues and people's disagreements. I think you started to hear it in some of the music. Was trying to expand, but how do you expand with a group of people who all more frequently than not have an agenda? They're working toward something else, or this is a temporary gig, there's somebody else on the phone.

Luckily I didn't stop my travels and generally living life, despite the tribulations of making rock music. So I have plenty more to tell of the twelve-year period since I left Van Halen, but only half of it has anything to do with the music or the musicians that I was working with. Had some high points, some not; some remedial work, just trying to catch up to where I had ended up last. Just trying to get people up to normal reading levels, much less exploring the classics, much less writing one of your own. We were still working on commas and periods.

Adventures In Hollywood

A few words about the movie project: You do a video, you're visualizing a song. My best videos, up until I did *California Girls/Gigolo,* were live on stage. *Jump* is nothing but live on stage. *Panama* is essentially live on stage. *Yankee Rose* is live on stage. Giving a face, a visage to what you're hearing.

The part I played in *Just a Gigolo* is not really a part, it's simply accessing an aspect of myself that reminds you of yourself. That's why I'm so popular, 'cause I remind you of *you.* I can never lose with this kind of a bet.

So performing on video is not acting. Acting is portraying a context that you would otherwise never be in. I'm not an actor. I just exaggerate myself to a degree and impale the various details of my surroundings, starting with the cast of characters and then all of their various contexts—Bernie at the burger stand, Louise at the record store, whatever.

Just a Gigolo is simply walking around skewering the various factions of show biz, of music business, myself included. When it was time to do a movie, part and parcel of the same. Just longer, more deluxe production values, a bigger cast, but all picked from the same patch.

I shopped the movie around, and landed it quickly because of the success of the videos.

How many times have you seen somebody stand up at the local watering hole, bleary-eyed, blotto, he goes, "Yo, Adrian!" Everybody in the place busts up 'cause you know exactly what he's referencing. Well, "Forget about it, Dave" from the opening of *Just a Gigolo* was the same. "Forget about it, Dave," you know, in that Brooklyn-Crooklyn accent. I'll still get in an elevator, and a complete stranger, three people behind me will say, "Forget about it, Dave."

I did a thing around '87, a big homecoming football game in the Midwest. I was invited to be part of half-time entertainment. As I came running out of the tunnel, a whole section of the stadium stood up—had to be ten thousand people—and yelled, "Forget about it, Dave!" We were clearly already on movie turf. The brass ring was firmly within reach.

The idea for the movie was basically a musical with a very left-of-center plot. There were a number of rewrites, but the general script for *Crazy from the Heat* was a story about Dave (and keep in mind all of these characters are right out of *California Girls*).

Dave has just finished a grueling tour around the world, shows up for a party at his evil manager Bernie Colon's house in Beverly Hills with his whole retinue, his pimp road manager Julius, the little Woody-Allen assistant named Stu, and so on. Bernie has figured a plot to steal Dave's money, needs him to go on a vacation to accomplish this, needs him out of the country.

We find a place on the map called the Dongo Islands. The whole team embarks on this vacation, and of course it's your worst Third World. The jeep breaks down in cannibal country, but we escape and are rescued by Madame Dugay and her senile husband. They're royalty who live in Deep South antebellum architecture on the other side of the island.

Meanwhile, Dave's original managers, who Bernie Colon stole Dave from, are now broke, despondent, desperate to find a way to warn Dave, because they're true-blue. In order to make the money for the plane flights to the Dongo Islands, they sign up for a sleep experiment, a thing they see in the want ads.

They go down to a clinic in the inner city, of course they can't sleep. So they go prowling around the building at night and they stumble upon a meeting taking place in another room. A Japanese business cartel is financing a series of successful underground experiments by a wild-eyed de-licensed scientist. The upshot of the experiment is they have found a way to isolate brain serum and they're going to sell rhythm to white people. Of course Bernie is involved in this. But there's some problem with crossing the races, so the brain serum has to come from a white guy with rhythm, and they can't think of anyone but Dave.

So a scheme is developed to kidnap Dave and take his brain serum so they can begin to synthesize the product and make millions selling rhythm to white people. In order to get rid of the body they're going to strap me to the ball that descends in Times Square on New Year's Eve and I'll be crushed, and on and on and on. All of it, of course, taken from real life.

CBS Pictures was in a state of flux that involved not just the company but the whole movie empire. Everybody had their own agendas to worry about. I was left pretty much to my own devices as far as writing the script, essentially producing the movie, having had a fair amount of experience with those videos.

Landed a 10-million-dollar budget for the movie, and there was to be a couple million-dollar director's fee. It was a *huge* deal, especially since I was first-time everything.

I was considered underground even though we had

sincerely an over-ground budget. We were assigned a staff of some four folks, all of them deadly earnest, with names like Bernie and Shelly. You could find them tomorrow probably at Morton's or Le Dôme. They were kind of going along with us because we were flavor of the week.

I had the fella who had done all of the production design for the movie *Arthur*. We couldn't afford to pay him the stupendous kinds of fees these folks get, but he took it for half price, and flew out his own staff, his own crew.

We would have big meetings and everybody's idea would be heard. We would bring in the production staff, set designers, editors and what-not, to sit and listen to the read-throughs. Before we had actors and actresses we would take different parts and read through it, and I would quiz even a truck driver on, "Well, what do you think of this part?" When you do that, you arrive at a loyalty that only comes from a married woman, and not aimed at her husband. It's solid.

We had a veteran casting director. We had been up all night working on the script. We had done up the inside of our office by ourselves with spray paint and posters and what-not. It did not look like anything Mike Ovitz would have anything to do with. I'd been eating powdered donuts because it reminded me of fourth grade. Powdered sugar all over the table, all over the floor. She sat down, we cleared a little space on the table for her to place eight-by-ten glossies. Later that day I was called into the dean's office, so to speak.

The production executive: "There's some rumor of drug use going on in the writing room. White powder was seen on the table." I replied: "One of my favorite confections is powdered donuts." I was dismissed with a gentle stare.

Promptly sent out one of the runners to buy a case of powdered donuts and kept them in the 'frigerator. Whenever we knew one of the production staff from CBS was coming over, we'd break out a couple of packs, rub powder all over our faces and our hands, down the front of our shirts, and sit around like nothing was wrong. You'd go to shake hands, your hand would be covered with powdered sugar.

Our writing sessions were like something out of *Hellzapoppin'*. Not that we were drinking and getting stoned; there was just so much noise and laughter and hilarity. It was something that everybody wanted to be part of. The writing session started at the end of the day. You had all the technical and step-by-step to do up until seven, eight o'clock in the evening, and then you would have your writing session for five hours. Most of the script was judged on the laugh meter. The secretaries would bring their Tupperware with their tuna salad dinners. That's how the writing sessions went. We was goin' places. We was ready for the big time. Hoped it was ready for us.

The entire album of *Eat 'Em and Smile* was designed to match up the scenes for the movie that never came to be because, unbeknownst to us, CBS Pictures was in trouble. If I remember correctly, we were about four weeks away from the start date. We had a cast. We had everything made, all of the costumes, et cetera. Every shot was storyboarded.

But CBS was changing hands, parts of it were being eliminated. They boiled the movie division, decided that they didn't want to be in the business anymore. There were some eight pictures I think that were green-lighted and setting up to go, ours being one of them.

Well, most directors have no day job, so to speak; they're entirely dependent on that movie deal at any given time. If the company goes out of business or sneaks out from under, you either don't have income to fight it, or you don't want to fight it 'cause you're liable to make an enemy or two, who may pop up down the line. So directors tend to go away quietly. I raised holy hell, "What do you mean? We just spent well over a year preparing this. I put a lot of things on hold for this." Worked harder than I'd ever worked in my life. Plenty of nights falling sleep in the office, then taking a cat bath in the room sink the next morning in preparation for the next casting call.

I sued CBS. I went to court, got the director's fee. Never did make the picture—made semi-efforts at shopping it to a couple other movie companies, but it was something that was born and bred out of imagination and vision. Ran into the usual blockage of "Well, we'd like to rewrite the script." "Well, we'd like to make another movie with you first, Dave." I shied away from that immediately. It just was not the right foundation for what I was trying to build. And again, I had no delusions that I'm an actor. I don't believe you can serve two masters equally. What I do is music. So it was an easy thing for me to walk away from the film.

In retrospect, the only downside of the whole adventure was when the Van Halens locked on to me in that all-too-familiar negative press campaign. The whole onus of "sellout," "left music to do a movie career." It was not my design at all. It was sidebar, just as my adventures have always been.

Krell Wars

There's an old science fiction movie from the fifties called *Forbidden Planet,* where the extinct inhabitants are called the Krell. So we started to call cocaine "Krell," gave it a science fiction name. We would stay up all night, well into the next day, having what we called Krell Wars. And the best Krell War was when Van Halen was opening for Black Sabbath, in 1978. Ozzy Osbourne and I had a major Krell War until about nine-thirty in the morning.

I said, "Oz, wake-up's in, like, thirty minutes. I've got to go clean up a little."

"Okay. We'll continue this later."

We drove from Memphis to Nashville. Checked into a hotel. It's an identical hotel, it's like a Marriott something-or-other, an atrium Marriott, with the interior balconies, everything's enclosed, the hanging gardens vibe. Just like every McDonald's you go to, it's identical.

It was noontime, and I went right into the bin, fell asleep. Got up, we opened, sold-out show, ten thousand of our closest friends. We're sitting backstage, and suddenly, two of the guys from Black Sabbath and some muscle burst through the door, "Where is Ozzy?"

This is not like a new question, to me. The guy had *no* idea where he was going, didn't know where he was while he was there, and couldn't tell you where he had been—a lot like Columbus.

I says, "What do you mean, where is Ozzy?"

"Ozzy hasn't shown up. We're not even sure he checked into the hotel. We can't find him anywhere. We can't do the show."

"Oh, man. Last I saw, he was heading for the limousines, back in Memphis. And I haven't seen him since. I turned belly-up, and I did my gig, and I have no idea where he is."

"Oh my God!"

Instantly, the police, the press, everybody's involved. Ozzy has disappeared! He's been kidnapped! By a cult! He's gone. His drinking problem loomed a little too large, and he's wandered off to some cave-like environment where he's been killed. Dead.

They popped back through the door thirty minutes later.

"No trace. No footsteps. Can you sing some of the Black Sabbath songs?"

"Fellas, I don't know the lyrics, I'm sorry."

"Oh my God."

Show is canceled. Refunds all around.

Everybody goes back to the hotel. *Major* press. Ozzy has disappeared. All night, a vigil. It's hell. The whole Sabbath band is in the lobby, sitting cross-legged, Indian-style, on the carpet, morose.

Six-thirty in the morning, Ozzy comes walking out of the elevator. He's back from the dead!

No he's not. This character had gone into the new hotel, reached into his pocket, pulled out the key from the last hotel, looked at the number, got into the elevator, went right up to that room. There happens to be a maid cleaning up the room.

He says, "Get out of here!" She runs off in terror, he closes the door and falls asleep.

This is my life.

We had to double around and make up the show. And I think that was the record, at that point. Some seven nights in a row. Seven shows in a row, with hops in between, which means six and eight hours on the tour bus, going to the next city.

PRACTICALITY

If you go anywhere where it's completely jungleness, you've got to take a big fat paperback, something by James Clavell, *Shogun,* or *Taipan,* something like six hundred pages long, or the complete works of Mark Twain. And start reading ten days in advance of the trip, 'cause you're gonna get the trots, no matter what. You're gonna get sick, you're gonna get dysentery. You're going to be trying to cope with the trail, with the boat, the back of the truck, whatever it is that you're in, and you're going to be miserable. You're going to go diving into your pack to discover exactly what humidity and daily rainstorms have in common with that new biodegradable, earth-watch, environmentally sensitive toilet tissue that you thought you had so carefully packed in that new Nalgene waterproof bag. It is at that single moment that you will be back to the front page of your book, because you're gonna shit faster than anybody can read.

TIARÉ

Last time I was in Tahiti they had just finished putting the first asphalt road, you know, like black tar, all the way around the perimeter of Mooréa Island, and it had been there for six months. And as I was walking alone, miles away from anybody or anything, I saw a little tiaré flower that had punched its way through hard-pack dirt, gravel and then blacktop tar and asphalt. And I thought, what kind of pressure can a flower exert against all of that?

Take your hand and try and be as gentle as that flower's maximum exertion. You can't do it. But the persistence defeated everything that any guy ever drew on a drawing board. It's not possible to be that gentle. But to maintain the persistence that allows you to push through gravel and blacktop. I've always tried to apply that to myself. One of the few times that I've seen it really vividly in front of me.

BEAUTY PAGEANT

I did a gig, it was like late '85, I was halftime entertainment at the Miss Mexico Beauty Pageant. It was in Mazatlán on the beach, about four hundred people on folding metal chairs in front of this ornate stage. They were broadcasting it on Channel 34, on a program called

"Siempre en Domingo," always on Sunday. In fact, they show it twice on Sunday. It's satellited to some 73, 74 million people around the world. I was halftime entertainment. I was going to get up and lip-synch "California Girls" and "Just a Gigolo."

There were maybe twenty-five contestants. And there was the bikini contest, and then you had the dancing in bikinis contest, and then you had the evening wear contest, which was I guess one cubic foot more material than the bikini contest. I did my halftime thing and joined the audience.

It was time for the dancing and evening wear portion of our program, and each girl would come out in her little sheath dress, miniskirt, vacuum-packed for your safety, one size fits all, and they all danced to the same loop of music.

Now, the PA system was not state of the art. It was about six years back in the rearview mirror. They're blaring it in an effort to play to all the people, but you're outdoors on the beach; you're fighting mother nature and her ocean for possession in the old auditory canal.

I'm sitting out there in the audience and I'm watching and I'm listening and I can't—it's *very* familiar—figure out what this song is, it's so damn familiar; it's blurbled and burping. The light comes on in my noggin. Some choreographer from Mexico City found the quintessential hard rock, dance groove, and looped it over and over again so that all twenty-five girls could get through their moves. "Miss Jalisco province," "Miss Monterrey," and I realized it was Ted Nugent playing "Wango Tango."

So I'm sitting there listening to Ted Nugent scream

"I'm a big salami, I'm a Maserati, I'm a real hotty, don't you really want me," and those gals are givin' it all they can give. I happen to look over to the side of the stage—and this is actually about a ten-foot-high stage, a ten-foot deck. If you raised your hand above your head, your hand would come about to where the shoes were. And the girls were all lined up and they were all wearing little miniskirts. "Look skyward, Luke; behold the Force." There it is in all your favorite colors of tricot and cotton blend, fairly bursting at the seams with ardor and enthusiasm. You don't need to speak español to know that, partner. These babes are putting off more smoke than the Branch Davidians. And every crew guy and everybody working the show, is right there within hallelujah distance, right? Not one is looking up. Everybody is glued to the television monitor.

I laughed, 'cause there it was, naked, hot, live and steaming in front of your filthy little eyes, right within grabbing distance. Not *one* of them was looking up at the real thing. Everybody was glued right to that screen, "Ooh, ahh," listening to "Wango Tango" at 180 decibels.

Catch The Cat

The beer was spilled on the barroom floor,
And the shop was shut for the night,
When, out past the window came a small gray mouse

Who sat in the pale moonlight.
And he drank all the beer off that barroom floor,
And back on his haunches he sat
And all through the night, we could hear that mouse roar:
"Where is that fuckin' cat?"

I can totally relate. How do you catch the cat? Well there's gotta be five, six different kinds of combatants . . . runners, sharpshooters, counterpunchers. Sharpshooter will always pick his shots; a runner will always run away from you; a counterpuncher waits for you to go first.

No. You wait. He'll present himself.

Nowhere Gets A Name

I use the term Zen or spirit and all of that classic quasi-religious cultish terminology because it gives a name to the place. Even Neil Young's song, one of my favorite songs, "Everybody Knows This Is Nowhere"—he gave nowhere a name. There's a comfort in that for me. Turns out, I'm damn close to a beginner on Zen thinking, but I arrived at it in the most classic fashion. There's no book that teaches you how to learn it. You simply have to think about it and experience—there's no answers. And that's what I did on the road.

I came up with a series of logical reasons why,

wherever, who, what, where and when, without knowing it. That's the ultimate way to come to know this kind of thinking. I dress it in normal language. I use my own words like *vibe*—so you get into your own groove. And then later on in life I read some books and it turns out, hey, I've been doing that for twenty years. I arrived at it in the most innocent fashion.

And because this kind of thinking is purely questions, really causes you to dwell, to consider and reconsider, and that's so out of the ordinary, everything is worn right on the sleeve or the lapel these days, that I wonder, am I getting too dense? Am I forcing the issue? Am I asking people to participate too much? I hope so. That's kind of rock 'n' roll, isn't it?

PUSS IN BOOT

First time I went to Paris, 1978, we couldn't wait to get to the prostitution district. The Rue Saint-Denis. This is where Napoleon's troops celebrated their victories, okay? History.

Keep in mind, I'm invoking the pre-eighties clause here. This was pre-AIDS, pre-politically correct, pre-everything.

So we went to the Rue Saint-Denis, and we all found company. I found a little gal, a little blonde with a Dutch boy haircut. We went upstairs into a little room; she had on these thigh-high boots, kind of beige color, black panties, took off everything except one boot.

I'm thinkin', "I have no idea what she's gonna do with this boot. Maybe I'm gonna do such-and-such, and then she's going to do somehow, I don't know . . . reach around with the leg and . . . with the boot . . . rub against with the other leg, and maybe my neck . . . I have no idea, but I'm in." I'm here for the duration. I'm the first treehouse you're going to run into after you crawl under the wire, honey.

And, there's the bell. We commence. The whole time, I'm thinkin', "Okay, now she's gonna do somethin' with the boot."

Everything's all done, everything's all finished up, I give her the cash, she takes it, puts it in the boot.

SHOWTIME

I always knew I was show people. "Hollywood, that's gooey bally-hooey Hollywood, where every young mechanic's a screen romantic, yesterday they said that you would not go far, now on your door's a big gold star." You're in show biz.

I would go watch the circus or particularly Cirque du Soleil, and I would get the biggest charge out of imagining how they lived, because it seemed like family: Long tables, everybody knows each other, everybody travels together, they date and marry each other, families, free-wheelers. How very exciting. And that's what we created with Van Halen. It wasn't just the show on stage, but the life.

A great sense of theater based on at least perceived shortcomings—no pun intended—same here. I'm no Caruso. There's no Valentino in my bathroom mirror. But it's not "make do," its "let's go." And it gave the overall proceedings a tone of *real* abandon, *really* fantasy, completely our own rules. The basic tenets of theater, and particularly comedy—you live in your own world with your own rules. This was another way of manifesting that. When you go on the road, it should be Gypsy Rose Lee meeting everybody. It should be the Marx Brothers in a car driving to Nacogdoches, Texas. It should be a review, all of us disenfranchised, unscrewed down, joining together under the flag of blood. And our blood is show business.

In 1978 we opened for everybody. We opened at Anaheim Stadium for Boston . . . I think Journey was on the bill, we were third or fourth, you know, young upstarts. People ask me, even now at the local cafeteria, "Hey, was that really you who parachuted into the stadium?" Well, we hired these four guys named the Sky Gods out of Lancaster, California, acrobatic parachutists. Had a big meeting with them—there's some 8 mm film somewhere of the meeting, a briefing: What kind of plane do you jump out of? What altitude was it? How fast was it going? Where did you learn to parachute? What's the name of the parachute? What's the temperature up there? What's the rate of descent? What kind of shoes do you wear? How much do they cost?

So you have 65 thousand people packed in the stadium. Two hours before the gig, a small van is parked right behind the stage, nobody pays any attention. The four of us are under a blanket in the back, wearing full parachute gear. Time for Van Halen to go on. People are getting nervous backstage and going, "Where's the band? Nobody can find the band, man, where's the band? Look! Look up in the sky . . ." and these four characters come piling out of the plane like they have never jumped before, arms and legs kicking and everything. They come sweeping over the stadium, wigs under the helmets, goggles and everything. They land right out in back of the stage, thousands of people can see it. They're whisked into this blue van, the van zooms up to the stage, we pop out, pulling off the identical goggles and jumpsuits, and run on stage. It was quite an entrance. People still ask, "Was that really you?"

I would run into guys like this reporter in Europe, in Germany, who had actually been in D-Day, Allied Invasion, a real parachutist. He came after me, guns-a-burnin'. "So what kind of parachute did you use?"

"Oh, Ram Air Square. I prefer the 6300 series. I get a little more drag."

"And where did you deploy?"

"Well, you know, ten thousand feet doesn't give you quite enough time. The difference between ten and thirteen is big—as you know . . ."

By the end of the night, we was drinking buddies for life. These kind of moves are what I call a sting, like the movie *The Sting*. Second best one was at the US Festival, 375 thousand people, top bill, highest paid band in the history of show business, *Guinness Book of World Records*. Did I say this already? I'll say it again regardless.

I said we should film backstage because we'll have a great backstage scene and show it on the big movie screens, on the side of the stage, and then we'll come on. "No, you can't do that. Too far away, too much cable, not enough people, too much power," you know. Said, "Great. Even better. We'll throw the best party anybody ever did throw, two weeks in advance, film that, put that on the screens, pretend that's backstage that very moment and then we'll run on." Cool.

Rented a sound stage, two hundred guests, everything from supermodels to midgets in cowboy uniforms with a sheep with a saddle, punk rockers, congressmen, bikers, you name it. The *best* party ever. Like Andy Warhol said, the best party you could imagine is where the least important—or least interesting—person there is you. This was it.

We scripted out a number of things. We had the local DJ, Pat Kelly, there saying, "Hey, we're backstage right here with Van Halen"—and a piece of pizza flies by—"Jesus!" The midget, the manager in the three-piece suit with the supermodel playing the video game. Astroturf, a Chinese buffet as big as a football field. We'd keep filming and filming little vignettes as well as . . . just as things occur.

The midgets get soused. One of the supermodels says to one, "Can you really ride that sheep?" He says, "Sure," he gets on the sheep, it goes straight into the buffet, the buffet caves in. Shot a scene where the DJ goes, "Okay, this is Dave's inner sanctum, his private dressing room. Not everybody is allowed in but I'm a pal, we can go in." Comes in, there's a blonde with her tush on the keys of a piano, and I'm like schtupping her and I've got my robe around my waist, and I turn and shove my hand in the lens total paparazzi-screw-you, "Hey, get out of here, get out of here," and he's pushed out.

Guaranteed, if we walked around long enough tomorrow afternoon, somebody will say, "Dave, were you really squeezing that blonde?"

Then everybody convenes inside, and Big Ed says, "Okay, guys, we gotta go on, it's showtime." The video finishes on the screens, we run out on stage, same clothes, confetti and all. Good sting.

The Race Across America in '85. Manager and I set it up beautifully. *PeeWee's Big Adventure* movie party is happening and all of the MTV VJs and people are there. So we set it up that I'm in the men's room when some of the VJs are in the men's room and the manager says, "I can't fuckin' believe it."

"Oh, no, man, somebody told you?"

"Yeah, man, somebody told me. Jesus Christ."

All the VJs are yelling, "What's going on?"

"Goddamn it, he bet his producer that he could drive his '51 Mercury low-rider convertible across the United States in three days or less in time for the MTV awards."

"No, really?"

"Well, you know, I like a good bet."

"It's a permanent convertible?"

"Yeah, well, makes it like a Bruce Springsteen song, you know."

"Hey, we got to cover this. We got to check this out. Jesus."

Me and Big Ed load into the car, big good-bye to the very well-attended press. Drive about six miles, pull into the side street, load the Mercury up onto a flatbed, put it under a tarp, guy drives it across country. I don't shave. Get on a bad airline, last class, wearing a hat and glasses. Fly to Baltimore. We get in the car. This is the dawn before the big arrival. We drive up around Jersey City, pull in, a little sleep in a motel, promptly lose the key to the car. Can't find the key to the car. Meanwhile, I'm in the bathroom on my knees rubbing dirt on my face so I have that weathered look. The maid just then walks through the door. We're frantic, there's a panic, because what is about to transpire is big time. We finally find the key.

As we're driving over the George Washington Bridge, there's a helicopter following us. We pull up in front of the Parker Meridian Hotel, which is all blocked off, blaring "New York, New York" on the car stereo, covered with grime except for the goggle marks. Pull up victorious, stagger out of the car, hug each other. That night lost fourteen awards in a row. Stole the show. Spent the night in the bathroom with the Go-Go's, doing everything you can imagine and then some.

These little tricks are show biz tricks that are larcenous at heart. There is larceny involved. It's a great word. It's not big like *manslaughter.* It's not little like *jaywalking.* It's *larceny.* And it's great to know these stories, I think, you'll like them even better when you understand that there *was* larceny involved. You'll respect us even more.

Did a trick when we released the album *Skyscraper.* We got a special consideration from Tower Records on Sunset Boulevard. They let us build a twenty-eight-foot mountain on top of the store. Same guys who built the Matterhorn for Disney. A major peak with six little platforms to stand on. So we could have little climberettes in bikinis with hard hats and little ice picks and a coil of rope on their shoulders, you know, kind of chipping at the mountain in slow motion. We knew that there was going to be a big syndicated radio confab held right next door in Spago. We didn't tell anybody, but we also hired the marching band from U.S.C. and positioned them about six blocks away, down near Barney's Beanery. And we said, "Oh, we're just going to play a little music in the parking lot, there will be a few people, we'll unveil the mountain that says Skyscraper."

Comes the right moment and—synchronize your watches, gentlemen—the band fires up, starts marching down Sunset Boulevard and traffic backs up, no shit, for three-and-a-half miles. The cops go nuts but they love it, 'cause this is show biz, this is why we're all in Hollywood anyway. As the band comes around the corner to the record store, I pop out of the top of the mountain and rappel upside down to one of the platforms, waving and yelling at the people, on the end of the rope. And the band played in the parking lot, pedestrians backed up for miles in every direction. Every nose was pressed against the window at Spago. I've never seen so many Oliver Peoples glasses reflected in one place. It was completely illegit, but in these kinds of cases, it's far better to ask for forgiveness than permission.

Around '80, '81, with Van Halen, we were doing many live interviews. Live interviews on radio up until then took the form of Sunday religious radio. "So you guys are in town to play a gig?" "Yeah, well, you know, we're really looking forward to it. My arm feels good, my curve ball's dropping just right. I just want to get out there and help the team, Bob." We pioneered the Gonzo spiel: "It's a barbecue, it's life, take the radio, press it against your body, now feel the sound of my voice as it travels up your spine into your filthy little mind." "Don't touch that dial, we're on all the other stations, or at least we should be, yours truly, David Lee Roth." And so on.

For about a four-, five-month period, I wore an Emiliano Zapata outfit, you know, the big hat and serape with double guns and bandoliers and cowboy boots with my spurs. We would go into a radio station and make a big funny joke of handcuffing the DJ to a pipe or something in the corner and they'd be going, "Ahh, this is so funny. Okay, Dave, let me go." I wouldn't let them go, and we'd run the show for an hour and a half. And just start flipping dials and carrying on, and the program directors, half the time they loved it. They let it go.

Just to even deepen the colors of the theater that was going on at the time, I hired two little guys, midgets, Jimmy and Danny, to be my bodyguards in the early eighties. They were both late of Ringling Brothers Barnum & Bailey Circus; they were clowns in the road show for a number of years. Great partiers, great hang at the bar, knew their way around the whole world, having been traveling show people for a number of years, so we went for it.

I have a great picture of myself shot from behind with the long blonde hair, the chaps, and in one hand a cigarette and the other hand a bottle of Jack Daniel's, going, "Ah, my people," being ushered into the backstage of Madison Square Garden by the two little guys who were wearing SWAT team uniforms, with tactical baseball hats, the dark blue Sam Brown utility belts, handcuffs, and everything, billy clubs dragging on the ground. They both have one hand in the small of my back, the other hand is gesturing "Get back, get back." It was very impressive.

Got them matching karate uniforms with black belts and sunglasses and everything. We had Secret Service outfits, little gray suits with mirror sunglasses . . . and they were actually my bodyguards. They would always walk in front of me to the gig, the hotel, the restaurants.

Once we rented a boat in Marina del Rey, one of these little travel yachts, for the evening. Set up the table for gambling, with ham and cheese sandwiches, drinks, overflowing cigarette butts . . . Got some bikini girls to sit at the table with us and the two dealers, with the croupier visors and the whole thing, the little guys.

Howard Stern was not yet Howard Stern when Van Halen did our famous *Life* magazine article. In the middle there's a double-page photo of my room—looked like an art installation, with all the stuff piled up and so forth, exploding suitcases. And all the details, the clothing strewn, the books, et cetera, the nylons hanging over the cowboy boots.

Howard was staying downstairs from us when we were at the Detroit Hilton. And he fondly tells a story of coming upstairs to our floor to complain about the noise at 5:30 in the morning, and having two midgets in SWAT team uniforms stop him at the elevator.

That same night some little groupie gal was carrying on with a member of the team behind the swinging utility doors for the express elevator on the floor that room service uses. Little glass windows about head height. I remember walking down the hall in my bath towel about four in the morning, and there's a bunch of people crowded around the windows watching this gal take care of this guy. And I was craning my neck to look over the shoulders and I felt a little tap around my beltline—it was Danny. So I picked him up and held him up to the window.

I asked him late one night on the tour bus, "What's it like being a little guy?" He said, "Dave, life for me is a series of assholes and elbows." Speaking physically, from his perspective, that's what he's looking at. Spiritually, of course, I could relate perfectly.

We had routines worked out like when they were wearing Secret Service suits, I would wear matching sunglasses, and we would walk into a room, lift the glasses up and casually look to the left and then put the glasses back down. Befuddled everybody, because how do you deal with a security guard who's crotch high?

You never really know somebody's personal history till you see it acted out. When we arrived to play Las Vegas, we were in the casino of a hotel, one of them shows up with his ex-wife, a show dancer from Vegas who's six-two. Watching them walk to the elevator was cool.

Same night, as I went up onto my floor to go to my room late, late, dawn time, little Danny had passed out at the blackjack table and one of the gals with merchandising carried him up to the floor, lost her strength and ended up dragging him by his arms to his room to put him to bed. All I saw were these little legs turning the corner. I knew I was in show business.

Flash forward to a few years later and a few words about props.

A giant inflatable microphone, the size of a Buick, would be thrown on stage at the end of the show. Somebody in Texas had thrown one of these supersize cowboy hats made out of foam rubber on stage, so we kept it, and I'd put the hat on and ride the microphone and go bouncing around on stage.

What this ultimately developed into was a sequence where the band would break into an instrumental and start doing some soloing, and I would be whisked backstage and hide in an equipment box and rushed out through the audience to where the sound platform was or lighting controls were. They would finish their opus on stage, and the spotlights would hit the center of the arena, and I would climb this ladder to the ceiling. I would get up to a platform and all these lights would go on and this platform would lower and it would turn out to be a boxing ring with regulation red, white and blue ropes. I'd be wearing a big robe with sparkledy boxing gloves. We would do a song and then out of the ceiling would come this surfboard, like eighteen feet, as big as a taxi, and it would lower down right next to the boxing ring. I would throw off the robe and the gloves and jump onto the surfboard and it would raise up, and I'd go surfing over the heads of the audience to the stage, and would be deposited there.

But there were times we couldn't use the surfboard, so for one tour we got an extra-super-large-size microphone and put it on a carriage. It took twelve big guys in hooded robes to carry it on their shoulders with a big parade saddle. And I'd get on the saddle and ride the microphone to the stage. While that was happening, two giant inflatable legs would come over the tops of the amplifier banks, wearing nylons and high heel shoes. They'd inflate like somebody was laying on their back with their butt against the back of the amplifier line, and their knees were on top of the amp stacks, and we'd ride the microphone straight at 'em.

The giant microphone, as well as the parade saddle, the inflatable legs, et cetera, all had to be designed and manufactured, okay? The best meeting was when I said, "Okay, we'll use the boxing ring again, but we should put four devils—statues of devils on each corner, like the album cover *A Little Ain't Enough.* And on cue, I want them to pee Jack Daniel's into the audience. There were several technical meetings involving prop managers, stage directors, experts.

They showed up a week later and said, "Okay, look we really talked about this. Our biggest hurdle here is that because of the sugar content of actual Jack Daniel's, you're going to foul the tube. So with this in mind, we came up with such-and-such a motor, with such-and-such a reservoir for the liquid, and it will come out in a spray.

I said: "No, no, no. I need a stream that goes at least fifteen feet before we move into spray."

"Yeah, but the heat of the engine—"

"I don't care about the heat of the engine. Invent a cooling system, and put it up the devil's ass."

Tens of thousands of dollars later, we have four gargoyle red devils on a Spielbergian level of excellence, and they peed Jack Daniel's a solid fifteen feet. Every night one of the crew guys would have to go out and clean out the tubes, so to speak, and load the reservoir. But for budgetary considerations purely, there are other forms of that very beverage we can use that are cheaper than Jack Daniel's. So he would go to the length of loading a bottle of Triple Rose Knoxville Especial into a big bottle of Jack Daniel's, knowing the press would all be sitting out there watching every move when he would go out and load up the devils. The word got around, and you would see people four meters away from the boxing ring catching it in their mouth, bathing in it, yelling "Heal me!"

That's entertainment.

A-105

Bought a couple of pairs of used cross-country skis, and boots, and bindings, because there was snow on the ground—we were doing a North American tour—and I would ski from the hotel to work.

One afternoon, Big Ed and I were skiing from the hotel to the arena in Erie, Pennsylvania. It was snowing. It looked like a Norman Rockwell painting; like a Christmas card.

There was one place with a light on. I said to Ed, "Hey, we're in front of the schedule. What say we stop over there and get a drink?"

Chained our skis up to a pole and walked into this old, old bar, like a union meeting hall from the twenties, the kind of place that echoes when you scrape your chair. Big, long bar, big mirror. One old gal sittin' at the bar, eatin' some potato chips, drinkin' a 7Up, watchin' the TV set.

And we sat down at the bar. I said to Ed, "I don't know a thing about Erie, Pennsylvania. And I'll bet you that gal, right there, has got a story to tell. Tell her to come on over to the table, we'll buy her another soda pop; let's hear her story. We all got one."

Ed goes over, he says, "Would you like to join us? We're strangers from a strange land."

She says, "Sure." Come on and set down; she's in her sixties; her name's Flo.

"Flo, how you doin'?"

"Oh, yeah, I was born and raised in Erie, Pennsylvania; raised my kids here, and everything."

"Really." She has no idea who we are. I'm wearin' my baseball hat and overalls.

I says, "Flo, would you like another 7Up?"

She says, "Sure."

I said, "Great." And I reach into my pocket and pull out a stack of quarters, I say, "You're music director tonight. You work the jukebox, and I'll go get you your soda pop."

She takes the quarters, walks over to the jukebox, and as we reconvene at the table, "Just a Gigolo" starts up on the jukebox.

So I'm watching her face for any crack in the woodwork whatsoever; she has no idea that's me.

Finally, Eddie leans over to her, and says, "Flo, do you know what this is, on the jukebox?"

She says, "Oh, sure."

He says, "What's that?"

She says, "This is A-105."

He says, "Well Flo, this fella here is A-105."

She goes, "Baloney."

"No really. His name's Dave Roth, he's the one singing this song."

She says, "Really? I listen to this song every night that I come in here, which is more nights than not."

I said, "Really?"

She says, "But I will tell you, son, there's one person in here who likes A-105 even more than me."

I said, "Really? And who would that be?"

She says, "His name's Sal, and he's ninety-five years old if he's a minute." She says, "He comes in here, and he doesn't talk to nobody, and he puts on A-105 at least five times a night. He just stares off into the space," she says, "I gotta level with ya, honey, I don't think it's so much he likes your song, as old Sal's kind of a gigolo himself."

I said to her, "Well, we're playing down at the local arena in just a few hours, Flo. Would you like to come to a rock show?"

She says, "Oh my, I've never been to one of those," she said, "but my son would probably know who you are."

I said, "Really? Is he a music fan?"

She goes, "Yeah."

"How old is he?"

She says, "Forty-five. He lives in San Diego. Do you know . . . have you ever heard of that?"

"Yes, I have." I said, "Flo, I'm going to send a limousine for you. Are you going to be here at the bar for a while?"

She says, "Sure."

We skied off to the arena, sent a limo back to pick her up, brought her in; she sat down backstage. Now we have eighty people on the road crew, right? Pirates, one and all. You know, guys who lose a tooth and then wear it from their ear. Nothin' but black T-shirts. Big guys, too, work-with-your-hands guys.

She never did see the show. She sat backstage in the hallway on a bench, and, one by one, and two by two, every single one of those pirate roadies found his way right up next to Flo, under her arm, and got ten-and-a-half-minutes' worth of mom. And I would walk by, and there would be a six-four truck driver, lookin' like Charlie Manson, chain smokin', and Flo would have her little arm around his shoulder, going, "And what happened then? What happened then, honey? Did she call you back?"

"Naw."

"Well, you know, sometimes that happens, honey."

A little mini-therapy.

She never saw the show. She had the time of her

life. She was in heaven. And every single one of the crew found his way to that bench . . . . "Yeah, I kind of miss *my* mom."

"Well, honey, I know what you're goin' through."

She came to every single concert I've ever played in Erie, Pennsylvania, since. Now she's in the computer, and we can call her up in advance. Just make sure she hasn't changed her address, and we send the limo for her. Picks up Flo, and she sits backstage. I don't think she's heard a song yet.

Heidi Fleiss

I've always had a fascination for the night world—the city's underbelly. The Henry Miller thing. I've also had a fascination for butch girls, or strippers, or prostitutes, or the dysfunctional types. Is this who I wake up with every morning? No. But I've always kept an open mind. That's where most people's imagination goes sooner or later.

So, my assistant, Ed, and I—this is about summer, 1993—come out of the famous Rainbow Bar and Grill on Sunset Boulevard, and right next door is the famous Roxy. There's a big door guy at the door of On the Rox, the club upstairs, and I says to Ed, "Hey, look, there's a function at the junction." Best up periscope.

"Can we get in?"

"Hey, Mr. Roth, sure, come on."

We take eight steps up the stairway, and there's this

great-lookin' blonde, sitting with legs akimbo. Now there's a great group therapy way of puttin' it. A little red dress, a little red skirt, little panties, and she's kinda lounging back. I said, "Whoa! This is a great island."

We walk inside. Girls outnumber the guys, three to one. Everybody's dressed up, lots of hair care products. I sit down, gal comes up, sits down next to me—like they say in *Mad Woman of Chaillot,* "She had a face of a person who had stood at the edge and looked over."

We commence to talk, and she's a great conversationalist; obviously has known many different kinds of people; you can know the whole world without leaving your room. I said, "Wow, you're fascinating. What's your name?"

She says, "Heidi. Heidi Fleiss."

I say, "How do you do?"

She says, "David, I'm a fan; this is my place, and my partner is Victoria Sellers . . . Peter Sellers's daughter. You're welcome here anytime."

I said, "Great. I plan on becoming a fixture."

I came back the next weekend, had a great time. The third time I came back, somebody graced me with the information that this was a menu, not a guest list.

I had no idea. I'm the only one in town who has no idea what this is about.

That night, she says, "Dave, we're closing up," L.A. time, you close at two, "Come on up to my house, gonna be a bunch of people."

I drove this woman from the bar up to the house. There's a colorful party; there's girls swimming naked in the pool. The girl I drove says, "Yeah, I'm a school teacher from Kansas, I'm just here to visit Heidi, my friend, for the weekend . . . ."

Next day, I found a purse in the backseat. I went digging in to find ID, and pull out a mirrored chrome hairbrush.

And I thought, "Ain't no school teacher carries around a hairbrush like this." It seemed to go perfectly with Heidi's mirrored cat-dish.

I became suddenly aware of who Heidi was. Yeah, I knew Heidi. But I didn't inhale.

"UNPLUGGED"

We become used to the idea of mild abuse, and then we begin to participate in it. The big thing about monkeys, chimpanzees, is taunting each other. This is why interactive video games where you compete with another human being are more popular than when you compete with the game itself. It's because you can taunt and abuse the other person when they lose, or as they are losing, in an effort to encourage more loss.

Want to know why "Unplugged" is so popular on the TV set? We're not there to see the winners. We know that Eric Clapton is going to swing, he's going to be up and surfing the first wave because he's based on acoustic music. He's like that designer popcorn they sell in Beverly Hills, it's black seeds, but it pops white. He comes from the blues, so we're aware that he's going to fly, it's going to be great. Aerosmith, the same thing. I saw their "Unplugged" thing—it was great, stellar performance!

They're also based on the blues, which is essentially acoustic music. That's not why we watch the program. We watch to see a band like Great White or Billy Squier crucify themselves. We watch to see a car crash. In aerospace it's called "auguring in." The bigger the divot left behind, the bigger the bonfire we're going to have. "Did you see Poison on 'Unplugged' last week? Oh my God, they sucked *so* bad."

"How bad?"

"Well, let me take two fucking hours and tell you."

Art And Commerce

What's art to me is based on a simple principle I read in a book a long time ago. It goes like this: Anything that doesn't have to do with survival or procreation is art. The reference goes like this: Caveman is chasin' the Cavewoman. He's got procreation in mind. He's just about to get to her, just about to grab her little tush. Suddenly they turn, and they see that there's a mammoth comin' out of the tree line, down into the clearing, dead straight for them. Suddenly, his mind's on survival. Mammoth comes hard-chargin' right up to the edge of a cliff, the guy and the gal duck out of the way, the beast plunges over the edge, a thousand feet, straight vertical, down to his demise. And the Caveman leans over the edge of the cliff, and gives him the finger.

That's art. Implied emotional content, a statement being made. An act of passion.

That old hackneyed phrase, "You've got to give the people what they want," is a move of business and commerce.

I learned business and commerce as a means of supporting my jones. My jones is art, in all its forms. And it is my every intention to keep it absolutely pure, in every step of the way. And the first temptation that will chase you down like a hungry animal is the desire, the perception in your mind that you have to be *something* instead of be *someone.*

You get caught up in "Well, what do the people want? What does somebody else want? What will appeal to somebody? What will be popular with somebody? What will generate a lot of money?" You will be creating something other than *pure* art. And it won't sound like it. It won't *look* like it, it won't *taste* like it, and it won't *smell* like it.

A Walk In The Park

I stopped to buy ten dollars' worth of bunk Jamaican reefer in Washington Square Park. I was walking with a girlfriend, we'd just finished sushi lunch, and I said, "Sugar, let's get a little dime's worth, we'll go up onto the roof and smoke a joint. We'll be romantic."

She says, "Great."

I'm not gonna smoke pot in the park, there's kids there, for chrissakes.

Little do I know that the French Connection is in full effect, and there's people in a third-floor brownstone with binoculars, and walkie-talkies, watching the dreads, who are sellin' these little bits and pieces. Thirty steps outside of the park, I got two guys on my case like white on rice.

"New York City Police," and the arm in the back, and they put me in a van with fourteen other characters, and we wait there for four hours, as one by one, they usher people into the precinct station. And you're on a chain gang—a single chain, with your left arm, or your right arm, depending on what side you're on—chained to the main. I'm hooked to a Jamaican dread named Tree. If you saw his haircut, you would know why he got that name.

Says, "Say, mon, I know who you are. You don't have to go t'rough dis. I give you my number, I deliver."

I've got a law student two seats behind me: "Hey, but if he doesn't deliver . . . I'll defend you."

We have a fashion photographer in the back of the Econoline, going, "Irregardless, we'll have great photos."

Now keep in mind that this Friday the Branch Davidians, the wackos in Waco, Texas, are threatening to torch the place, finally. And that Monday morning is the Rodney King verdict, part two. So you have a nation in tension, in anxiety mode. Okay?

So out of the tree line and down into the clearing wanders Diamond Dave. I'm halftime comedic relief. Now if you're gonna be a true rock star, you gotta have one drug bust on your résumé. And it's best if it's a light one. Well, there's nothing lighter than ten dollars' worth of bunk Jamaican reefer, picked up on the hoof in Washington Square Park. So you have this guy holding up a plastic bag the size of a saddle blanket, on CNN International, this tiny, little thimble-size plunket of pot.

CNN International, for forty-eight hours, all Saturday, all Sunday, every thirty minutes, there's a picture of Dave. It was right out of Tom Wolfe's *Bonfire of the Vanities*—Sherman McCoy, who fell into the machine.

So we march into the station, not thinking that there's gonna be a hundred twenty members of the fourth estate waiting for my most imminent arrival.

Howard Stern calls me up the next morning, he says, "So Dave, you lookin' for publicity?"

I said, "Howard, this is a thirty-five-dollar pot bust. It's a hundred dollars if your dog poops on the sidewalk. If I was looking for publicity, I would have pooped on the sidewalk."

Two months later, he says, "So what's the outcome?"

I say, "Well, since the wackos in Waco, the only difference between me and the Branch Davidians is they stopped smokin' two months ago."

What's curious—and these are barometric readings of placement, you know, somewhere in the hierarchy, the social caste—I'm not on the A list of anything. But for ten dollars' worth of bad guage, I'm on CNN International every thirty minutes.

RECREATION DIRECTOR

My best recreation director was named Paul. I had met him at a Club Med in Tahiti. He was entertainment director for the whole village, you know, 750 people from all over the world, and he's responsible for the entertainment; whether it's the show at night, skits and shtick, or clowning on the beach during the day. I hired him on as recreational director.

He would have theme nights, like waffle house night, where we would come off stage and he would have hired twelve bikini models from Hawaiian Tropic in Lakeland, Florida, and gone to the local Waffle House, it's like a Denny's, rented uniforms, got menus. You would walk in, and there'd be two lines of girls in these sickening orange and green uniforms, like corn-dog waitresses, handing you one-page laminated menus. And there was a huge buffet of all the worst American trash food you can imagine; waffles, fries, hush puppies, tomato sandwiches, the kind where you got to roll up your sleeves and put your elbows into the sink so when you bite into it, the juice runs down your forearms into the sink. Or we would have Arabian nights and there would be sand all over the floor of the dressing room. And he would have gone to a costume store in Omaha and come up with eight Scheherazade outfits. Everyone would show up on the bus later with glitter all over their jeans.

Holidays were particularly popular. Consider the black Christmas tree! Getting ready for the tour, one of the recreational directors and half a dozen roadies are standing around trying to figure out what to do for Christmas because we're going to rehearse through the holidays. Big sound stage, the Raleigh, big enough for a blimp.

They said, "Yeah, we're trying to think of what to do for Christmas."

I said, "Simple, what's the biggest tree we can possibly get?"

"There's one place that Bobby knows has a tree that's about forty-five feet." Now, that's pretty fucking big, really big. Count that ten feet is as high as a basketball hoop, four basketball hoops high, that's a pretty big tree.

I said, "Super. Buy it and paint it black."

I come back at 5:30 in the morning. Here's a recreational director wearing lawyer loafers and silk pants with a dozen roadies, seven cases of black spray paint, spraying a forty-five-foot tree. We used a forklift to pull it upright, stabilized it.

I said, "Cool. He knows when you've been sleeping, he knows when you're awake, so be good for goodness sake. What if you've been bad?"

Eddie from Bensonhurst says, "Well, you get coal. You get a lump of coal."

I said, "Great. Find enough coal and barbed wire to dress the entire tree, and that's what we'll put under it for presents."

A day later, I have no idea where in Southern California, they come up with lumps of coal the size of bowling balls, dressed out the tree, wrapped it all in black barbed wire, hung red lights, put a Jewish star on top. This was recreation.

In the wake of the specialists, the road crew got involved.

Rudy, the guitar tech, invented the Later. Kind of a

fruit drink loaded with rum or vodka or something. We would have these parties, especially if you're playing multiple nights in a city, two, three nights at the local arena. After the first night we'd have a big party. Then he invented Super Laters, 'cause they'd make you later for the dance than you ever thought you'd be.

We had to build him a special road case, like six-and-a-half feet tall. It opened up like a closet, with three big sections, containing three industrial-strength blenders, circuit breakers, a car stereo, mixing gear, disco lights and ice buckets. It was called Raving Rude's Libation Station. The biggest road case anyone had ever seen! And we would set up a tent, open air, and have one rompin' stompin' barbecue. More about this later!

Everybody values their free time or their off time *supremely* because you work so hard when you're on the road. You develop what it is that takes you away, your passport. For me, I always take my bicycles or cross-country skis. Golf is very, very popular on the road. It's a meditational sport; you really drift away, you lose yourself in the art form.

Not unusual to have six buses pull up in front of a hotel 5:30 in the morning, pending a day off, and nine guys on the crew would get off their buses with full-blast golf bags, two-tone golf shoes, a pair of shorts and jack-boots, a headband and twenty-seven hundred bucks' worth of golf clubs.

You got to know all the cool golf courses all over the world. In Japan, the golf course outside of Osaka is super-high tech. You don't carry your golf clubs; nobody does. There's a little track, like the railing at a dog track, and there are these little electric holding carts that are connected. You put the bag of golf clubs on the thing, and it runs down the track to the next hole. And there are attendants at every hole wearing white uniforms. Every hole has a drink stand and a food place.

Or the course near Louisville, Kentucky, where a farmer built himself a pitch-and-put, three-par, out on the great rolling hills. There's a little shack with a coffee can. It's fifty cents to play the holes, it's another fifty cents if you rent one of the clubs. There's a dozen clubs leaning against the wall. There's nobody there; he's out cutting hay rows. There's a little sign—handwritten—it says it's on the honor system.

One of my best pals on the road, Brian, runs the sound. He started running monitors and working on PA systems, sleeping in the back of the van on the first Bad Company tour in the early seventies. He knows every fishing area of every city, of every burg, of every village and hamlet in the free world. He's toured everywhere you could possibly think of. So he brings his poles and his tackle box. No matter where you pull up, you could look out your window at eight o'clock in the morning on a day off and there's Brian waiting for the next taxi to take him over to the little river twenty minutes away, or over to the pond a half hour to the left. And he *always* came back with fish, and we would prevail on the kitchen to cook it up for him, or Big Ed would cook it. Everybody had a thing.

We had one barbecue in the parking lot, forget where it was, but some of the guys had played at a golf course, made friends with everybody behind the counter. Cool—not only are you invited to come to the show, but we're having a little hang in the parking lot. Raving Rude's Libation Station in full effect.

These fellas who worked at the golf course showed up. They had a whole duffel bag, old used golf balls that had been dredged up out of the lake. So while some people are playing cards, and some others are watching the TV or confabbing, four guys over on the little hillock underneath the street light were whacking golf balls toward the hotel.

"Okay. Off the Buick, across the grassy knoll, and straight up into the stop sign."

What was an extra attraction is that our friends, the folks who would come out to visit for a long weekend or a few days, would ask ahead, "Hey, I see on the itinerary that I'm going to be there for a day off. Is Big Ed cooking? We going to be out in the parking lot?"

"Oh yeah."

"Great, 'cause I want to help Ed cook."

People would fly 2,800 miles into the middle of suburban nowhere and look forward to sitting Indian-style in a parking lot at three in the morning.

"So you guys are having a hang, huh? Can I help?"

"Well, yeah, sure."

" 'Cause I want to help Rude mix drinks."

About half the time you'd smell it before you heard it. You'd be in your room, you're just waking up, it's five, six o'clock in the evening, and you'd smell ribs. You'd look out, there's thirty people milling around, setting up cheap-shit chaise lounges, lawn chairs.

Rudy and I celebrated our twenty-second year of working together not long ago. We drank Super Laters. But, you know, in a lot of places it's hard to find the piña colada mix or pure Cuban cane juice, or Myers's rum—not the six-year, the twelve-year. In a lot of places it's tough to find ice. So, we self-contained: We built Raving

Rude's Libation Station. No longer were we dependent on the promoter to provide blenders.

Each night would be a different drink depending on where you were. If you're down in Georgia . . . Peach Later. So it was as the natives do—somewhat.

It reached a level whereby Rude, who had a lot of responsibilities on stage and stuff, would have to leave earlier for the hotel than the band in order to set up the station, so we'd have to hire extra union guys to finish his job for him. We'd put him in a limousine, send him off to the hotel to set up, loaded down with all the provisions that the promoters' caterers supplied. He would order up a bushel of peaches, cracked ice.

It was come one, come all. The new crew guys, or some union guys, would say, "Whoa, what's with him?" They're watching a crew technician get into a stretch limousine and take off before anybody else was finished. "Who does he think he is?"

"Hey, man, that's Raving Rude."

You'd walk into the parking lot or the room and say, "Rude, man, you look a little tired tonight. What's up?"

"Oh, goddamn it, I spent half the day trying to locate strawberries. But I got 'em."

He had been riding around in the limousine trying to locate strawberries in Kenosha.

Rude looked like a defensive tackle. Perennial smile, always ready to do, always ready to go, lot of want-to.

"Atlanta Peach Super Later. So I guess we're using glasses instead of paper."

"Probably the best idea, Dave."

We'd get moonshine in from this one particular truck driver, he'd show up with a case, that shit would take the wax off the inside of the cup. You'd be spittin' out wax from a single gulp. You could strip the deck of a Boston Whaler with that shit. You couldn't use normal paper cups 'cause it ate through the wax.

And at these affairs were local radio people, local newspaper people, promotion people, groupies, building people, police, paramedics, caterers, all kinds of people. If you got through one-and-a-half Peach Laters, everybody was the best of pals.

Travels With Dave

In 1978 when we started touring with Van Halen in a considered fashion, we would take breaks like every three months, a ten-day break, figure a week off with a couple of travel days on either end. I couldn't wait to see the world. Material goods beyond a cool pair of shoes or a stack of new tapes were of little interest to me. I wanted to go break bread with all different kinds of people, preferably in dramatic geography. I love dramatic weather, snow and cold, heat and humidity, rainstorms and so forth.

In 1979, I purposely went to the South Pacific during rainy season. Nobody goes there then. Tahiti is one small little island with two hundred other little islands in the archipelago, and each one is connected by puddle jumpers, twin-engine something or others, usually prewar. And it's a ten-minute hop, a thirty-minute hop, a forty-five-minute hop, you land at Papeete Airport, mainland of Tahiti. You can drive all the way around the edge of Tahiti in two hours.

I went during rainy season 'cause that was part of *Treasure Island* too. That's part of *Moby Dick.* Commenced adding up a list of stamps in the passport that ultimately included all throughout Tahiti, the South Pacific, the West Indies, all throughout Mexico, South America, New Guinea, the Amazon, the high Himalayas.

I've climbed in the fifteen greatest climbing areas in the United States alone. I'm only an advanced intermediate, at best, but I've climbed in fifteen other countries as well. Everywhere from Finland to Rio de Janeiro, to Yosemite in northern California. Going out at night, lowering ropes from the top of the old stone berths in Schweinfurt, Germany, where they serviced all of the submarines during World War II.

I started going to Club Meds as I progressively became more and more isolated from the general neighborhood. The more records you sell, the more isolated you are; the less people address you directly or say what's really on their mind. People develop different agendas and preconceptions, and you become very isolated in your fame.

Extreme example of that—and I went through a phase of this for a handful of years, where you can't go to the 7-Eleven anymore, baseball hat or not. Super-fame means somebody tapping you on the shoulder for an interview, for an autograph in the middle of a movie. Super-fame means somebody following you into the bathroom and knocking on the door to the stall. Super-fame means your number is passed around, and you get all kinds of calls at bizarre times of day or night, and you have to change your phone number every two months.

The beauty of the Club Med for me was that I had contact with all different kinds of people on a very equal level. I always had a running four-day start on the overall game because nobody knew who I was. I looked like I worked there. Just another long-haired guy with the bathing suit. Indeed, if anybody ever asked me I'd tell them I was in telecommunications or something really abstract. Fractal bioengineering, you know, who really wants to get into that? You're going to move right to "Great, what are your hobbies?" You tell people, "Oh, I'm in telecommunications," they don't really want to know what that is, sounds too vague. They'll ask you something like, "So how's business?" "Doing pretty good." "Great." You're done, next subject. I find that very refreshing.

It's a great balancing factor when everybody's in a bathing suit. When everybody's sunburned. When you take away all the royal scepters and the feathers and the holy robes and all of the talismans, it's all just "nobody in here but us chickens." So I would track around to the different Club Meds for that very reason. Keep in mind that Club Med in the early eighties was a much wilder affair than the family scenario which exists today.

It was also a great place to work outward, because most people would go to a Club Med and stay within that little village, that little compound. They might take a proscribed sightseeing trip to see the pyramid for half a day. Or to go see the ancient burial site for three hours, complete with monologue from the driver in broken English. Or today is shopping day for trinkets to bring back to the other sorority sisters or the other guys at Salomon Brothers, whatever. A T-shirt that says, "My uncle went to Cancún and all he brought back was this lousy T-shirt."

Haiti was hoppin'. You had people from all over the world going there because it's French-spoken, directly; after that is Creole, and then English. The cost was zilch because it was a dictatorship; it was wildly corrupt. I think it's the second-poorest country in the world, certainly the poorest nation in this hemisphere. I've always been socially conscious, but there were periods of time when the world simply revolved around me. It's part of James Bond to go to a dictatorship in a Third-World country and gamble there. How many James Bond movies have you seen where he's sitting across from the Idi Amin knockoff, gambling in some quasi-African somewhere—somewhere between St. Tropez and Uganda, with a name like Zerimba? That was part of it.

Did you ever read Graham Greene's *The Comedians*? It was written, I believe, in the sixties, about Haiti and all of the carryings on. It was very much like Cuba was in the forties and the fifties, with the gambling, the nightlife, fancy hotels and spurious characters of all types. The Oloffson Hotel rose up in the middle of Port-au-Prince, a tremendous slum. But the Oloffson Hotel was antebellum, it was deep Old South with the white latticework and the white columns and the balconies. You would go to the Oloffson Hotel to drink mint juleps or something that no guy in Pearl Jam would ever admit to having. It was right out of the movies, it was out of all those spy movies.

There was one fellow, his name was Prosper, and he

always wore an ice-cream white suit, with a gold chain cross for his watch pocket and a monocle with a gold rim and a chain. He always carried a black polished ebony cane with a gold top, white shoes, always immaculate. A little bit of jewelry and a shaved head. This was like 1982. And it was a military dictatorship, complete with their own death squads, the *tonton macoute.* Everybody was being listened to and watched. There were all kinds of deals going on.

Remember *The Godfather,* Part 2, when they're in Cuba right before the revolution? Same thing: Same floor shows, same hotel life surrounded by abject poverty, same people, whether it was congressmen or Eurotrash party people or industrialists. A lot of show people passed through there.

We'd be invited to ride around in Baby Doc Duvalier's big cigarette speed boat, painted gloss black, called the *Executioner.* To me at the time, all of this was out of *Dr. No.* I had blinders on to the social conditions around me.

I can bond with anybody, so I got to know all the homeboys workin' the bar and stuff over at the hotel. They invited me to the Birthday of the Devil. This was right around November 1st. So Big Eddie, my assistant, and I got in a jeep with two bar guys, drove into the interior of Haiti.

Now, the Birthday of the Devil is based on one concept: Haiti is 80 percent Catholic and 100 percent voodoo. They practice Catholicism, in its infinite varieties, but they *all* practice voodoo, to some extent. It's African.

Cut to: Me and Ed, two white guys, maybe three hundred blacks. This crowd comprised of every village within spitting distance who has sent the main priest and his assistant, the local voodoo sect. They've been pounding drums since dawn. Everybody's sweating, everybody's bleary-eyed, everybody's carrying on . . . and us.

Everybody there works at the local hotels, so they're wearing gear that they've stolen from the hotels. The main priest is wearing a paper Fourth-of-July Uncle Sam hat, red, white and blue, with Christmas tree tinsel wrapped around his neck. He's totally delirious from rum and whatever, and dancing all night. The main priestess has on a muumuu and one of those transparent blue plastic sun visors, with the digital lights that go blink-blink-blink-blink, all the way across, and it says Miami.

They're dancing around inside this hut, and they're sacrificing chickens. Read: the guy smacks the chicken on the head with the flat side of a machete blade, a couple of times, stuns it, puts it in his mouth, feathers and all, and each of the other priests dance up, in delirium, and tear off a piece of the chicken and chew it up and swallow feathers, bones and all, till ultimately there's nothing left but the rib cage and the neck bones, which they place in the middle of the hut, on the sand, and then draw a sand figure, Lazulee, the goddess of this and that.

We watch this for a couple of hours. I says, "Ed, I need a little breather." There's tension in the air.

There's got to be fifty different drums going, going, going. We go out, and we sit next to this little toolshed. After a few minutes, the drums stop, and everybody starts coming out of the shack toward the toolshed.

I said, "Oh no. We're in for it now." I have no idea what's gonna happen.

I notice that behind us there's now lights in the shack. It's one of those rough-hewn shacks, where there's space in between the boards, and I can see candlelight.

Lo and behold, the doors open up very slowly and ceremoniously, they surround us—this is right out of Monty Python—and the doors open up, and six guys come walking out, very slowly, backwards, with a child's coffin—which symbolizes the Birth of the Devil. He's born, and progressively gets younger, somehow, and dies . . . it's abstract. The Devil is born backwards.

A procession is formed, and we march down the two-lane blacktop, in the pitch-black. Drums are beating, everybody's chanting, six guys carrying a child's coffin backwards. And we dance and march for almost two miles down two-lane blacktop, in the middle of nowhere.

Every now and then, a bus will go by. Probably carrying some tourists to the local hotel.

Oh my God, can you imagine what those tourists thought? As we danced by? We danced almost two miles down two-lane blacktop, to a graveyard. Danced on the graves, until dawn, to the drums, and then fell asleep in the bushes. Everybody.

I woke up in the bushes, about ten o'clock, the next morning. Ed and I found our way back home with some people who had a jeep. They took us back to the beach road; from there, we walked.

Birthday of the Devil.

I had a plan, you know, that I was gonna call my girlfriend Casey, and tell her, "You gotta come on down to Haiti."

Next day, found the bar guy who had taken us to the

ceremony, and I said, "You know the priestess, the one with the Miami hat?"

He said, "Oh yeah."

I said, "I'd like to cut a little deal."

Paid her eighty dollars to make a blessing to one of the goddesses for success in romance. Made a blessing for me.

It worked, but to this day, I have a problem eating chicken.

Do you know the story of Toussaint L'Ouverture? The Imperial Royal Palace in Haiti was an identical replica of the White House in Washington but maybe 20 percent the size. And out in front is a big statue of Toussaint L'Ouverture, the great liberator; *l'ouverture,* the opening. He was the first black liberator in history, led the slaves in an uprising. But then there are those in the know, expatriates and people who explain that no, because slaves only had first names, they called him L'Ouverture because of the gap between his two front teeth. They could have called him Toussaint Letterman.

So all of this digested equally explains a lot of the character of the place at the time. Great weather. Blistering sun every day, very little rain. The AIDS thing was still something in the back of a magazine every now and then; that whole scare had not reared its ugly head. Everywhere that you would go, like the Oloffson Hotel, would be Prosper, sitting alone at a table, drinking a little espresso, looking off into the distance in his ice-cream suit.

He knew everybody's names before you knew his. Walked up to the table, "Mr. Lee Roth, it's a pleasure to meet you. My name is Prosper. I'm one of the neighborhood here. Welcome to our little island," this kind of thing. He knew everybody. Everybody knew Prosper. And it was well known that he was the eyes and the ears of the dictator.

He was watching us. Everybody knew, but it was never discussed. Any function, there was Prosper.

Well, when Baby Doc was run out of office, they started exchanging government heads. Two years later after I stopped going to Haiti, I opened up the newspaper, who's the new president? Prosper. There he is with his Miami dental work and his little French monocle. He became the acting president for a while, and then they deposed him, too.

I did spend one Christmas in Haiti. I guess this would be about '83. I got on my bicycle, left the hotel, went way off into the hills on a dirt road. I had taken some bread, a little ham. I remember I also had a little package of cream cheese, the kind that comes in a wheel made of tiny little triangular packages.

I had finished my lunch, I was headed back. There was an old fellow, looked to be in his eighties, standing by the road. Begging is a way of life for a lot of folks—put his hand out as I was going by. I didn't have any money, but I had some of the cream cheese left, so I gave him that. He stood there and looked at it, and he started to get tears in his eyes, and he looked up at me to see if I was joking. Slowly, he got down in that little Third-World squat where you sit on your heels, opened up one little triangular square of the cream cheese and started eating it, bit by bit, with his fingers. And then he licked the paper until it was spotlessly clean. The whole time he had tears in his eyes.

When I saw that, I decided that was going to be the last time I went to Haiti. It really drove it home where I actually was. That this was *not* a place to go looking for merriment.

It was around this time—hang it on a hook called Haiti—that the world, to an *increasingly lesser* degree, revolved around myself, "the Atomic Punk," "nobody rules these streets at night but me," " 'cause I'm on fire." After enough mileage, enough distance, you can't help but become aware of what's around you, the tepee next door, so to speak. My lyrics and my general tone began to alter subtly. I started writing titles like "Fair Warning" or "Mean Streets." Those were not celebration songs.

Went to New Guinea with a girlfriend at the time. We determined that we were gonna cross over the Star Mountains, down into the Sepik River. We trained for that for a year, running. "Honey, look, there's no moon, it's freezing cold, it's pouring rain, it's five-thirty in the morning, let's practice setting up the tent!"

I never had my thirtieth birthday. I planned this accordingly. Crossed the international dateline—you have to fly to Sydney, before you go from Sydney to Port Moresby, New Guinea. Cross the international dateline, you lose a day. My birthday's October tenth; we left on the ninth, landed on the eleventh. I never turned thirty.

Visited a village called Dabarap—there's maybe forty people there: Bones in the nose, little gourd on the dick, and that's it. All natives in the highland jungles of New Guinea speak pidgin, which you can get, literally, a dictionary for, from the Missionary Aviation Society. It sounds like John Wayne Indian-talk: "No spittum betel juice here. You go-um long way lik-lik."

Well "lik-lik" is how you say "little," if you've got a face full of betel nut, and you're stoned out of your mind and have been for the last eight years, up there in the highland jungle.

Betel nut comes from the areca palm tree. What you do is chew the betel nuts, like wood pulp, tastes like a number two pencil, and then you take one of these tendrils that's pepper-hot, and you dip it in powdered bird shit, give it a little taste. It makes your spit really bloody, viscous red.

Every tribe has its own way of spitting out betel juice. Some tribes spit it in an aimed stream, some just kind of let it dribble off the chin, and others do like I do with sunflower seeds, where you just take a mouthful, chew it up into a big, woody pulp, and you get this big cloud of pulp and spit. If you buy something like a billum bag—which is a carry bag, made of woven twine, made from wood bark—depending on the red drips on the billum bag, you can tell which tribe it was made by. Because those who dribble it, the bag has got a certain character to it: It's straight line dribbles. Those who blow out wood pulp in a big viscous cloud, half the bag will be colored red.

Got to the village called Dabarap. Now, the first thing you always do when you visit the highland jungles: You sit in the long hut, the elders gather, and they bring out a little wooden plank with some natural tobacco that they grow, and a couple of copies of the *Post Courier News,* which is printed out of Port Moresby, the only jetport there.

So they break out the little piece of wood, with the newspaper, and the natural tobacco, I say "Hey, I recognize this. I know just how to do this." After a fashion.

And they commence to tell us their most prideful story. You exchange your best stories.

They commenced to tell us their best story, *Da Bik Pella Balais Mixmaster Bilong Jesus.* This is pidgin. You can buy this dictionary at Pickwick Books. All the natives speak at least fifty words of pidgin, even though they have seven hundred dialects of their own.

Okay. Well, it took a couple of hours, and a few cigarettes. We began to get it. Bik Pella: This comes from Australians Mick Leahy and the Taylor boys, who first investigated New Guinea, in what, 1928?

What's more Australian than "Well, you're certainly a big fella, aren't ya?"

So anything big is a *Bik Pella.* You've got a face full of betel nut, anything big is *Bik pella.* Bik pella pig, bik pella mon, bik pella tree . . .

"Well, you're certainly a big fella, aren't you?"

Balais means balance: Birds balance in the air, fish balance in the water. You gotta kinda take it in context.

Mixmaster: Slang for egg beater. That flies. A helicopter! Old world Australia. *Bilong,* Possessive: Belongs to; *Jesus* is Jesus.

Turns out they're describing the first helicopter they had ever seen, that had landed in their village clearing and deposited missionaries. Baptist missionaries, with Bibles.

Anyway, you'll see signs in the airport that say "No spittum betel juice floor." Because everybody, all the government workers in Morseby chew it all day. The only place you see cars is in Port Moresby. And *every* car has a red spray going from the driver's side window all the way to the back bumper.

Betel nut is like mediocre pot, with a mild tea caffeine

buzz that kills your appetite. You could eat if you wanted to, but you don't think of it. And you can work or hold conversation just fine, but if you're just going to sit on a hillock, underneath the tree, and look off into the distance, you could knock out seven hours without even a blink.

It dyes your teeth bloody red. It's like in the musical *South Pacific*. Bloody Mary? She sings the famous song, "Bali Ha'i." She's Bloody Mary, because her teeth are dyed red from betel nut. Betel nut is *the* drug of choice of most of the free world. Or unfree world.

I remember coming back from a vacation like this, when I was in Van Halen, '82, '83. Valerie Bertinelli—there was always a little conflict between us—said, "So where did you go on vacation this time, Dave?"

I said, "We went to Tahiti, and we climbed Mount Bali Ha'i. Have you ever heard of it?"

She said, "No."

I said, "Like in the musical *South Pacific*. Bloody Mary, the little lady in the muumuu with the dyed red teeth points and says, 'This is where you will find your love.' She sings, 'Bali Ha'i is callin . . . Bali Ha'i beckons you . . . ' are you familiar with that?"

She's an actress: "No."

I said, "Okay. Led Zeppelin. 'The Immigrant Song.' You know, when they go 'Ah . . . aaah . . . ahh . . . ' "

She says, "Yeah."

I said, "Well, they stole that from *South Pacific*."

I'm sure, to this day, she thinks Led Zeppelin wrote *South Pacific*.

We'd just finished a South American tour, winding up in Argentina, late '83. I said to Big Ed, "We're going to have to fly across it anyway to get to Los Angeles, so why don't we go to the Amazon?"

He said, "Great, I've always wanted to go to Africa." The Amazon seemed close enough. We flew to Manaus at the headwaters. Well, Manaus is a big name on a little map, but when you go there it's like the worst end of Hong Kong at the turn of the century. Everybody's living on little houseboats, but these boats are nothing but a roof and a hull with pillars, and you sleep in hammocks, it's open air. The boats are parked six and eight deep, you have to walk across other people's boats to get to the wharf. Everything looks like the 1920s.

We saw one body float by in the water. Another guy, while we were provisioning, was just dead on the stairway at the top of the wharf, somebody put a newspaper over him. Everybody's sick. Everybody's got the dysentery, the trots, doing the Pepto-Biz waltz. I'm sick to death. I got the bacteria, stung by something, whatever. I lost close to fifteen pounds in a week, most of it dehydration.

We're trying to provision in Manaus. You get so used to a sporting goods store in America, "Umm, I'm going to need a 90 percent diethyl-toluamide for the mosquitoes because I'm going bass fishing in Oregon. I need some Merrell boots insteps, you know, that are waterproof but that have venting holes. I need Gore-Tex without the nylon for the pants but with nylon . . . " not in Manaus.

Four weeks later, we're a million miles up the dead-empty Amazon river, it's like every book you ever read. Ed's making an omelette out of a can of what we think is Spam but in Portuguese is dog food. There was no picture.

We're shopping up stuff in open-air markets, this is total pirateville.

Ed would go into these bars where there would be these guys literally with striped T-shirts and a buck knife, missing fingers and this kind of thing. Says, "Who's going toward Iquitos?" "Who's headed up the river for a month, two months?" We had two cases of Chesterfield cigarettes with us because that's who sponsored the latest Van Halen tour. Came up with these two guys, early thirties, we get out on their boat, the *Marcia,* complete *African Queen*, a hull and a flat roof. Little gas generator blew up the first night, but we're not turning back because I'm dreadfully ill, we're committed. We're going to do it by candlelight.

Second night out I seriously think I'm going to die. I'm having convulsions, contractions where everything clenches. We're not quite out of city limits so to speak, there's a little infirmary we pull into. Eddie has to literally carry me into the infirmary. There's no chairs. Everybody's sitting on the cement floor. It's a Friday night. There's a little stainless steel table, there's bloody bandages in the corner, and so I sit on the table, and I'm having contractions lasting maybe twelve seconds apiece, can't breath or anything.

At that moment two jungle federales wearing the blue khaki uniforms with the jackboots and the hats—but the boots are unlaced, their guns are swiveled around behind them, their hats are topsy-turvy—bring in what came to be known as "the dead woman." Woman in her forties, obviously shantytown from the way she's dressed, completely covered in dirt and mud, not breathing, nothing. Probably got hit by a car; they found her in a ditch. She was drinking Cachaca. I think it was called *pinga*, I'm not sure. Thirty cents a quarter. Nonsolid rocket fuel.

One's got her arms, the other's got her by the ankles, and they just throw her on the floor, right next to me. I see this veritable death in front of me, and I've got tears in my eyes and I'm thinking, "What an awful way to go, man, I should have been eaten by a fish or fell over something big, but just to shit myself to death . . . "

Nurse comes in, doesn't speak English. One of the boat guys, guys with me, speaks English. She recognizes the symptoms instantly. She produces a syringe the size of a Chevy piston, and the needle is just a little bit smaller than your average lead pencil.

The nurse steps between the dead woman and myself sitting on this table, and I hurt so bad I'm crying. This is not a colorful exit. I'm thinking these things consciously, 'cause I'm lookin' at the gate. The nurse puts that needle in my arm. Eddie stabilizes me because I'm still having contractions. There's a lot of juice in the syringe, looks like a third of a quart's worth of something. So it's going to take a minute to get it all in. And as the nurse is a few seconds into the shot, the dead woman comes to life. Suddenly it's apparent right away to all of us because everybody knows what *pinga* is, which in Spanish slang means dick. *Pinga* in the Amazon is thirty cents a quart with a screw top on it, and it should have a shark on the label. She became comatose on *pinga,* got hit by a car out on the dirt road, she was already somnambulant, wound up in the ditch, and that's where they found her. Threw her in the back of the police truck and drove her to the infirmary.

The nurse becomes frantic, she's babbling in jungle

Portuguese; my interpreter guy is trying to interpret back and forth; Ed's trying to stabilize my arm; I'm still having convulsions. The nurse climbs onto the table where I'm sitting to get away from the dead woman because she's starting to thrash. So Eddie, who's like defensive tackle material, puts his foot on her neck to keep her from hitting me or the nurse because I'm getting a major shot here, the mother of all shots. At that precise moment the two cops happen to walk back into this little tiny room, see what's happening and start to arrest Ed.

The interpreter's going crazy trying to explain to the guys who have their hats on sideways. Because *they* have been drinking *pinga.* These guys are stumbling around with their shirttails out. They're going to arrest Ed; the dead lady is thrashing around like a bad day of bass fishing. And I started to laugh. Yeah, I survived.

One night a few weeks later it's full moon, we're in the middle of nowhere. I mean, we haven't seen another human being in eight days. Ten, eleven o'clock at night and a canoe goes by. This is like the Twilight Zone.

"Did you hear that?"

"No. Well, yeah, but did you?"

"I just saw a canoe go by with a little outrigger engine, tiny, handmade. I swear to God I saw eight people in that canoe."

"No."

A few minutes later another canoe goes by. And then another canoe goes by. They're going to a party. They takin' back streets, but they're goin' to a function at the junction. I can tell from the hum of the engine. I can smell it.

Well, in our boat the *Marcia,* we were dragging a little canoe behind us. We pile in; me, Ed, our interpreter Paul, the two boat guys. We take my giant stereo along, my total shoulder motor. Head up the river in the middle of nowhere. About twenty minutes later there's light burning, music playing, people laughing. We pull up, and there's a shack.

Well, come on in! There's maybe eighty folks there, all jungle people. Not bones in the nose, but there's very few shirts. The boss of the place is named Nail, I don't know how to say it in Portuguese. Named Nail because he has had seventeen children. Almost everybody in the place was one of Nail's kids. They had a little battery-driven stereo, so we put their tapes in my stereo, and we rocked out till dawn.

Everybody gets totally slam-dunked on *pinga*, dance and dance and dance. The sun's coming up, five of us pile back into our little dugout canoe—I mean the water is literally a quarter-inch below the rim of the boat—with the stereo, totally soused, in piranha-filled waters. Head out into the river, get into the current, and realize we forgot the oars. Everybody from the soiree is of course on the shore cheering and clapping. We're drifting sideways in slow current. They're holding up the oars and laughing and cheering.

We drifted and drifted, and you might splash your hands in the water a little bit trying to redirect the boat. About twenty minutes later we pass the *Marcia.* We keep going for another hour, hour and a half, before we get close enough to shore to jump out. We had to walk back through the jungle towing the boat in the mud. I think we made it like by lunchtime. Best damn party I ever been to.

Day after day, having to fish up dinner . . . and breakfast. You sit up on top of the boat with duct tape around your wrists and a long-sleeve shirt around your neck and duct tape around your ankles drenched in 90 percent DEET to keep the mosquitos out. The piranha would bite your hook in half, not the line, your hook. Their bottom jaw distends, and it shears. It'd bite a bass hook in half. Long about your fourth, sixth hook, 3:30 in the morning, you're sweatin', one becomes somewhat frustrated.

Due to piranha, I went swimming maybe twice, and it was a quick in and out. Take a bath Cong style, where you squat down, and somebody dumps a bucket. My toenails turned coal black. When I finally got back to New York, two months later, I went right to the hospital for tropical diseases. Everybody looked and rubbed their chin and palpated, did some blood work, some paperwork. I went to three different doctors. Third one says, "Wait one minute." Gets a scalpel, starts scraping the toenail, it was compressed grime from never getting off the boat.

Isolation is a sweet drug. It can be very frightening but that is also alluring. I told my manager at the time I was going up the Amazon. He said, "Great, just give me a call every few days." Sorry about that.

At some point we wound up at a tiny little village called Juarini. It's not even on the map. Seventy-five people. Whole village turns out to see whoever we were. They killed a cow for dinner. They had a guitar, I played blues. And they had a shortwave radio. The only thing they ever really listened to was from Manaus, and that was weather reports more than anything else. It was always the same weather: It's going to rain, then it's going to be fuckin' hot, and then it's going to rain like crazy, then it's going to be hot again. But it's radio; it's the future. So they listened.

At dawn the next day, while we're on the boat sleeping, word comes down, says, "You see some crazy white boys on a boat called the *Marcia*, tell them to phone home." So over the shortwave we got in touch with Manaus, who hooked me up on the telephone with the manager. "Hey, the guy who owns Apple Computers is throwing a huge outdoor music festival, and he wants Van Halen to top bill."

I said, "Why are you calling me out here?"

He says, "He's offering a million and a half dollars for one show."

I said, "Is he offering that to anybody else?"

He said, "I think he offered it to David Bowie."

I said, "And how long is David Bowie supposed to play?"

He said, "Two hours."

I said, "Tell him we'll take it but for an hour and a half."

Floated about another four days up river and wound up at a little mining camp where some German geologists were doing surveys. Gave the boat guys the rest of our cigarettes, and hitched a ride on a little twin-prop plane with four German geologists. Pilot wore a cowboy hat. Took off from a dirt strip in the middle of a thunderstorm. Sounded and looked like God was coming home to dinner early and boy, was he pissed! Flew over the jungle for hours and hours. As the sun was coming up, landing in Manaus, there was wreckage of a plane still smoking that had crashed trying to land, flew over it by fifty feet maximum, landed, and began a search in earnest for somebody who could explain my black toenails.

I went to the Himalayas, in 1991, after I had made the video for *Just Like Paradise,* which featured climbing in Yosemite.

Dangling around at two thousand feet on the face of Half Dome shooting parts of that video. I got to work with some super-climbers, Dave Breashears—at the time the only American to have summited Everest twice, and Mike Wiess super-technician, super-outdoor climber. They've worked together on many films.

Renny Harlin later directed *Cliffhanger,* a movie they worked on. I would run into him occasionally, and he freely admitted that he stole his opening scenes from watching my video, *Just Like Paradise.* He said to me in that little accent of his, "David, I did not have respects for you until I went into the mountains and experience what you do. Now I have much respects for you."

I said to him, "Renny, I'm flattered and I just wanted to tell you that I used to have no respect for you and your work, and I still have no respect for you and your work. But thanks for the compliment." He was flabbergasted.

Anyway, I went climbing in the Himalayas with Dave and Mike. Mike brought his wife, who's not a climber, but she came along. And we went and climbed Lobuché Peak. It's about 23 thousand feet.

Denver, Colorado, is one mile high, á la Mile High Stadium. You start gettin' a little short of breath at five thousand feet. Most people feel a little headache come on, a little malaise. Feel a little apathetic, slow, can't really put thoughts together as quickly, short-term memory difficulty—now I'm describing most of the Midwest, or at least most of my friends. Around fifteen thousand feet, you start battling altitude sickness.

I flew to the other side of the world on my own. You fly from Los Angeles to Tokyo, and then from Tokyo to Bangkok, and spend the night in Bangkok, and then go to Kathmandu. Got together there. Provision up the rest of the food and so forth. Get the climbing permits. You have to pay for permits to go on to the mountain, at least so there's a record of your last name if you don't come back.

Kathmandu hasn't changed since the twelfth century, except now every fourth street corner has got a guy with no socks and a knock-off Armani T-shirt with a jacket with the sleeves pushed up going, "Hey, got some hash, dude." The rest of them are fellows walking around, in the traditional loincloth and their version of dreadlocks. It's still like going back in time.

From there you fly to Lukla, which is at the base of the Khumbu Valley, a huge vista that contains the mountains you've been looking at in school books but can't remember how to spell the names. Ama Dablam, Lhotse, Lhotse Shar, Nuptse, Everest. Everest was about a day, two day's slow, easy walk across the valley from the mountain that we were working on. You work your way up that valley, before you get to the mountain that you're going to climb.

But the adventure starts in Lukla. You go to the little airport in Kathmandu, and you wait for either the plane or the helicopter to fly you in to Lukla which is perched on the side of a mountain, it's a tiny village, every house there is made out of wooden boards and slats, candlelight lanterns, little dirt trails.

You head up this dirt trail that's two feet wide with an eleven-hundred-foot drop-off—Empire State Building is eleven hundred feet tall, okay? That's *nothing* in the Himalayas. That does not qualify as big air, that's just *walking* space. You run in to little kids walking along carrying their body weight in firewood in a handmade hemp bag on their back, and the string goes around their forehead, and they're *dancing* up the trail to school.

As you go into this valley and back in time, you've got to realize that all those little wooden huts that you see, the lantern in that hut, all of the rugs, whatever, were carried up here on somebody's back. There is a kind of hamlet when you get up to fifteen thousand feet, the last highest point of real civilization.

It's called Namché. The Namché Bazaar is very famous. It's what Shangri-La is based on from James Hilton's *Lost Horizon.* You see all the mountains all around. There's nothing like it on earth.

There's a generator; they have some electricity. But keep in mind that every pole that the wire is running on for electricity to the generator was carried up, out from Kathmandu for four weeks, 'cause no wood grows up there. Not unusual for a little kid to walk out of Namché at fifteen thousand feet for four, five, six days just to pick firewood and carry it back up.

In Namché, there's this fellow, has a teahouse. It's very simple. It's like something out of *Lonesome Dove.* A little cot you can rent for a few bucks. A "shower" downstairs, a wooden box about the size of a telephone booth. He boils up about ten, fifteen gallons of water, let's you know when it's all ready. You go down into that shower stall, and it's fuckin' cold. It's way zero, and the wind blows, and it's dry, and you're dehydrated, and you've got altitude sickness. You pull a string, and it's got a bucket that sits on the end of the pipe over your head with holes punched in the bottom. Even though the water's boiling, the pipes are so cold that by the time it travels five feet, comes out the bottom of the bucket, it's just right. It was the first shower in two weeks that any of us had taken. It was like, wow, high tech.

He had a little bit of solar power going on up there, some panels that a Japanese climbing expedition had left behind. He had had a microwave oven brought up out of Kathmandu, something that was shipped through India or Thailand. It was his prized possession. This was kept in a wooden-board room where everything was cooked on a stove that was stoked with wood fire. Again, think cowboy. Big iron stove that you kept throwing wood and kindling into, and everything was cooked on top of this stove or baked in the fire. Make popcorn, you know, with a big skillet and a top on, 'cause you can transport corn kernels. They do well with the weather and last forever.

The Sherpas are a high-altitude group of people used to living in that oxygenless environment. Once *you* get to fifteen thousand feet, things start to go wrong. You begin to dehydrate severely, on a regular basis. You have to quadruple your water intake, and even then your body goes into supplementary overdrive—Jesus, the brain's drying out, force more fluid there, and you start getting cerebral edema, you have a headache twenty-six hours a day. Your hands and your feet start to swell, extremities start drying out. Body goes haywire; can't sleep more than three hours at a hit, if that.

As you're making passage up from there, you start making mistakes. People aren't thinking straight, they walk off of a trail, and they have the length of the World Trade Center to consider their error. People who go for a simple trek—you'll run into a fair amount of people who will go as high as Namché, they don't pack right, they're not dressed for it, they make mistakes with the medicine kit. Somebody gets hurt, twists a knee, there's no infirmary to go to, there's no stretcher, there's no ambulance, there's no paramedics. You just spent two weeks walking up the *Wizard of Oz* mountain and just sprained your knee or busted it so bad that you can barely move from your sleeping bag, you're in trouble.

You'll see the French Puma helicopters owned by the Nepalese government go up and down that valley once every couple days. But the helicopter you see going up that valley is coming to pick up the guy who broke his pelvis six days ago, not the guy who snapped his arm in three places yesterday. He's got some cassette time to put in with the old Walkman before his ticket home arrives. You can be up there for a couple of weeks, it doesn't matter what's wrong with you. You know, there's an order, everybody's in trouble.

And your body starts deteriorating at fifteen thousand feet, just disintegrates. Too much stress, whether it's the sun, the lack of the oxygen, the stress on your body of maneuvering up there, much less maneuvering through bad conditions. You lose your appetite, you lose your thirst, so everything is force feeding, and naturally, you can't get enough in. If you get a cut, it's not going to start healing until you're back in Kathmandu. If you get a cold, it's for a long time. You'll notice that your fingernails don't grow as fast after fifteen thousand feet.

Fillings will pop out of your teeth 'cause different tissues and surfaces swell and contract, depending on temperature.

There's three drinks in the Himalayas: First and most popular is called *chhang*. It's made out of yak milk, very carefully diluted, then left to ferment. It's really sour, kind of a dish-water taste, and it smells rank. You can smell when somebody's been drinking *chhang* from twelve meters away. It's really strong, like wine. A lot of people up in the high mountains start drinking it right at breakfast. It will take the cold off.

Tomba is fermented millet, grain. If you just let it sit, it will start to create its own heat. So what you do is, you put it in open jars and wrap the jars in towels and then stick the towels into the bottom of a sleeping bag and let it sit for about three weeks to a couple months. It starts to smell rich and sour. All of your Sherpas, the guys working the rope team and stuff, their sleeping bags smell like *tomba*. It's the one reuseable booze I've ever seen, 'cause *tomba* is literally sopping grain. You fill a cup up with it, you pour boiling water into the cup, let it sit for a minute, and then with a straw, suck out all of the liquid. You can refill that cup four or five times. It's alcohol. Throw away the grain or feed it to the yaks, start all over.

The third and most popular drink is tea, *chaya.* They buy big kilo bricks of Chinese and Tibetan tea. Super strong. Not unusual for a Sherpa to drink between ten and fifteen cups of this stuff a day—food being at a premium, the firewood to cook it being almost nonexistent. So they start drinking tea in the morning with a little bit of flat bread, whatever, ready to climb the mountain. A little *chhang* to cut the cold. But you can hit overload pretty quick. As you're climbing, once you start from base camp, if you're working with a lot of Sherpas, not unusual to come up over a little ledge and find somebody bolted to the ice ledge, dead asleep, in the snow drift, sleeping off that little extra *chhang*.

All of this has to be packed with you, 'cause over fifteen thousand feet nothing's growing, no animals exist except for one kind of big, black bird. They're like myna birds, huge black ravens called goraks. You have to hide all your food from the goraks 'cause they'll eat right through the bottom of your sleeping bag. You try and stash food, got something left over from a can of something so you put it in a plastic Ziploc, wrap it up in a sweater and stick it in the bottom of your sleeping bag, by the time you come back at the end of the day, the goraks have chewed through the bottom of your sleeping bag and made off with everything, including the Ziploc.

You set up your base camp depending on what approach you're going to take to climb that given mountain. When Edmund Hillary did it in the fifties on Everest, he took a couple hundred guys with him, bringing food, shelter, stoves, medical supplies. I think the world's record was some 350 people, either a Japanese or a Korean attempt on Everest. Set up a whole city at base camp, and from there you move two-thirds of your gear to Camp 2 and from Camp 2, you move two-thirds of that gear to Camp 3, and so on up the hill. I think there's five basic camps on Everest, and that's called siege tactic, alpine climbing.

What we did was called super-alpine, which means there's no going back from camp to camp. You set up base camp and then you go 1, 2, 3 to the top, and you don't carry enough food or shelter or supplies to be able to retreat and try again. Hillary would go out for a day—people still do this, more often than not—set up ropes, put in bolts, set in ladders, et cetera. You spend the day doing that and then retreat to the previous camp, spend the night, advance your stuff a little more, then set up another camp. You can always retreat if the weather becomes too rough, or you miscalculated your timing. You retreat to the previous camp.

In super-alpine, you don't do that. You take limited weight. The three of us did the climb with one Sherpa going from base camp, 'cause we carried just enough gear, just enough food to try and summit within three days going out of base camp.

We advanced. We were up around 22 thousand feet. It gets to be twenty below zero. You have to carve out an ice ledge. There's certain hours of the day when the sun is out that you have to stay away from your tent because ice boulders are melting and rolling off, smashing all in their way. We almost made the summit; we were within three hours of topping out. We could have made it, there was just enough daylight, but we would have had to spend the night there up on the peak, and we didn't have bivouac gear, we didn't bring any kind of overnight gear with us. That's what pure super-alpine is, a gamble; you either make it completely or you don't at all. We could have summitted and spent the night there huddled together like dogs, but that's when it becomes a lose-your-fingers-or-your-toes kind of an adventure. So we retreated. It was the worst snow conditions they'd had in years, which I didn't realize 'cause it was my first Himalayan experience going into that kind of winter. Everybody was scared. When we got back the Sherpas were crying and praying. That was the first winter ascent on Lobuché peak ever attempted.

You bring everything with you. It's like going to the moon. Even food for the yaks. You bring grain, sacks of grain on a yak. What you do is you make lumps of it about the size of a softball, you mix gravel with it. Nothing grows over fifteen grand, so you take little gravel pebbles, kind of heat it all up into a mush, make big lumps out of it the size of a softball. You grab a yak by its bottom lip, it opens up its mouth, you ram your hand down its throat up to your shoulder, pushing the ball of grain down his gullet. The grain works as—I don't know, it's like fiber I guess, just kind of grinds everything up in his stomach. That's how you feed them every day.

It's very common when you dig out a ledge on the side of an ice cliff, ice melts when the sun comes up and the temperature goes up a few degrees, big showers, little avalanches, rock boulders the size of a bowling ball to the size of a 'frigerator will go rushing by.

So everything has to be bolted in and tied in, everything of value goes into the sleeping bag with you so that you can keep it workable. You spend a lot of time melting snow, 'cause there's so little oxygen, it'll take you an hour to boil water. Fire burns at such a low temperature 'cause there's no breathability. Once you've melted that snow for drinking water, put it in your little bottles, you stick them in the sleeping bag so they don't turn into giant popsicles. Same with your boots, your boot liners, your gloves, any technical working gear, 'cause everything else is going to freeze up inside that tent. It's like sleeping in an ice chest. Everybody's uncomfortable 'cause nobody can sleep and everybody's a little scared, everybody's got headaches and stomachaches.

A great deal of what Himalayan climbing turns out to be is not the technical difficulty of the actual climb itself. If those exact same mountains were located in Northern California, and we were climbing in springtime—the technical difficulty of most of those mountains would be not at all undoable. Think of it as a simple football game; throw the ball, catch the ball, kick the ball. That's all nice and fine if it's springtime and you smell the grass that's just been cut. You're well-fed, well-slept, you kissed somebody good-bye when you went off to the playing field, you're going to see them when you come home—that's easy.

But what if you're playing that same game at twenty below with sixty-mile-an-hour winds? Whoa! Now we're talking Himalayan ball. What if you haven't been eating right for a month, and you're miserable and you're dehydrated, and your head feels like its going to explode, and your hands don't work right, same thing with your feet. Now the game becomes more complicated. What if you had to carry your uniform on your back for two weeks to the big game uphill, in the mud? Now that simple game of ball becomes a little more convoluted.

Okay? So you're fine, you're up, you're playing ball, you got the game going despite all those other distractions. Just before the big kickoff, you discover that you're missing one of your shoes. What do you do? That's Himalayan ball. Or instead of the USC Mighty Trojans with the guy on the white horse, you've got a great big white yak. That yak is carrying all of the Gatorade for the whole game, as well as the water, the salt tablets, et cetera. That yak decides he's not a football fan after all, runs head first into a boulder and trashes everything on his back into splinters. Now what? That's what Himalayan climbing is about.

The actual move of climbing from this rock to that rock, if you did it just after you woke up refreshed and full of breakfast in Pasadena, California, is very different than after two weeks of walking up steep stairways in super frigid climate. After a point, even the yaks give up. They get scared too. They don't want to cross those little suspension bridges. They'd do anything—they'll put their body sideways and refuse to move.

I had three cassette tapes with me. I had started off with more, but one of the yaks smashed all the packs off of his back, rolled over on it, destroyed everything except for a blues classics tape, a country western tape, and an Aerosmith tape. Nothing gets a yak over a suspension bridge faster than "Back in the Saddle Again" by Aerosmith. Had a little handheld tape recorder with a single speaker in it that we could listen to around the campfire, weight being of absolute paramount importance. You'll find people who are going to make super-alpine ascents in wintertime on big mountains literally pulling the metal grommets out of their boots, pulling the metal ends off of shoelaces, pulling handles off of a hammer, in order to lighten the weight.

You start ridge walking above twenty thousand feet. Just put your hands in praying position and pretend that's the mountain. It's like walking up the edge of a razor blade. You put one foot on one side of the ridge, and one foot on the other side of the ridge, and you start making your way up. And that's how you're coming back down, except you're gonna be doin' it backwards. 'Cause you're gonna pound in an ice bolt or an ice axe into the snow and you rappel, with the rope going through your belt line and down to the next guy. But the next guy is so far behind you, you can't even see him. The guy up in front of you is so far ahead of you, you can't see him, it's snowing, it's whiteout. You're going to back down that ridge with one foot on either side of the ridge backwards, at twenty-three thousand feet. And if you fall off the side and your rope doesn't hold, you're going to take a vertical drop the height of nine times the Empire State Building before you go boom.

That's what makes that kind of climbing so severe; it's the commitment. It will test your human emotion to its absolute maximum. 'Cause nobody's thinking straight and everybody knows it. Man, it'd take you forty-five minutes to put your boots on. *No exaggeration.* And you're working as fast as you can. You pull on a sock; you gotta rest. You pull on another sock; you feel like quitting. You question everything. You go to dig around in your bag to find the boot liner, by the time you find the liner, you're out of gas, you gotta rest again. Get one boot liner on, you forget what's next. Oh, right—the other boot liner. Take you ten minutes to come back to what it is you were doing initially. Were we making breakfast? No, we had breakfast. Did I clean it up and put the pots away and pans away? I think so. Let me check. I forgot where I put them, and on and on. Not unusual at all, forty-five minutes to put on your boots before you're even out of the tent. Everybody's operating like underwater.

You're climbing in a place where your climbing

permit is printed on a piece of handmade pulp paper, using a wooden press with a turn-screw wheel to make pressure that is no different than what Gutenberg used to make his Bibles back in the 1400s. No different. They make pulp, beat it with a stick, flatten it out, dry it and make it into paper. That's what your climbing permit is printed on.

I'd go back in an instant.

My one regret out of all of this is that after my Himalayas trip, I started paying attention to what management and some agent or promoter or what the accountant or the lawyer thought would be appropriate to do for music, in terms of, "Well, you gotta do this now." "Well, we gotta pursue this now." "Well, we gotta do this now."

I came back from the Himalayas, I was surrounded by some people who were frantic to make more money, frantic to expand, to tour bigger and so on. For some reason I started to pay attention to that. I should have stayed on the mountain. I should have stayed out at sea. I should have stayed in my little tree house in the South Pacific. I should have found me a girlfriend and gone off back to the Indies somewhere. I just started spinning my wheels, trying to be what somebody else thought I should be. Write, record, tour, and repeat. What a morbid waste of fucking time, trying to put gas in some asshole's Mercedes. A Mercedes that I gave him, by the way.

Brass Attack

After the '94 *Filthy Little Mouth* tour, I decided to pick up the ball where I had left it a few seasons ago. Which was with the brass attack. The saxophone was the original fuzz tone instrument, man. Did you ever see that vein on the side of somebody's neck? That's the barometer of soul power! That's the barometer of soul volume. That's what you set your watch to. How big that vein is on the side of your head.

When you get somebody really blowing brass that vein goes all the way from the collar top to where your hat finishes. I first discovered that vein by watching Al Hirt blow in a still photograph in *Playboy* magazine back in the early sixties. Miles Davis had that vein. The only other option is to do what Dizzy Gillespie did with his cheeks, and I only do that when I smoke pot.

It's natural. I'm not trying to move uptown when I go with brass. It's more downtown. It's razz. It's either lazy milk with a little shot of scotch in it at 4:30 in the morning, where the notes fairly drip out of the horn bell, or it's screaming hot rockin' Edgar Winter. Or sassy hot sauce King Curtis. Or slow smoke in flat air from Miles Davis.

We keep reading about celebrating the difference, celebrating the difference. So where's *your* black bass player? It's just pretty basic, all right? You've got a Presbyterian bass player, you've got a Christian Science bass player, you got a Jewish bass player and you've got a black bass player. Who's the best? Riiite. . . .

I'm celebrating the difference. If you take a band

that's primarily Afro-centric, it's going to sound very different from a band that's primarily Latino. And I have done both. I know it for a fact. I've got it on tape. I have returned, sire, with photos.

So I put together the Super Band. Because in a day and age when everybody's proclaiming the value of our rich, ethnic, diversified cultural tapestry, how come it's still all-white bands and all-black bands? Well, we've got these cool spices. Let's mix them together. I put together the Super Band for one song: "Ice Cream Man." This was the brass rendition. Before it was power trio with yours truly toasting up front on the first Van Halen record, 1978. It's an old, old blues written by John Brim and performed by Elmore James. It's that sassy, barrel-house, Baby-let-me-bang-your-box, Moms Mabley, Live at the Apollo, somewhere between the thirties and the fifties-ism. That fits with my spiritual content perfectly. Also fits with my choice of shoes.

I contacted Omar Hakim, drummer extraordinaire, along with my good pal Nile Rodgers, who had produced my last album, *Filthy Little Mouth.* That caused a stir in and of itself, because Chic is the Led Zeppelin of dance music. All dance roads will lead back to Chic. Yes, James Brown did the chicken scratch. Yes, somebody did the hand claps. Yeah, somebody had three chicks going "Shoop, shoop" before Chic. But Chic combined them all into one easily digestible pill.

So, big stir. David Lee? Viking thug pop riff god of whatever is having a black man produce his record? Oh, they squealed like wieners on the barbecue. I knew we were onto something great. That's rock 'n' roll. The sentiment, the attitude, the spirit, the why, comes long before "the how."

Nile and Omar put together a super band. It was jazzbos and clear-cut players like Greg Phillingaines on piano. Greg was music director for the Jacksons' road tours and such, fifteen to eighteen musicians on stage. Who's gonna run that? Who runs the rehearsals? Who exercises the horse? Who's responsible for his feed, come race day? Greg Phillingaines. When Barb Streisand looks off into the upper left-hand corner of the page and starts singing "People . . . people who need people . . ." and there's one piano in the background, you'd better not fuck up that one piano. Talk about stress gig! Catastrophe beckons at the end of every third bar. This is Greg.

Edgar Winter did the brass charts. Edgar's background is based in rhythm and blues. Beaumont, Texas. That funk zone thang. We gave that song a more traditional reading than early Van Halen had. I made a video of "Ice Cream Man"—all of this out of my pocket—because people in the music industry love to do what's been done before. When somebody in the studio says, "Sounds like a hit," the translation is: "This sounds like a hit that's already on the radio." We love to hear what we heard before, especially when it's successful.

But trying to explain an all-black band to the powers that be, on the heels of rock, is like trying to describe colors. Try to describe blue to somebody over the phone. And have a good time, on me.

Made my own video, having come from the College of Experience. Knew how to cut every corner in the game. Did it in black-and-white. Looks like something from PBS—*Birth of the Blues.* My sister Allison designed all the clothes: suspenders, high-waisted pleats, two-tone shoes, you know, just short of *Guys and Dolls*. It looked like the real thing if this was 1944.

I assembled the band all at once in the big Sony studio on West 54th Street. It's about the size of half a football field. When I approached Sony—old school—they said, "Who's paying for this?"

I said, "I am."

They said: "Okay, Shorty, cut across. You can skip second base on us." A number of people at Sony were super-gracious and gave me super deals. Very cool. Because many times on my brief but colorful tenure out here on the pitch I've begun to think they don't make 'em like that no more. I'm here to tell you they do. Sitting behind desks at Sony.

Anyway, it's a major room, the size of three basketball courts, which is what I needed to assemble the band, shoot the video and record the music. So I assembled the band, April '95, including the three female backup singers, in the studio. I was there to lead. More than just sing. I was there to motivate and mobilize.

They were baffled and astonished and quiet at first, because I was gonna record this "live." What if there's bleed-through on the 24-track console where you'll hear drums coming through the microphone of the trumpet? Cool. My favorite jeans have holes in 'em. The sound should spill over the edges of your turntable. The way you achieve that is old-school recording style. What do you think when Aretha sings, "R-E-S-P-E-C-T?" You do pay r-e-s-p-e-c-t because you can hear the drum track ripping through her vocal microphone and you can hear the guitar player off in the distance over her vocal mike which has an echoing kind of room sound that's different on the direct mike that's on the guitar. Magic.

I demanded that approach. These guys had played for everyone, Sting, George Benson, Eric Clapton and on and on, and nobody could remember the last time they had performed with a whole band in a studio. This was great. I had so much fun. We were in there easily for ten hours, maybe one break. We didn't take breaks. The gig was the break. It's an art form. Keep everyone excited and, to a degree, competitive.

I created an atmosphere where everybody was firing on all cylinders. Ideas, creative thoughts were encouraged, even demanded. Have an idea? Let's hear it. We'd take votes. Jesus Christ, when was the last time they took a vote in the rhythm section on a Pete Gabriel disc? I'd say, "Let's take a vote," and everyone would look astonished.

The vocal, one take. We'd play the whole song all the way through. No stopee-startee. No compiling, okay? The vocal, flat notes included, is straight ahead, die-rect. It just came out beautifully. I hired Howard Bingham, Muhammad Ali's photographer, to shoot the session. There's one of me falling under the piano. It was sensational.

The song was never put to a disc. It was never released. The video exists. Never released. I can't be concerned with that. It was a complete project. I always did figure, "Build it and they will come." Don't try and figure out what will make them come and build that. I have to follow my heart. Some day it will be in a movie, or on a greatest hits album; it may be on a new record. It'll exist because it's stellar.

I have easily a hundred songs like this that I've done over the years. Everything you can think of: dance music, blues vibe, country, instrumentals, whatever. I'm always compiling and recording classic tunes, and whatever will be will be. If I have to spend every penny that I own to do this, well, this is what I do. I did this when I signed up. It may cost me everything—"Ice Cream Man" cost more than a quarter of a million dollars—but this is what I do.

I guess one of the resultant tributes was when Edward Van Halen, in a confiding conversation before the big catastrophe at the MTV Awards, said, "I'm jealous of you."

I asked: "Why?"

He said: "Because you go out and do exactly what you want to do. I'm working for my brother, my agent, my manager, everybody. Even when it cost you money in record sales you still did it. I never did that, and I'm pissed."

I started doing these projects in 1985, right after I left Van Halen. My taste in music is across the board. It is alternately a boon and a curse. A boon and a bane. I could walk into any record store and be smilin'. There's a store in Greenwich Village that specializes in movie sound tracks. You can leave me in there for a whole weekend. Heavy rock, bootlegs from Japan, . . . oh yeah. We have been going through all the disco clearing houses where all the DJs do all the latest cuts. Searching for a five-volume set of the re-mixes of the old-school dance tunes from Studio 54. Not available to mortals. You can leave me in Prime Cuts, a DJ clearinghouse in L.A. I could be in there for nine hours.

So I just started doing a variety of things. It was an open field, especially since I had done *Gigolo* and *California Girls* and scored with that; got a new white suit and a German car out of it. Great. I pursued things that I had a familiarity with. Funk, soul. I grew up with that. The keystones of my life are based on Al Green songs. "Trouble Man" and James Brown's haircut.

I always said I want to be free-form. Make hybrids. There's a lot of times I'm just trying to "get it right." Let's see if we can get that down thing that John Lee Hooker had. Let's try and get that blues phrase just the way it should oughta. Other times, take the music past where you found it. Go down into the uncharted territory. Be bold!

I always wanted to combine. The Beatles taught me that. They started just like I did, indoctrinated into black music. First three, four albums, half of each was cover tunes. "You Really Got a Hold on Me" . . . we didn't know that was Smokey! "Twist and Shout." "Mister Postman." "Roll Over Beethoven" . . . which is not a white expression. From there they began to weld together all the different parts that they found in the musical junkyard. French music with cockney, beer songs with that Major Lance fake cha-cha. The rhumba beat on "And I Love Her."

They welded it all together and then they started walkin' orchestras in and brass sections and oompah bands and old-school Brit vaudeville. This was my blueprint. Rolling Stones, same-same. Bolting country western into delta blues into Chuck Berry get-in-the-car-Maybelline into Elvis meets Cochran. Wayne or Eddie? Beautiful. This, too, was my map. Their specialty was this kind of conglomeration. Like Jimi Hendrix bolting trad folk strumming into the blues.

I have compiled hundreds of songs, completely and

comprehensibly. I believe that even the Polaroids have to be stellar. I insist.

Nineteen ninety-five. If y'all want to eat rabbit, you gotta hunt where rabbit is. Don't go down to the gulf and fish for rabbit. You won't catch one.

What's brass country? What's sexy-funny? Sophisticado downtown funk? Las Vegas! That's how I learned it. That's where I learned that kind of sass and brass and upward mobility with some Alphabet district thrown in to temper the taste. It's Sammy Davis, Jr., on a live album saying: "Ladies and gentlemen"—he's hoarse after two shows—"I just want you to know before we carry on here, we're recording this show live here at the fabulous Sands Hotel, it's 5:30 in the morning, and we're still rockin'."

Okay, sign me up for that. The mind-set was: We're gonna take over Las Vegas. We're going to own Las Vegas. We're going to trundle through those streets like Hannibal and his elephants. We're not going to arrive politely.

The show was designed to update Vegas to our sense of humor. I don't mean a kitsch sense of humor, like when you look at the cover of a Sammy Davis album and admire his pegged trousers . . . "I'd like to get some pegged trousers and wear them to the party tonight, it'll be funny." No, no. Let's not be funny about it. Let's contain humor but we're sexy motherfuckers. Let's have the humor, be competitive with the Dennis Millers and the Lenny Bruces, whoever is incisive, whoever's right on target. Let's be there.

In terms of music, let's be right there with who's

hot shit right now, not who was hot shit then. Let's keep the theater of it: The California Girls—*anti*-bimbos. Broadway, theatrical, costuming, dancing. Not project girls in bicycle pants and Doc Martens squatting and puffing and huffing. Something new.

It was off the map. It was stellar. Just in concept, because nobody has tried it in years and years. Everybody assumes the traditional frock. You become as the Romans do. I have no interest in becoming a Roman or doing as they do.

Call goes out: Who do we get? If you want to record, want to do a video, all the facilities are in Miami Beach. Miami is a burgeoning music scene packed with live bands.

There are many cover bands in Miami Beach playing every hotel, every bar. There were a dozen of us before the dancers—we had a six-piece brass section, bass, drums, congas, keyboard, guitar player, female vocalist, myself, two dancers . . . fifteen. That's a respectable troupe.

Most of them, paying the bills and putting a little grease on the table for the kids by playing clubs and bars exactly as I did. These are the folks who sit in when it's time for Julio to make his 113th album. These are the folks he hires. The keystones of Gloria Estefan's brass section, Teddy Mulet, trumpet and trombone man, Randy Barlow, trumpet, they've been playing with her since 1976. Teddy did the charts for the brass.

Olbin Burgos is the drummer for Gloria. He was not until the musical director for Gloria's band came to one of my rehearsals, saw the band and hired half my boys! They were perfectly ready to stick with me, but I said,

"Hey, I truly believe the Promised Land is out there. I think the world is curved, and we can beat the monsoons to the punch. But who knows . . . ?"

We approached the appropriate agents for Las Vegas, and it was essentially downhill from there. They had no idea. Right away they didn't understand the humor.

We showed up with pictures of the California Girls dressed like Betty Grable, with the shorts and what-not, this was not bikini girls, this was forties. I'm in the picture, too. They refused to use the photo because the girls' legs are the focal point. Keep in mind they're wearing short shorts. Not bikinis, no topless, no nothing. They look like they are out of Busby Berkeley. That's how my sister Al designed it. To be interruptive, but inviting.

The agents were flipped. As in: "We're not sure about this; there's nudity." What? It's legs.

"Well, Las Vegas is very family-oriented." How do you think those families got started? You think they *prayed* themselves into pregnancy?

I was aware that this wasn't the Rat Pack's Las Vegas anymore. But I assumed there would be a place, a single spot, where we could base our operations. I explained it comprehensively. "Guys, we're a seed, not a flower. We're gonna do two, three, four hundred people a night. That's all. Just like old Van Halen did. But out of that four hundred that you put in front of us, three hundred will tell a friend and say 'You gotta go.'

"But they're not all gonna come back. There's not gonna be seven hundred tomorrow night. It's gonna take a couple, three years. And at the end of it, we'll *own* Las Vegas."

Of course, the agent didn't tell this to the hotel people. They're looking for instant success, instant sellout. They were very disconcerted. We were pulling three or four hundred people. The audience was going hysterical. They were loving the show. The media was going wild. But it was only three, four hundred people a show.

Let me put in my time. I have no delusions. This was a *complete* left-hand turn. When you saw the show, you got it right away: "Ah, there's a symmetry to this. This is not spastic, erratic behavior. This is very clearly connected in a straight line. This is Dave's humor. Look at those California Girls. Listen to that music. It's brass but it fuckin' humps your rope."

The agent had not explained that to management, allowed them to labor under an illusion. At the end of several engagements we had miffed everybody in Vegas on the management end. Audience was lovin' it. My sense of humor can be based on these jokes: "Look at my girls dance. Turn your shorts into grilled cheese. More moves than O.J.'s defense team. Hot enough to convince Michael Jackson to quit the Boy Scouts and shakin' harder than Ted Kennedy reaching for his breakfast beer."

Boom! You're outta here!

I thought it was hilarious. So did the audience. But management would say: "We don't want you to use the *F* word." Oh my God. I'm sitting there with adults and we're talking about the *F* word as if we don't all use it twenty times a day?

I played a little joke while the band played a detective theme. I said, "Yeah, I got busted for rape not long ago. I don't know if you're aware of that. But I got a good lawyer. I got Cochran and the boys. We plea-bargained it down to tailgating. They've got me doing civic service now. I'm working with kids. . . ."

It's the kind of humor that makes you feel like you're inhaling fishbones. You squirm, learn, burn, churn and laugh. My most favoritist kind. But they cut the girls out of the photo, and there was just a little picture of my face, cut just enough to show some bangs. It looked like Pat Boone. I said to myself, "My God, I wouldn't even go to this fuckin' show if I saw this advertisement."

What I had done, with the band, was again, old school. Nine times out of ten, say Tom Jones or somebody will show up, have a music director. He'll hire a brass section from the city, have one day's rehearsal—they sight-read the music—and they're very good. But nothing replaces mileage. So we rehearsed for three months, five and six days a week.

The rehearsals took place in a warehouse in Miami Beach. It was hot. It was humid. It was great. Everybody couldn't wait to get there early and leave late. It started to become the thang. It was like some kind of underground circus. Cafe society started calling up. We'd have people sitting on these old couches in this warehouse. We'd fill up the trashcans with all kinds of booze and let in forty or fifty on Friday and Saturday nights and do our real show. The band was like three feet away from you if you were sitting on the first couch. People just had the greatest time.

Up close and personal. I would improvise all of my stuff, find my way, how to make a joke, how to kill time. And everybody loved it because it was right out of Spanky and Our Gang. Buckwheat's in charge of the burlap curtain. The rope breaks. Spanky is playing the part of Santa Claus. When the rope breaks he plummets into the birthday cake. Everbody assumes that's part of the show and instantly decides to come to the next one. It was spectacular. One of the most memorable experiences in music I've ever had.

A typical set of the Mambo Slammers—we were billed as David Lee and His Blues-Bustin' Mambo Slammers—would go something like this: Fire up with "Mambo Caliente" from *The Mambo Kings,* right into James Brown's "Livin' in America," which swings into "I Ain't Got Nuthin' but the Blues," done Mose Allison junkie style, which moves into Miles Davis with the detective rap, which goes into "Panama," which goes into "Ice Cream Man." All of it the wildest barbecue you'd ever want to go to if you was dressed up.

People were astonished. These were classic Van Halen fans who came to the Vegas show not knowing at all what to expect. They flipped out. Because of the musicality, the overall over-the-topism, the enthusiasm and the optimism. It was all right there. It made perfect sense.

Well. The agent hooks us up with one hotel, Caesar's Palace Lake Tahoe in October. Which turns out to be the hump month. There's *nobody* up there. Classic agent bullshit. Before the snow there is nothing goin' on. So of course we pull our three, four hundred people. The hotel people start to freak out. Plus I use the *F* word. By the way, I took my little rape joke from Rodney Dangerfield, from a tape of his live comedy routine in 1961. The more people got upset about that joke, the less I told anybody that fact. Because I took a particular personal amusement in knowing that we have come exactly no distance since 1961. A joke he was telling in that *same city* in 1961.

In Las Vegas we played Bally's, went from there to the MGM Grand. Wound up playing there from Christmas Eve through New Year's. Anyway, Las Vegas did to me, ultimately, what it did to Bugsy Siegal. There's no plaque for Moe Green, and there is not one for me either.

We live in a culture now that's based on infantilism. If you have a six-year-old you have to settle for the kind of entertainment a six-year-old appreciates. That's already backfiring. The six-year-olds are no longer six. By the time you read this that six-year-old is now seven. MGM Grand just had to close down their theme park. I was kicked out, the theme park was kept. Turns out God's got a sense of humor. Vegas is not about children. You can bring children but it's not about them. If I go to the Mustang Ranch, there's a Gymboree?

We want to go to Vegas. But there's gotta be an inducement. There's gotta be something more than another theme park. That's for kids. My inner child wants to get laid.

Reunion Blues

So what's so difficult about a reunion with these guys? I don't have to love them. I don't have to love you to make great music with you. You think all seventy-five people in the New York Philharmonic love each other? You think they even fucking know each other's names?

Anyway, I called Edward Van Halen when I finished the bulk of this manuscript. I said, "Ed, I want to be at peace. That's all. I have no agenda other than that. I'm not trying to get back in. You guys are solvent, no more of this quarreling."

He said, "Yeah, I feel the same way." I didn't realize that he felt the same way because at that time he was looking to throw out Michael Anthony and was rehearsing other bass players.

On the first day that we talked, he said, "Yeah, we always thought about using you to spice up the album, the *Greatest Hits* album." Hmmm. Spice? I'm the rice.

I show up, first day in the studio, first thing I hear from Ed is, "No matter what happens, we're going to be friends, right?"

Well, if this was *Donny Brasco,* you'd be dead by the next scene. If this was *The Godfather,* based purely on that single sentence, I would have sicced Luca Brasi on you. But I close my eyes, I invite denial into the atrium, and I hear this four times a day, from then on, "No matter what happens, we're going to be friends, right?"

Okay. So there's a plan afoot. It doesn't take Sherlock Holmes to begin to discern a pattern. Their whole thing becomes hyper-strategic. Now, with a rock band you cannot strategize anything beyond, "Okay, we'll release the single four weeks in advance to pressure the sales." You can't fool with the team, you can't start strategizing how the songs are written. You can't hire a marketing image consultant. You can't find somebody to teach you how to dance on stage as a singer. You either got it or you don't.

I say to the fellows, "Great. I haven't sung in six

months." I had finished the Las Vegas engagement. Edward's very concerned, "Geez, are you able to sing a whole song? Would you be even able to go on the road?"

I told him, "Ed, I did nine nights in a row. It's an hour-and-forty-minute show, no drum solo, no guitar solo, no bass solo, no break. On stage the entire time, and that doesn't mean you can mope around 1969-style in between songs and go, 'All right! All right!' No, no. That don't fly. You're on, one hundred percent.

"However," I said, "I haven't sung in six months. In order to get the muscles going (the producer's not going to show up for another month), let's rev up a dozen or so of the classic old VH tunes. Everybody knows every note, every move, everything. You don't have to think, no mind." Let me relate Ed's reply in identically the same manner that it was spoken to me with their management in attendance:

"No fucking goddamn fucking way. We're not going to retrace any fucking old steps. We're not going to do any old songs or anything that even remotely sounds like any old songs. We're going to write a fucking set of songs where it doesn't matter who the fucking singer is or how he fucking sings it, it's just going to be a good fucking song that anybody can sing. We're not going to do anything with any weird lyrics. We're going to do something where the lyrics are the lyrics that anybody could write, and we're going to go from there."

At that moment I thought: Okay, I could convene a band—I know many musicians—we'd learn fifteen Van Halen songs in four days. I'd put my mileage roadwork in early afternoons before I'd go down to the Van Halen camp. But I also figured that news would get out quick, don't want to create any kind of foment, I'm going to back off from that, so I chose to tough it out.

Trouble is, you can't sing an unwritten song. You can't build muscles on an unwritten song. The lyrics aren't in place. You don't know what the next lyric is, and I'm not going to know until the producer is in there. He's going to earn his percentage, because he's going to make as much as me in the end. So let's have some of that melodic expertise. Cool.

Work on some plays that you already know, guys, that's how you build the team. But when we actually began rehearsing I was banished to a storeroom in the back of the studio, a windowless cement box where I could see nothing and hear nothing except over my headsets. They would push a button to talk to me. They would run through these new songs and I would sing along back there in my cement bunker.

So I brought in five potted palm trees and some clamp lights, oranges and yellows, and made a little Club Dave with a big glass ashtray I stole from a British hotel.

Hey, if I'm working Ice Station Zebra I'm gonna make it comfortable. All right, this is a test. God and his five angels are testing me. The potted palms. Oh, my God. Alex Van Halen screaming at Big Ed as they bring these things in. My guys take pride in their stuff because it's colorful, it's eccentric. We built an oasis, and we said all were invited. Where do you think the crew hung out when we took a break? Club Dave.

"What the fuck is this fucking goddamn fucking bullshit. We're motherfucking forty-year-olds. What is this fucking palm tree horseshit? This is fucking work, man. This is motherfucking business, okay?" That's Alex Van Halen speaking.

And I stay cool. I start showing up with my lyrics, and they're dismissed out of hand, one right after another. Edward Van Halen would hold the paper in front of his face, stare right into the middle and go, "I don't know."

Edward doesn't read. It's a muscle he doesn't use. He can't read a whole set of my lyrics in seven seconds. Some of my stuff you'll still be figuring out seven years later. It's designed to do that. There's some substance there, you know. So first Edward puts me in a room where I've got to make my own environment, now he's looking at the middle of a page, lookin' to put the thumb on me.

From the very first day in the studio I say, "Is this just two songs? Because if it is, let's not fool people, allow them to think that more is coming. Because we all know we're going to sell a lot more records if people think there's going to be a tour, so let's not lie to them."

"No, Dave, we're taking it step-by-step, little baby steps," he says, "but I'm telling you, I'm not looking for another singer."

Next day, literally, all over the press, there's an announcement from Van Halens' management they're auditioning new singers, they're leading a search for a new singer.

I asked, "Ed, what is this?" He replied, "Oh, the manager, he's just out of line. I'll call him."

Well, we went through a dozen episodes like that because this manager has toiled away in abject obscurity for his whole career. He comes from obscurity. Now he gets his fifteen seconds of real media attention.

Now *both* Edward and Alex are demanding rewrites; a brand new addition to the process. We're getting ready to record, the producer is just now showing up, and in they walk in with Desmond Childs, some character who writes lyrics for Bon Jovi. They had written a whole song, lyrically and melodically, over the telephone; the producer, Glenn Ballard, Edward Van Halen and Desmond Childs. They brought it in, said, "Sing this."

Well, I'm sorry, Desmond Childs for Bon Jovi may be the exact right thing. For Van Halen it's syphilis. Any amount kills the entire organism. Okay? These sanguine, sissified, grew-up-way-too-close-to-mommy lyrics. It sounded awful but even then I tried to sing some of it.

Wasn't right. And keep in mind that while all of this is going on, not a single photograph had been taken in a three-month period. Nothing. Look at the album cover, not a single photograph nowhere.

Half of the *Greatest Hits* album is some other singer, pictures of guitars, and in some of the albums I understand they packaged guitar picks for children. What's the next album going to come with? An apology? No pictures. No photos. This was once the greatest visual entity. That was something that I presided over for all those early years.

So, I'm in the middle of all this. The manager is having a ball. He's had more publicity than he's had in his entire life or ever will again. And it was their idea to do the MTV appearance. I said at the time, "Great, what a beautiful way to sell records, what a great advertisement to sell records. But you're also allowing people to labor under an illusion that we're reconvening." Still, some people think that's not lying.

Said to myself at the time, "I don't want to do any press because, frankly, I'm embarrassed. Everybody in the entire planet knows they ain't going to find anybody better than me for this group, ever."

We go to New York. The day of the MTV awards—at precisely six o'clock in the morning, Ed Van Halen calls me. I'm staying at another hotel.

Let's just address six o'clock in the morning. Abuse is the lowest form of fisticuffs. He thinks he's going to wake me up and ruin my day. Trouble is, I'm excited, I'm in great shape, I've been up since 5:30, I'm drinking a cup of coffee and I'm about to go rock climbing in Central Park. I got James Brown on the stereo. I just read my little Zen chapter. I'm on fire. I am ready.

The phone rings, I casually reach for it. Ed, screaming, at me over the line. Screaming, "Goddamn it, I'm sick of this fucking bullshit. I told them when they did that special tribute to you on MTV where they showed bits and pieces of your videos, I said to them, 'Fuck that. Fuck you. I ain't no fucking backup guitar player.' Who the fuck thinks they're the star of this show? If you think you're the star of this fucking show, then you walk out there on your fucking own. I'd rather go home anyway. Tomorrow is my kid Wolfie's first day at school and I'd much rather be there," on and on.

I replied, "Ed, I have talked to nobody at all. Nobody. All of this is unsolicited. People are very excited that the band is back together. You guys have been together for ten years. I'm the, quote-unquote, new addition."

Well, quite obviously, the Mighty Edward is terrified that somehow all of this attendant publicity and excitement over my reconvening with the band is somehow going to overshadow his musical brilliance. As if. As if anybody in the fucking solar system thinks of Eddie V. as a backup guitar player. If somebody does, well, then I'm the singer for Up With People.

He's been up all night. His plane landed at 6:30 the previous evening. It's now 6:00 in the morning, okay? He's screaming beyond real.

Well, that night a limo pulls up at my hotel and I climb into a car full of scorpions: The manager is there. Van Halens are there. The security guys are there.

First thing out of Edward Van Halen's mouth is, "Fuck this shit, man. I'd rather be fucking home. I want to see Wolfie go to his first day of school." And on he goes, slamming, slamming the whole way to Radio City Music Hall.

Edward: "Look, all we're going to fucking do is we're going to just fucking walk out there and fucking give away the award and when we talk to the press all we're going to fucking talk about is the two new songs and that's fucking it." This is all I'm hearing on the seven-block ride.

Me: "But, guys, you can't get up in front of a press corps and just not answer. They're going to ask you what happened to the other singer. They're going to ask you about me. The tour. They're going to ask you about everything *but* those two songs."

Edward: "Fuck them. We're talking about the two songs and that's it."

We get to the Awards, the audience is unsuspecting. Edward is pissed, miserable, that "my-shorts-are-too-tight" face on the front of his head. We walk out on stage and the place goes ballistic, nuclear, off the map. Eddie and his brother are astonished. They had no idea. Well, I see those smiles. . . .

The Van Halens freeze. Edward puts his sunglasses on. He's visibly angry. Visibly. He's the only angry person in the whole tri-state area, next to his brother.

And the audience is going nuts. So I go to work. It's not something I think about. For me this is natural, this is freewheeling. I smile. Well, everybody is suitably ecstatic but not quite fucking ecstatic enough for a VH gig, so let me put the hip swivel on you, boom! Now you're standing up, aren't you? Yeah, that's what you came for, isn't it? T-shirts in the foyer!

Everybody in the audience stands up. Every alternative rocker, every three-piece suiter from the record companies, all the MTV people, everybody is on their feet. And everybody's having a ball. The people are screaming and yelling, and the Van Halens are balled up like pill bugs, angry faces, exchanging glances.

Well, this is what was planned. Ed Van Halen, as per six in the morning, had every intention of disassembling this gorgeous parade. And of course I interjected a few things besides the plain old banal libretto that's being read on a cue card.

The people from MTV had said to me, "You know, Dave, you could freestyle on this a little bit if you want." "That's why I'm here, guys, 'cuz you can depend on me," and they were looking forward to it. I was the one guy out of the whole show who did it.

The first thing I said to the audience, "God, a lot has changed. For starters, whoever thought that we would be standing on stage here again ten years after the fact?" That statement caused the guys to physically separate from me on stage. For the last decade it's entirely been the Eddie Van Halen show. He's very fond of saying, "This is my band." And with previous singers it was. Absolutely. No competition. No encroachment at all.

With me in the band, it's one of those miraculous 97-97 deals. It's 97 percent you and 97 percent moi. Is it Mick or Keith? I don't know.

I'm currently the fun part, and I'll always be the fun part. I ran into one of the current managers not terribly long ago, and he said, "Hey, Dave, you know, it's just another chapter."

And I told him, "No. Classic VH is the whole book, all right? The rest of *you* are just disposable chapters."

Just before we had walked on stage, Alex Van Halen turned to me and said, "Milk it, Dave. Milk it for all it's worth." And I thought to myself—just as they're announcing us—is he setting me up?

Edward stomps off the stage. Now it's time to go visit the press, which is in several different tents: domestic, international, "Entertainment Tonight," whatever.

Earlier I had said to them, "Guys, this is very, very dangerous. This is a minefield."

"Why? Why is it dangerous? Don't worry about it."

I said, "Because I don't know that we have the same opinions and answers to a given question." Edward said, "What do you mean?" I said, "What if they ask, 'Are you guys going on tour and can we expect more records and what-not?' What would you guys say to that question?"

Ed replied, "Well, we just say baby steps, we're going to take it step by step, see how it goes. Let's just not get too excited here."

I said, "My answer would be different. I got three answers to that one question: Let's go, let's go, let's fucking go. I'm packed. I'll wear these clothes. By the way, I'm not real good with baby steps. My specialty is ass-kicking. Does that sound unreasonable? It may well be, but I guarantee you, you will find no reasonable man on top of big mountains, but that's where I'm going."

In every sense of the word they were shocked. "You can't say that."

"Then don't put me in front of the press."

By now they're really furious. We march into the first media tent, and the press starts going to town. First question is from Stuttering John from the Howard Stern program. There's forty people in the tent. He asks Ed Van Halen, "So do you like Howard Stern?" Knowing full well Howard's taken an ax to these guys a decade.

"Oh, yeah," says Ed, "We kind of like Howard, he's a good disc jockey," whatever, and it's obviously false. He's got a look of distress and anxiety.

I lean over to the mike when he's done and say, "Howard Stern represents something very important in our society, because the powers that be, of censorship and restriction, are wielding their sword out upon the field even as we speak. There must exist a Howard or somebody like him at any given time or else the other guys aren't going to stop at the door."

The Van Halens forcefully pull me away from the microphone, à la the Three Stooges, and one of them puts his hand over my mouth—I don't remember which one. A reporter asks, "Are you guys looking for another singer?" The brothers say, "No, no, that's just rumor and gossip."

The press come after them like hammerheads, literally yelling—I've never heard the press talk to an artist like this—"Bullshit! Bullshit! It came from your manager and he's standing right there." The manager ducks out of the tent like a ferret. Now the Van Halens realize they are no longer in control.

So Ed Van Halen resorts to tragedy as his form of self-expression. "All right, I've had enough of this. Enough of this, okay? We're not going on tour. We're not going to be doing any shows. We're not going to do anything. Even if we were thinking about it, we'd have to go and make a whole new album first, and we're taking it step by step, okay? And by the way, I've got to have a hip replacement, and it's just like Bo Jackson, see, and I hurt it jumping up and down on stage."

The room goes dead. I've never seen the air sucked out of a room like that. He goes into this self-tragedy mode to get attention and kills the entire moment.

When, he says, "We'd have to make a new record," this is all news to me. I'm thinking, why, before the *Greatest Hits* even comes out do you tell people you'll have to buy another record? But I be cool.

We go to the international press tent. Same thing happens: Ed goes into his "my tragic life" routine, kills the room, and somebody asks, "So what about Sammy Hagar? He's just gone?" Ed replies, "Yeah, screw him, he quit, he bailed, man, fuck him." Well, he didn't quit. They connived and created a scenario to make him quit. Made it untenable; he had to bail.

So I said to the press, "Wait a minute, wait a minute. Right now Sam is pissed, tomorrow he's going to be even more pissed. But in a month or two there's going to be a patch of blue, the light's going to come in, he's going to look around and see his pretty new wife, his pretty new daughter, look around and realize he's living in Hawaii. He's going to put his shoulder to the stone, he's going to push and push, and soon that stone will move, and all the light will come into the house. But, hey, what the fuck do I know about losing a high-profile gig?" The crowd loves it.

I looked around and the Van Halens had already left the stage, disappeared. I took Edward aside in between that tent and the next one. I said, "Now is not the time to start addressing a whole lot of personal issues. We created a scenario, we have invited a whole lot of people to celebrate and now is not the time to bring everybody down and start talking about your hip. It's selfish."

He said, "Hey, man, this is my fucking life. I'll say whatever the fuck I want, all right? It's my fucking hip, I need fucking hip surgery."

I said to him, "Fuck that, it's bad manners. You're also talking about things that I have no idea about. Don't put me up in front of the international press and start talking about plans I have no idea even existed."

He turns to me and says, "Nobody ever fucking talks to me like that. You ever fucking talk to me like that, I'm going to kick you in your fucking balls. You fucking hear me?" I begin to think we got a problem here. We've got somebody who's off on cloud cuckoo land.

I take a few steps down the hallway. Alex Van Halen, who's been on his feet for all of twenty minutes now, collapses. He can't stay on his feet for more than thirty minutes at a hit. Turns out that three degenerated discs in his neck are giving him a lot of trouble. He collapses against the wall, he has to go down into the fetal position. It's like he's having a seizure.

I walk over to see what's happening with Al. Their immediate thing is to block off everybody and do nothing. I'm stopped by Van Halen security, hand on my chest, "Stand back." He recovers after about fifteen minutes, but the remaining two interviews he has to sit down, and Edward is beyond himself now.

Kurt Loder of MTV says, "Ed, can we look forward to a tour?"

Ed replies, "Hey, man, fuck that shit. We're not in it for the fucking money. We're not a fucking nostalgia band, man. We're not here to just make a fast buck and fuck off like KISS."

Kurt comes over to me and says, "What about you, Dave?"

I say, "Kurt, aside from cosmetically, I haven't changed a bit. Let's go. You got a car? What's the first city? I'll buy some clothes on the way. I'll borrow some Spandex pants from one of my girlfriends. I'll pick up a local T-shirt that says Chicago when we're in Chicago, I'm cool. Can I get some pot? It's not critical."

We leave from the press conferences to head for the limos and there's thousands of fans, screaming and hysterical. Alex comes up to me and says, "Dave, remember how you used to jump up and down on the limos, you know, get the crowd going crazy after a concert?"

I say, "Yeah."

He says, "Go ahead. Jump up on top of the limo. Get them going. Get them going."

And I thought to myself, it's obvious now, isn't it, you're setting me up.

Get into the limo, everyone's pissed, silent, except me. I know what's up with them.

On the way back Ed says, "Say, Dave"—that fake little boy innocent voice—"got one of those cigars?" He's talking about a fifty dollar Cuban cigar. I says, "Yeah, Joey Sas in the other car has them. When we pull up in front of your hotel, I'll get Joey Sas to pull one out of the bag, you bet." We get out of the car, go over to Joey. Get the cigar, go over and hand it to Ed. I literally turn to say something to somebody on my right. When I look back all of them have walked into their hotel. Marched Girl Scout style.

I go to the Alanis Morissette party, it's a very comfortable environment, it's packed. All the suits from Time Warner, everybody's there. I see my friend Ingrid. She's there with her partner Chris. They run clubs, and she's kind of the reigning social whatever of South Beach. And she don't drink.

We're sitting and talking, I says, "You guys going to be here for a while? Because I'd like to go call Eddie V. and say come on down." The call is made. "Nah, he don't wanna to come down."

I go home, there's a message on my answering machine at the hotel room from Edward. "Hey, man, we've got to fucking talk. This is bullshit, man," da-da-da-da-da, on and on. "Hey, man, if you ever fucking talk to me like that again I'm going to kick your fucking balls. I run into you, you better wear a cup. I'm going to kick you in your nuts."

Let's just stop and consider this. The whole thing of balls, dicks and nuts and kicking and slamming comes up again and again. What does that tell you? You've got a macho thing going here, to say the least.

Well, judging by the time that the phone call came in, because the answering machine says 11:45 in the evening, that little prick was smoking my cigar when he made the call.

Three weeks went by, not a call, not a word, nothing. Finally I phoned Warner Brothers and said, "Are we doing the video for the *Greatest Hits* package?" They say, "Yeah, we're shooting in a couple of days."

Yeah. Can I see the treatment? Sure. Sends me this treatment, where I am relegated to being an image on a screen in the background, while the band jams in the foreground.

It was going to be Alex Van Halen's way of putting the thumb on the classic Van Halen legend. It's just the way he scraped the album clean of anything interesting and colorful. He was going to do that with video. And at that point I said no, just no.

I had known all the way along that they had another singer waiting in the wings. He's also represented by their manager. Nothing goes on in Los Angeles that I don't hear about. It's a small shop, we all share the same computer programmers, the same drum roadies, the same rehearsal spaces, the same guys who sell us recording tape. They're all fans, so I know right away they've got this other character waiting in the background. They would never have been as abusive to me, especially their manager, had they not figured that they had another guy. Okay?

So I wrote an open letter to the media. I waited, and up until the night before I sent out the letter the manager was calling me, telling me, "Oh, no, Ed just wants to see how it goes. He really likes you. He's really happy with the arrangement. And by the way, I'd like to get my 17-percent commission off the top of your advance. Don't get excited, Dave, no need to go to the press, no need to talk to anybody. Ed's a little upset but, hey, he hasn't made any decisions. So don't go to the press."

Enough's enough. The next day I sent out my letter explaining they never had any intention of doing anything beyond the two new songs. I sent out my letter, and it has been angry, vitriolic bullshit coming from their side ever since. It's still all "I hate Dave and I'm going to do everything I can to make you hate him." So what else is new?

Not long ago, around midnight, Big Ed and I are strolling in New York, Fifth Avenue, really empty, dead. A minivan comes screeching up to the curb, a guy leans out the window and yells, "Diamond Dave!" I look over and he's got a carload of shooters—paparazzi. "Yeah?" And I don't stop walking. He turns and he said something to the gang in the van. They all put their cameras down.

I said to Big Ed, "Did you know those guys?" He says, "I recognize the driver, he's paparazzi. He was at the Howard Stern thing." They put their cameras down respectfully and looked and smiled out the window, and the guy said, "Class act, Dave, you did it right." Drove off and not a frame was shot. That's *my* barometer.

Flexible

There is a statue of a Buddha in my driveway
Rigid and stiff
That's where the birds shit

And he deserves it
Me, like a blade of grass
I bend profoundly
No raindrops on me
The wind blows 'round me

All The Girls I've Loved Before

We called my great grandmother on my mother's side "Big Grandma." She came from Russia, and she lived until I was eight years old. She never told anybody exactly how old she was, but my mother remembered her describing how when she was a little girl in Russia, her first inklings of what America was about was a fella, the boss, the President. He wore a top hat, had a beard. And of course she was talking about Abe Lincoln.

The sense of history that runs in the family probably comes from my mother's side, tracked all the way back to that. My mother would get stars in her eyes when she'd tell that story to me. From the time that I can remember, my mother was always dragging me around by the wrist to go see Paul Revere's birthplace or where the Minutemen came from, or where the Battle of Concord took place.

It was my mother who gave me the appreciation for history. I have a real fascination with "what came before." Later on I learned the saying that "the end of your game depends entirely upon your beginning." I saw a bus disgorge a whole bunch of kids the other day so they could stand in line to get into Planet Hollywood. And I said to a ten-year-old, "Hey, man, do you know who Arnold Schwarzenegger is?" He lit up. He positively knew; he could probably spell it! Then I asked him, "Do you know who Beethoven is?" I think he thought of the dog in another movie.

There's a small conceptual leap to be made here. I was given a super appreciation of reading, and I think that this ties in with it as well. It was my mother—once my dad was through pounding the syllables and *The Cat in the Hat* into me—who would sit with me endlessly. We'd go through magazines, books, you name it, and to this day I'm a constant reader. I'll read the back of a cereal box. I'll stop and look at a street sign.

All this led to a fascination with the graphic arts, print art, photographic art. Anything that is coming off the printed page I learned a reverence for. My mother's sensibilities were way asthetic as opposed to disciplinary. She was the one who'd say: "Oooh, ahhh, isn't that great? Isn't that amazing?" And of course you're gonna agree with your mom. It was my pop who said: "Now I'm gonna teach you how to get there from here." My mother was the one who sat me down in front of the TV set to watch the Olympics. And she said: "The gymnasts got the best bodies."

It was my pop who showed up one day when I was eleven and said: "They're called parallel bars and you're gonna learn how to use them. Let's go to the garage." The combination was killer-diller.

I was in a New York deli getting breakfast not long ago. I had my baseball cap and my sunglasses on—my urban camouflage, you know—and the fella behind the counter said something and I started laughing out loud. Three people turned around and said, "Diamond Dave!" That laugh I got from my mother. It is . . . celebrative.

I was walking down the street one night and there was a homeless guy fixing up his cardboard boxes. I stopped and said, "I need a little bit of good luck. Here's a five dollar bill. Now you gotta wish me luck."

He said, "Why would you want to give me this much, man?"

I replied, "From what I hear, this is where God lives." That attitude I got from my mom.

There's a photo in this book captioned "Whose pants are worse?" Well, at the end of the proverbial menu, I want to be able to say: "Well, I tried *everything* on it." Of course those pants look dumb, ten years later. They're supposed to. Otherwise, why bother to progress? Why change? I got that from my mom. The eye for the detail.

Her influence has fallen onto my sisters as well. Lisa was my best pal from the word go and still is to this very day. She's about to graduate college for I think the eighth time. I won't tell you how old she is, cuz she could pull a Cameron Crowe, go right back to high school tomorrow and you wouldn't be able to tell the difference. Unless you were male and you'd be chasin' her. When we were kids, we played King Arthur's Court together, Jesse James, Captain John Smith and Pocohontas. We adored each other, still do. She is my guru. A lot of my philosophy or my little poems come directly from her soul.

My sister Allison is a designer, a graduate of the Art Design Institute. Hands-on, lets-make-it-happen kind of gal, she worked on several of my videos, costumes and such. The aesthetic eye. I remember sitting with her when she was a little kid. She asked me, "What should I do in the future . . . got any recommendations?" I said, "Yeah. There's three countries you gotta visit: America, Europe and New York City." It was my mother who sat me on her knee back when and said, "This is a picture of Morocco, this is a picture of Africa." Both of which she had been to. And that idea of travel, seeing the rest of the world, there's five sides to every coin, that comes from the women's side of the family.

There's also a very strong sense of contact in my family. I'm always grabbin' the elbow of your jacket, kickin' your shoe or hittin' you on the shoulder. That comes from my mom. The only thing that ever settled hyperactive little Diamond Dave down was when I would sit with my mom and watch television or read and she would scratch my back. Today? Scratch my back and you get the whole story. If you scratch my back for an hour, you get all my money.

So when it came time for me to start socializing with women in a little more adult sense, I was ready to go. I love women. Get along with women great. Had maybe three really good love affairs in my life. The first was when I was seventeen or eighteen. Sweet little R-lene Recindez, in Pasadena. Lived around the corner. Still owns the best Mexican restaurant on the left-hand side of the map, within walking distance of my house.

We used to sit in my Opel Kadett station wagon and listen to "Smoke on the Water," and make out like every high school kid. At that time I was too young to get into clubs or bars—in L.A. you have to be twenty-one. She was twenty-one at the time. And one of R-lene's cousins introduced me to one of the places where I could get in. Little gal with a navy crewcut, back in the very early seventies. She introduced me to—what shall we call it?—the k.d. lang school of approach. She introduced me to Women Who Love Women, and the Women Who Love Them Too.

The only places that I would go were the lesbian bars, the women's places, because the gals had food in their clubs and bars. If you had food, well, it was really a restaurant with dancing, right Your Honor? It was me, the door guy, and two hundred and eighty of our best girlfriends. I've always had appreciation for that side of the tribe cuz it's given me great access to the way a woman thinks, without all the usual subtext. "Why is he lookin' at me like that?" And same-same here: "Why is she lookin' at *me* like that? Uhh oh." It's the old *When Harry Met Sally* thing. Is it possible for a guy to hang with a gal without absolute sexual context?

So now you combine a lot of these elements; a sense of what is romantic and what is out of a book. What love is all about for me is, depends on it taking a very dramatic and very poetic form.

In the mid-eighties I was doing a commercial for MTV. I was sitting with two pretty gals, on-camera. When they finished the take I turned and asked one of the gals, Kelly, "Hey, would you like to have lunch one of these days?" She said, "Certainly," gave me her phone number.

Couple days later, not long after I had tipped the voodoo priestess in Haiti, I picked up the phone, called her, and said, "Kelly, this is David Lee, and I'm here to collect on that lunch offer." She said, "Great. Where are we going to have lunch?" And I said, "How about Port-au-Prince?"

There was a long silence and then she said, "What do you mean?" I said, "Because that's where I am right now. Accent on the 'right now' because there's a limousine headed for your apartment even as we speak. The driver's got a pre-paid airplane ticket in the glove compartment and I've got a hotel room with your name written over the door. If you like, just get in the car, and there I are. If, not, just send him away and I'll catch up with you when I get back home." She got in the car and, unfortunately, about a year-and-a-half later, we both got out. I gotta go find that Haitian priestess again. . . .

What's the best vacation? I'm fairly upwardly mobile, seen big boats and long skinny airplanes that can make it there in half the time, but probably the most exciting time I had was with a pretty gal from Dallas who I had met somewhere along the way. Let's call her Casey. She was bouncin' around from one job to another. Strong-willed gal. Her father was a geologist, raced bicycles in the sixties. Teeny, tiny little gal made of swag steel wire. And a laugh a lot like Mom's. Best trip we ever took we called "Keep Tahiti on your left."

A friend of mine, Gianni, who is full Tahitian, makes his living carving outrigger canoes in the ancient tradition. His father taught him how to build a house without using nails, in the ancient way. Twice a year, the Japanese fly him to the art museum in Tokyo. He sets up, carves a canoe out of a single log, builds an outrigger. They pay to watch him do it. And that pays for the rest of the year. Also paid for the materials he used to build a little tree house that hangs out over the beach. Thatched roof, no windows, little platform, mattress and a Coleman lantern.

So Casey and I paddled one of Gianni's outrigger canoes for a good sixty miles around the coast of Moorea. "Keep Moorea on the left." See a nice spot, pull up to the beach, put on your best, cleanest Bruce Lee T-shirt, check in for the evening. I'll chase down something for dinner, build the fire, you go get permission from the lady of the house, lady of the shack.

If all of this sounds very romanticized, it's because I designed it specifically to be just that. As much as possible without affectation.

These are all the girls I've loved before.

Coda

Radio personalities can be merciless for whatever reason. You'll be caught in the snow in a record company representative's little Dodge outside of Lynchburg, Tennessee, or Racine, listening to the radio station. You'll hear the morning team; you're thirty minutes late, no fault of your own. They'll say "Well, looks like David Lee's getting a little too big for his britches. I guess if he's a little more late, we're just gonna have to . . . " You know, it just goes on. They will turn on you.

There are some DJs who are known for being really acerbic. There was a morning team in Tampa, Florida, around 1992. Getting to their station meant going across the Three Mile Bridge. It's one of these bridges built over the swamp. It's eighteen feet above the most ginormous prehistoric swamp turf you can imagine. So on this day somebody leans over to pull out their cigarette lighter and slam-dunks a Volvo in front and causes a twenty-seven-car pileup on this long bridge, and everybody's backed up from here to Boston in the boiling hot sun. Traffic is dead-stopped. How do you even get a tow truck in there? You'd have to bring it in with a helicopter. I still to this day don't know what they do, disassemble all the cars piece by piece and take them away on a barge?

Luckily we're in a limousine with a telephone. So we call the radio station 'cause they're starting to get a little scratchy, they're going, "Man, David Lee is twenty minutes late. Who does he think he is?" Got them on the phone and said, "Hey guys." They said, "Hold on, Dave, we want to hear this. We'll put it live on the air."

"Hey, I'm out here on Three Mile Bridge. Traffic's backed up from here to Australia. I'll tell you what I'm gonna do. I'm gonna run it in, 'cause I figured we got only two more miles to go. And if you can send out the radio station van, tell the police, they'll let you through to the head of the bridge, 'cause I'm gonna go for it."

"This is amazing, ladies and gentlemen, he's gonna run it in."

All of a sudden we got the halo back.

The DJ is pleased. "Folks, this is amazing. David

Lee wants to be on the station so bad he's gonna run it in. We know there's a lot of you out there on the bridge right now listening to this station, so I want you to give him your support."

Literally hundreds of cars started honking their horns. The station starts playing my music. Everybody puts their stereo volume control on "stun," and the whole bridge is vibrating to "Just Like Paradise." It's 95 degrees, saturation humidity, which means there's no air, just moisture.

I get out of the car, take off my shirt, stick it in my back pocket and start jogging. There's thousands of arms sticking out the windows of these bumper-to-bumper cars, so I'm fivin' 'em every eight paces. And the music is honking and the people are on top of their cars, cheering. It's like a bad outtake from *Rocky.* When I get to the head of the bridge, my arms are sore from high-fiving three thousand hands. I get to the end of the bridge and there's the station's "Action Van," waiting for me with the doors open. They have an ice-cold beer and a wet towel waiting. The driver has a cellular phone, and he says, "We got him in the van!"

That's the kind of scenario when Double D out-alternatives the alternative. What's alternative? Just follow your own package. Groove to your own drummer.

I don't recommend that anybody follow this book as a blueprint for anything. Picasso said, "Computers are useless; they supply only answers." There's no answers here. This is not a computer. This is me telling stories. It's a needed job description. I certainly know a lot of the questions now, and I pose them with my stories. Everything here is a question. Don't run out and do as I did, but please do buy the book.

As far as stretching the truth, no. Told it just as I remembered it, which is all a body can do. Tall tales are tall right from the go. I tell the truth but I try to tell it well.

Everything with me has to be dramatic. Everything with me has to be full of emotion and drive and tragedy and catastrophe, valor and victory. Not to the extent of feeling a deathly sense of loss because somebody butted in front of me in the movie line, but in the spirit of living large. Every day I rejoice about something and I'm totally delighted and I'm the most fortunate guy on earth.

I tell this story now, equal parts to re-live it, as well as to preserve it. It's a story that we all participated in to one extent or another. You're gonna recognize yourself or somebody that you knew, sooner than halfway through this book. It's a story worth hearing. It was certainly worth telling. And way more worth than anything, living. But if any one of you drowns in the shipping channel, don't come to me. You've been warned.

I've lambasted managers and agents, lawyers and accountants, but you know what? There's a lot of good eggs out there too. And in order to arrive at this place that I currently dwell in, you're gonna have to have a half a dozen managers and agents and accountants and lawyers and in betweens. It's how you're gonna learn. It's the *only* way that you're gonna learn. And God bless, you should arrive at the shores of someone who's really good, 'cause they're out there—just mostly not.

The two co-conspirators who are the dearest to my heart after all is said and did up to this point, I'm figured we're barely at halftime, is Big Ed—Ed Anderson—and my assistant Steve Martin; we've been working together the better part of two decades. Those two guys and I grew up together, we put in some of the best years of our lives together, at the same time, at the same place, on the same bus. Often with the same girl, turns out.

If you're looking for weights and measures and actual numbers here and times and instances, believe me, I read where one of these porno stars is going to do his book. If you want weights and measures, he's gonna far outdistance four of me.

If you're looking for exacting history to the month, to the year, that's not how I remember it.

This is not a recitation of what I did, you already know that I did it. This is *why* I did it or how it was done—nine-and-a-half times out of ten, being clearly not what you expected. Me neither.

Perhaps if you know a little more how the artist lived, you get a little deeper experience when you listen to the music or you look at a photograph or you see a video. Sheds a little light, or, even better, confuses it, throws a little shadow. Now you're really intrigued.

As opposed to doing an interview: "Okay, let's go song by song. What is this one about, Dave? Okay, and where did the inspiration come from?" Well that's not how you tell stories with friends, around dinner or a campfire. You tell stories that indicate a mood, an attitude, a conflict, a drive, instances that illustrate. That's what this book, this entire experience has been about for me. This is where the music came from. The music always came first.

This book is not for simple spectators. If you can get from front to back, you will have learned, felt and experienced much of what I did. Maybe you'll laugh, or feel some wistfulness. Some of it might get you horny, and some of it might just piss you off. Now that's a story.

FEATURING

Gretchen
YOUNG
HYPERION

Eddie
ANDERSON

Steve
MARTIN

Anthony
VAN SLYKE
SPEED GRAPHICS

Kendall
MIGLIOZZI

Amanda
CAGAN
MSO

Neil
ZLOZOWER

Amy
WILLIAMS

Michael
MIGLIOZZI

Mitch
SCHNEIDER
MSO

Arlett
VEREECKE

Henry
ROLLINS

Nick & Robin
BAKAY

Dr. Nathan
ROTH

Sibyl
ROTH

Lisa
ROTH

Allison
ROTH

And of course,
BUCKWHEAT

!

CAST OF CHARACTERS

"Ravin' Rude's Libation Station"
Gil Traub • Harvey Schaps
Howard Stern • Mrs. Pitts
Pamela Peters • James Sheftel
Steve Mandel • Malissa Daniel
Irv's Burgers • Lathum Nelson
Jerry Edelstein • Perozzi & Hillman
Jason Binn • Club Med
Kevin Brail • Pink Pony
Nelson Place Hotel • Heidi Fleiss
Alan Hart • Kieren McClelland
Lisa Luke • The Starwood
R-Lene • Patrick & Diane Whitley
GO's • Chuck Norris • Lori Yedid
Crazy Girls • Larry Wagner
The Vault • Danny Rodgers
Jimmy Briscoe • Sylvia Gobels
Studio 54 • Gloria Balanay
Margaret Robely • Gazzari's
Roz Fox • Jerry Perzigian
Jerry Kramer • Dottie Bittle
Rainbow Bar and Grill
Tyler Hart • Bruce Lee
Ron Agnew • Whisky A Go-Go
Mario Maglieri • CBGB's
Shane Kauhane • Lea Sullivan
Roadies all over the World
Rob Marchner • Kristie Canavan

Steve Vando • Paul Silveira
Teagan Clive • Cliff Walker
Ted Templeman • Mo Ostin
James Hunting • Adjetey Osekre
Gary & Trina Tole • Pink's Hot Dogs
Tony Caputo • George Arcaro
Jonathan Shlafer • Joe Volpicelli
Stan Swantek • Sabrina Guinness
Tim Moore • Shanna Cordell
Uncle Manny • Lisa Slaughter
Kevin Brady • Louis Prima
The Beverly Club • Fred Norris

Vince Lombardi • Mike Weiss
Tony Vescio • Mike Weber
Café Tabac • Doug Burch
Gregg "Big G" Emerson
William "Count" Basie • Thor Moss
Joe Frilot • Jason Becker
Cecilia Levin • Cigar Warehouse
"Sweet" Connie • Bill Gazzari
V.I.P. Lounge • Nile Rodgers
Oscar Wilde • Oh My Darlin' Music
Joe & Arlene Sas • Flash Dancers
Petit' Louis • Warren Kaye
Benny & Sarah Urquidez
Paulie Zink • Larry Hostler
Bob Rock • Billy Sheehan
Theo Westenberger • Greg Gorman
Alex Hall • Chaz & Tina Evans
01 Gallery • Ron Kauk
Eat 'Em And Smile Band
Steve & Tracy Gemza • Gail Liss
Brian Hendry • Mambo Slammers
Andy Gaspar • Chris "Tramp" Olson
Clementine Anderson
Billie Holiday • John Mullin
Galen Rowell • Werner Braun
J.R. Ahlijian • Tammy • 6th Pct.
Washington Square Park
Eric Stiller • Marc Elfenbaum
Johnny Britt • Art Fruend • 13th Pct.
Henry Miller • Steve Gerardi
The Bulldog • Renata Elden

The Raleigh • Robin Quivers
Stuttering JJJJohn Melendez
Gary Dell' Abate • Bowery Bar
Peter Braglia • The Palms
Le Madri • John Weinel
Bud Tunick • Toni Basil
Café WHA? • Larry Wagner
Jackie "The Joke Man" Martling
The Palm L.A. & N.Y.

CAST OF CHARACTERS

Sylvie Simmons • Immigrant Grocer
Helmut Newton • Caroline Bon
Ron Voltz • Danny Pearl
Chris Simpson • Juan Turros
Carl Scott • Todd Jensen
Hank McAllen • Curt Gathje
Joe Cordano • Preston Sturges
Sal from Brooklyn • Roger Maris
Ed Parker • Mike Sprague
Allen Ginsberg • John Steinbeck
Nigel Buchan • Joan Milligan
Marcus "Conan" Silveira
Steve Lemon • Huck Finn
Vo Nguyen Giap • Gary Mardling
Muhammad Ali • Sean Webb
The Gang at Peter's Backyard
Jennifer Lang • T.J. Thompson
Jennifer Suskin • Joe Davola
Scott Ward • Mickey Mantle
Brett Tuggle • Miles Davis
"Opie" • Tecumseh Sherman
Paul Childs • George Patton
"Smile with Lyle" • John Fedele
Nancy Grossi • Zane Paite
Groupe Mobile 3 • Jeff McHarg
Jeff "Cowboy" Adams • Spy
John Campion • Bob Arcaro
Janine Lindemulder • Jay Block
Elvis Presley • Kerry Simon
Radio Directé • Ed Joseph
Pat "PK" Kelly • Mary Abate
Denise Pantos • Debbie "Doo"

Ikkyu • Catherine Guinness
John Hankinson • Carlo Gambino
The Hit Factory • Joe Galdo
Rich Hilton • Joe Holmes
Terry Kilgore • Karen Valdez
Johnny Weissmuller • Frank Trejo
John Copani • Peter Copani
Michael Bernard • Kenneth Zarrilli

Sony Music Studios • Jake Hooker
Blue Man Group • Jana Rajlich
David Breashears • Steve Vai
Butch Frilot • Andre McDougall
Craig Sherwood • Steve Hunter
Joseph Papp • "Cosmo" Wilson
Jeff Hendrickson • Kenny Donato
Liz Rosenberg • "Big Bad Bill"
Jules Zalon • Damon Zumwalt
Pete Kranske • "Big Fred" Bailey
"Wazotta" • "Rocket" Ritchotte
Sammy Figueroa • Travis Tritt
Eddie Martinez • Willie Weeks
Tony Gundin • Miko Brando
2 Guys Who Do Ads, Inc.
Ernest Hemingway • Brian Mann
Toby Fleming • Wax • John Itsell
Lisa Robinson • Rodney Johnson
Noboru Kataoka • Sid McGinnis
Tom Trumble • Grisel Dominguez
Laurie Quigley • Jim Hagopian
Gregg Bissonette • Teddy Mulet
Randy Barlow • Matais Oxidine
Kirsten Steinhauer • Hina
Jack Gulick • Mark Alger
William Hames • MTV • Rob Manley

Jack Lapp • Matt Bissonette
Richard E. Aaron • Nick Didlick
Dennis "Cricket" Brunken
Mike "Coach" Andy • Mike Burgess
The Germano Family • Sid Payne
Ed "Zed" Wannebo • Ted Shaw
John Robinson • Kenny Richards
Greg Mastrogiovanni • John Pochna
Carlos Guitarlos • "Top Jimmy"
Stuart Maltz • Elmer Valentine
Sigmund Freud • Al Grissinger
Robin Clark • Maryel Epps
Tawatha Agee • Ray Brinker
Brenda White-King • Tony Beard

CAST OF CHARACTERS

Larry Aberman • John Regan
Tracy Wormworth • Carl Wilson
Kevin Dillon • Brigitte Friang
James Newton Howard • Jeff Bova
Jesse Harms • The Waters Family
The Crowell Sisters • Abel Rocha
Yoshi Ohara • Marcelo Silveira
Edgar Winter • John Michalak
Marion Meadows • Earl Gardner
Alex Harding • Steve Scales
Howard & Nellie Bazzell
Omar Hakim • Greg Phillinganes
Scott Lochmus • Jennifer Laboe
Tasco • Crescent Moon Studios
Rudy Leiren • Leonard Bernstein
Javier Garza • Otto Printing
Neil Preston • Pablo Flores
Phil Guiliano • South Beach Studios
Ron Bergman • Eleanor Lehner
Muddy Waters • Carol Wong
Alan Baker • C.L.S. Transportation
Danny Davenport • Bruce Gilmer

Andrea & Alison Sacerdote
Brooks Ogden • Mike Comisky
Ian Huckabee • Gary Weinberger
Alex "Scratch" Moore • John Irey
Martha Schultz • Rene Simpson
Steve Lawler • Townsend Wessinger
Dan Barry • Jim Mercante
Tom Mercante • "Jungle Studs"
Larry Butler • Michael Buffer
Steve Campbell • Bill Cassel
"Doc" Whiley • Mitchielous
Skip Collins • Brett Cervantes
Larry Dana • Tracy Fredrick
Brad Nye • Jim Harbin • Paul Lewis
Tom Bates • Saladang • Andy Martin
Rick Mason • Reagan Miller
Mike Moorhead • Tony Nackley
Flo-Jo • Artisan Sound Recorders

Jim Putnam • Scott Dopson
Jim "Spook" Roldan • Babe Ruth
Khatmandu • Gene Langley
Harry Repas • Bill Wight
Dennis McCubbin • Roy Snyder
Tennessee Williams • Liz Hill
Johnny Roberts • Kevin Sims
Jim Beck • Howard Bingham
John Bleich • VH-1 • Bobby Melatti
Lloyd Dray • Kelly Loudon
Donny Marr • Eugene Holmes
Jerry Mendoza • Buster LaFroscia
Tequila Mockingbird • Susan Green
Jack Kerouac • Randy Staub
Michael Papale • Marko Babineau
Laura Rice • Coco Chanel
Louis Reard • Tadashi Yamashita
Steven Greenberg • Guadeloupe
Fernando Perez • Linda Skitzki
Steve Yarbrough • Joe Mooney
Jim Cone • Edmund Campion
Rick Hutton • Mick Panasci
Todd Mackler • Jimmie Haskell
Jon Lowry • John Guest

Lonnie "Doc" Brown • Merida
Steve Perzigian • Jerry May
Keith Mitchell • Dan Koniar
Showco • Michael Caron
Mario Leccese • Bob Huckaba
Andy Warhol • David Grenier
Audio Analysts • Randy Townsend
Bill Miller • Mike Mota • Keith Kevan
Bobby Velloza • Jeff Wiesner
John Brim • Dwane Warner
Bat McGrath • St. Tropez
Joanie Turnbull • Dana Vanella
Hadden Hippsley • Mark Griffiss
Mountain Productions • Dave Reuss
Robert Sebree • Showlites
Bernadette O'Brien • Paul Starr

CAST OF CHARACTERS

Mark Duffield • Dave Larrinaga
Bob Kelley • Mike Auerbach
Jerry Matteri • Jane Holman
Ken Tudhope • Robin Lemon
Dick Yost • Dave Jellison
Elwood Francis • Chaos
Hank McHugh • Willie Werns
Brian Murphy • Continental Burger
Raul Vega • Mark Spring
Jeffrey Jah • Mijares • Jim McNeill
Jim Norman • Maryland Sound
Andy Charal • Scott Richards
Paul Giansante • Don Whetsel
Frank Geroski • Flo & A-105
Dave Lucas • Silvano Monasterios
The Roxy • Steve Sybesma
Bernie Thoren • Bally's Las Vegas

Scott Graves • Olbin Burgos
Joe Mullin • Knute Rockne
Danny O' Bryen • Rusty Lowrey
Roy Compton • Vari-Lites
Quinn's • Louis Armstrong
Ron Stern • Jim Evans • John Scher
Jim Koplik • Sunset Sound
Paul Elliott • Andy Jones
Tommy's Nº5 • Karen Cohen
Susan Klusendorf • Arny Grant
Tony Ruffino • Paul Lewis
Steve Campbell • Jose Arredondo
Todd Frank • Gary Berwin
Mike Huber • Marjorie Sexton
Doug Goldstein • John Odom
Kenny Pinnel • Charlie Hernandez
Mary Jean Valente • Bali
Les Midgley • Frank Barsalona
Jane Geraghty • Barbara Skydel
Mike Hirsh • Fred Saunders
MGM Grand Las Vegas
Gordon Paterson • Nicole Miller
Diane Arbus • Chris Willoughby

Mike Zarembsky • Greg Willis
Steve Walker • In-N-Out Burger
Gary Passanisi • Mike Smith
George Englis • Charlie Horky
The Crew at Mates • Don Fox
Sonny Hughes • Ted Cohen
Diane Livingston • Valerie Treat
Eric Pearce • Scott Barnett
Nancy Griffin • Madonna
Phillip McArthur • Lenny Waronker
Burnettes Barbecue • Don Law
Jules Belkin • Club Madonna
Tom Caggiano • Jack Boyle
Blake Dewberry • Jim Neal
Criteria Recording Studio
Toni "Bis" Kelleher • Barry Fey
Christopher Cross • Dean Parks
Bill Graham • Debbie Kresh
Gary Rudell • Louis Messina
Rick Franks • Ron Strong
Rick Seireeni • Rich Mayne
John Adams • Wilson Howard
The Power Station • Joe Bush
Maria Parkinson • Bill Reid
Dave Williams • Martinique
Rock-It Cargo • Les Martin
Le Parker Meridien • Jim Lenahan
Irv Zuckerman • Carl Ingels
Robert Lombard • Ron Delsener
Paul Mortensen • Ed Warner
Terry Gilbert • Cindy Beaumariage
Second Ave. Deli • Nancy Mraz
Ken Parkin • Pablo Picasso
Electric Ladyland • Pam Sparks
Stacey Harper • Larry Magid
Ron Cohen • Deborah Schulman
Phil Ealy • Jerry Mickelson
Jerry Harvey • Stan Schiller
Danielle Harris • Plaza Hotel
Dave TV

Photo Credits

"MY OTHER BOAT IS A AIRCRAFT CARRIER"
"NO RISK, NO ROCK"
"My other vine is a Porsche" "This kid does more by 9 am..."
"Haiti '84"
"Look at that ankle.
She Wants it. Dirty Girl."

Taken by:
EDDIE ANDERSON

"AND NOW FOR YOUR QUESTION..."
"PARIS, FRANCE 1992"
"Some people see a therapist about their fetishes"
"Wait. Let me turn my radio down"
"I never consciously sat down and decided"

Taken by:
JIM HAGOPIAN

"VAN HALEN'S CURRENT MANAGEMENT TEAM"
"One second later, her body just sucked in the bikini..."
"ANYBODY GOT A CIGARETTE?"
Taken by:
YOSHI OHARA

"ROCK'S ROWDIEST ROGUES"
"THERE ARE CERTAIN MOMENTS THAT REMIND YOU..."
"WE WERE LATER MARRIED IN A SMALL PRIVATE..."
"Arena security did
a great job..."
"wouldn't You?"
"I AM THE GREAT, AND POWERFUL, OZ"

Taken by:
THEO WESTENBERGER
GAMMA-LIAISON
life magazine, c, time inc. reprinted with permission

"YES I GOT A MOTHERFUCKING WHIST
"THEN THE OLD GUY GOES..."
"BACKSTAGE U.S. FESTIVAL 83"
"This is the grown up version of the little boy..."
"Just like this and then I spin around..."
"Okay, Number B-27, Who has B-27!"
"You'd expect to find
Howard Stern here"
"What's going on with
the girl on the steps..."
"Holy Shit McDonald'
coffee is hot"
"I played the part of Buck..."
"THESE OTHER
TWO GUYS
LOOK SO GODDAMN
FAMILIAR"
"IT APPEARS TO BE
SOME SORT OF SIGNAL, SIR"
"I RUINED HER FOR OTHER ME
"However, the clear and present danger here is .
"It starts with tiny multi-colored chaser lights .
"Let's put it this way..."
"MANY WOMEN
PREFER NOT EATI
FROM THE MENU.
"I DON'T THINK MOST
PEOPLE FEEL PLEASURE...
"WHEN WE WERE KINGS"
"Whose pants are worse?"
"Who says I don't
play an instrument?"
"Are those buttons
well placed or what?"
"ARE YOU TALKIN' TO ME!?"

Taken by:
NEIL ZLOZOWER

"I Get It"

Taken by:
NICK DIDLICK

Photo Credits

"THE SPOT NEAR THE TOE ON THE SOLE OF THE SHOE..."

...would later become important because of DNA"

Taken by:
HOWARD BINGHAM

"LOBUCHE PEAK, HIMALAYAS 1991, 21,00 FEET"

Taken by:
DAVID BREASHEARS

"CAPTAIN'S LOG, STARDATE 2960..."

Taken by:
GREG GORMAN

"ONLY THE SEA WILL TELL"

Taken by:
CHRIS SIMPSON

"PEOPLE OF EARTH"

Taken by:
RICHARD E. AARON
THUNDER THUMBS INT'L

"NEW YEAR'S EVE? TRY A TYPICAL TUESDAY"

Taken by:
DAVE JELLISON

"AIR ROTH"

"THAT'S ME JUST A LITTLE LEFT OF CENTER"

"NO STARBUCKS NEXT 700 MILES"

"proof that kids do just fine without..."

"No one packs a canoe like my Mom!"

"Kayak around Manhattan; All the way around"

"All I'm saying is the guy right behind me ..."

"'Big' Ed and me somewhere in the South Pacific"

"PAPUA NEW GUINEA"

"VAN HALEN WORLD TOUR 1984"

"LAS VEGAS DAVID LEE ROTH"

"BEEN THERE"

From the:
DLR ARCHIVES
permission granted by diamond dave enterprises